Psychodrama since Moreno

J.L. Moreno is the pioneering figure in psychodrama, whose ideas and practice have made an immense contribution to the whole field of psychotherapy. In this book, internationally recognised practitioners of the psychodramatic method, many trained by Moreno himself, discuss innovations in the theory and practice of psychodrama since Moreno's death in 1974.

The book examines Moreno's seminal theoretical contributions to psychotherapy – practical ideas which explain processes between and within individuals and emphasise both the transpersonal or psychospiritual and the conscious or cognitive approach to an individual's problems. The contributors describe how they themselves have taken these key concepts and developed them in their own practice of psychodrama. They show how each concept inspires their clinical work, enabling the reader to understand in a direct and practical way how Moreno's ideas can be applied in therapeutic work. Each chapter is given an extra dimension by Ken Sprague's montage illustrations, commissioned specially for this book.

Stimulating and informative, *Psychodrama Since Moreno* provides a re-evaluation of the place of J.L. Moreno in the development of group psychotherapy and also shows how psychodramatists today are continuing to develop his ideas and take his method of psychodrama into new and exciting fields. It gives a clear picture of the breadth and originality of Moreno's ideas and will be invaluable to practising psychodramatists, other group psychotherapists and mental health professionals.

Paul Holmes is a psychodramatist in private practice and Consultant Child and Adolescent Psychiatrist in the National Health Service. **Marcia Karp** is Co-Director of Training, Holwell Centre for Psychodrama, Devon, and Honorary President of the British Psychodrama Association. The late **Michael Watson** was Principal Psychotherapist (Psychodrama) for North Staffordshire Health Authority.

Psychodrama since Moreno

Innovations in theory and practice

Edited by
Paul Holmes,
Marcia Karp
and Michael Watson

Foreword by Zerka T. Moreno
Montage illustrations by Ken Sprague

London and New York

First published 1994
by Routledge
11 New Fetter Lane, London EC4P 4EE

Simultaneously published in the USA and Canada
by Routledge
29 West 35th Street, New York, NY 10001

Permission to quote from *Four Quartets*, by T.S. Eliot, by Faber and Faber Limited.

Typeset in Times by J&L Composition Ltd, Filey, North Yorkshire

Printed and bound in Great Britain by
Biddles Ltd, Guildford and King's Lynn

British Library Cataloguing in Publication Data
A catalogue record for this book is available from the British Library.

Library of Congress Cataloging in Publication Data
A catalogue record for this book has been requested.

ISBN 0-415-09350-3 (hbk)
ISBN 0-415-09351-1 (pbk)

Contents

Contributors

Adam Blatner, MD, TEP, Board Certified in Child and Adult Psychiatry, is an Associate Professor on the faculty of the University of Louisville School of Medicine, Kentucky, and is the author of the well-known books *Acting-In* and *Foundations of Psychodrama*, and, with his wife Allee, *The Art of Play*. Through writing and teaching he continues to develop the theoretical foundations of psychodrama and its practical applications in society.

Leif Dag Blomkvist, TEP, is a psychodramatist certified by the American and Nordic Boards of Examiners in Psychodrama. He is the Director of the Swedish Moreno Institute and founded a hospital Psychodrama Department in Lund, Sweden, where he worked for ten years. He is a contributing author in Sweden, Germany and the USA in the specialist area of surplus reality.

Dalmiro M. Bustos qualified as a medical doctor in 1956 and worked as a psychiatrist in mental hospitals in the USA from 1957 to 1962. He is Professor of Psychopathology, Psychotherapy and Depth Psychology at the University of Cordoba in Argentina. He trained as a psychodramatist with J.L. and Zerka Moreno at Beacon, New York, and is the Director of the J.L. Moreno Institute in Buenos Aires and São Paulo. He is the author of nine books on psychodrama and conducts training groups in South America and Europe.

Linnea Carlson-Sabelli, PhD, TEP, is Director of the Psychodrama Program at Rush–Presbyterian St Luke's Medical Center, Chicago. She is known for her pioneering work enriching sociometry by mathematically quantified contradiction, ambiguity and ambivalence in interpersonal relationships. The Rush Psychodrama Program sponsors a broad range of educational and clinical activities, including a certified programme in Therapeutic Children's Theatre, and offers a unique opportunity to integrate psychodrama training with post-graduate education in nursing.

Max Clayton, BA(Hons), ThD, TEP, is the Director of the Australian College of Psychodrama in Melbourne. He was trained as a psychodramatist at the Moreno Institute in Beacon, New York, between 1967 and 1973. He was founding director of the Psychodrama Institute of Western Australia in 1971 and of the Wasley Centre in Perth in 1975. In 1980 he founded the Australian and New Zealand Psychodrama Association and was its first President. He regularly conducts training workshops in psychodrama and group work in Australia, New Zealand and Europe.

Ann E. Hale, MA, TEP, is the Director of the American Sociometric Institute, Roanoke, Virginia, and the current President of the American Society of Group Psychotherapy and Psychodrama. She is the author of *Conducting Clinical Sociometric Explorations* (at present under revision) and is the Editor of the Student Edition of J.L. Moreno's book *Who Shall Survive*, published in 1993.

Paul Holmes, PhD, MRCPsych, is a psychodramatist in private practice and a consultant child and adolescent psychiatrist in the National Health Service. He was co-editor (with Marcia Karp) of the book *Psychodrama: Inspiration and Technique*. His book *The Inner World Outside: Object Relations Theory and Psychodrama* reflects his interest in the integration of the theories of psychodrama, psychoanalysis and family therapy. He is active in the development of psychodrama training standards through his work on committees of the British Psychodrama Association, the UK Council for Psychotherapy and through his work in Western Europe and Russia.

Marcia Karp, MA, TEP, is the pioneer of psychodrama in Great Britain and is known in many countries as one of the world's top practitioners and trainers. She completed her training as a Director of Psychodrama with J.L. and Zerka Moreno at the Moreno Institute and is now Co-Director of Training, the Holwell Centre for Psychodrama. Marcia also works as a lecturer, writer and crisis intervener and has set up a psychotherapy practice in a Devon general practitioner service which involves both doctors and patients. She is the Honorary President of the British Psychodrama Association and a Fellow of the American Society for Group Psychotherapy and Psychodrama. She co-edited the book *Psychodrama: Inspiration and Technique*.

Peter Felix Kellermann, PhD, is a clinical psychologist and Director of the Jerusalem Center for Psychodrama and Group Work. He was trained at the Moreno Institute in Beacon, New York, and was awarded the Zerka T. Moreno Award in 1993. He is the author of the book *Focus on Psychodrama*, which presents a systematic analysis of the essential therapeutic ingredients of psychodrama. He now teaches psychodrama in Israel, as well as in Scandinavia.

Martti Lindqvist is a sociodrama director, writer and trainer who lives in Mantyharju, Finland. He has a doctorate in theology and his academic fields include social ethics and bioethics. He has worked as a columnist for the leading Finnish newspaper *Helsingin Sanomat* for seventeen years. Martti Lindqvist has acted as the Chairman of the Finnish Psychodrama Association and is at present chairing the ethical committee of that Association. He has published twenty books and received awards for his publishing both from the state and church in Finland.

René F. Marineau, PhD, is a psychoanalyst and psychodramatist. He is a Professor of Psychology at the University of Quebec, Trois-Rivières, where he specialises in history and epistemology of psychotherapy. He is an original member of the International Association of the History of Psychoanalysis and the author of the biography of J.L. Moreno. He is the founder and Director of the Centre International de Psychothérapie Expressive, where he practices and teaches an approach that integrates the theories of Moreno, Freud, Reich and Rogers.

Jonathan D. Moreno, TEP, is professor of Paediatrics and of Medicine (Bioethics) and Director of the Division of Humanities at the State University of New York Health Science Centre, Brooklyn. He has published widely on subjects in bioethics, and has conducted psychodrama workshops in the United States and abroad for many years. He is a Fellow of the American Society of Group Psychotherapy and Psychodrama.

Zerka T. Moreno is the doyenne of psychodrama practice, who has trained group psychotherapists and psychodramatists in many countries. Until 1982 she directed the Moreno Institute in Beacon, New York (founded by her husband, J.L. Moreno) – the original and world centre of psychodrama. She has served as President of the American Society of Group Psychotherapy and Psychodrama.

Thomas Rützel, Diploma Psychologist in Germany, works in private practice as a psychotherapist and is a certified psychodrama leader from the Swedish Moreno Institute. He has contributed articles in German on archetypes in the psychology of men's issues.

Hector Sabelli, MD, PhD, has degrees from the University of Buenos Aires and was formerly Professor and Chairman of the University of Rosario in Argentina. He is currently Professor of Pharmacology and Psychiatry at Rush University in Chicago. His research ranges from the biochemistry of depression, to mathematical methods in sociometry, and from electrocardiography to dramatherapy. Among other awards in psychiatry, he has received the Zerka T. Moreno Award.

Ken Sprague has become an inspiration to many in taking psychodrama beyond the clinic. He travels regularly training social workers, businessmen, trade unionists, church groups, and men's groups in Finland, Norway and other countries. He is Co-Director of the Holwell Centre and is a certified Sociodrama Director with the Australian and New Zealand Psychodrama Association. Ken is a printmaker and illustrated the book *Psychodrama: Inspiration and Technique*, as well as contributing a chapter describing his clinical work as a psychodramatist.

Michael Watson, MA, Cert Ed, Dip Psych, tragically died during the last stages of the production of this book. He was Principal Psychotherapist (Psychodrama) in the Department of Psychotherapy in the North Staffs. Health Authority. He was a Registered Primary Trainer and Practitioner with the British Psychodrama Association, of which he was at his death Chair. His main interest was in integrating psychodrama with other forms of psychotherapy, and with colleagues he ran diploma courses in Integrative Psychodrama and Integrative Psychotherapy.

Mónica Zuretti, MD, is a graduate of the Medical School of the Universidad Nacional in Buenos Aires. She trained as a psychodramatist at the Moreno Institute in New York with J.L. and Zerka Moreno. In Argentina she has worked both in state hospitals and private practice in her institute, The Zerka Moreno Centre for Psychodrama and Sociodrama. She has also trained psychodramatists on all five continents. She is a founder member of the Sociedad Argentina de Psicodrama and Vice-President of the International Association of Group Psychotherapy. She is the author of many articles and books on psychodrama and sociodrama, including *Sangre, odio y amor* and *El color de la mezcla*.

Foreword

Zerka T. Moreno

Turning the pages of this book, pondering, I wonder: what would Moreno think about this, his offspring's product? He would be delighted to know and it might even humble him, that he continues to occupy and stimulate those who come after him. He would say, as he often did after a satisfactory piece of his own work was accomplished: 'Wir haben's herrlich weit gebracht'. (We have brought it excellently far).

As a thinker, Moreno is often declared to be unclear; some of his postulates are not framed in terms normally understood by those who practise critical thinking. For those, the poetic–inspirational aspect of his work clouds his scientific exposition. As the personal part of my relationship with him recedes in time, the totality of this man's being emerges more and more for me. It was his spirit that captivated me from the start. I was young, naive and even ignorant, but something about the way he was wrapped itself around me, awed and inspired me and drew me to him. I told myself: 'This man is a genius. I am not likely to meet his equal in this lifetime.'

My sense is that Moreno did not belong in this time or place; if anything, he belonged to the ages. He was not of this family or that family, not of a single nationality or possibly even a single gender as his sensibility was often what we designate as female. Touchingly, Doris Twitchell Allen spoke of him as being 'an element, like the sky or the ocean'. It may well be one reason why he was so misunderstood, at least in his earlier years; but then, all who are of that nature are misunderstood. Yet, curiously, on some levels, he was almost primitive in spite of that very great gift of 'seeing people'.

He helped people to go beyond the mundane, to expand; that is what he meant when he said to Freud: 'I teach people to dream again'. He meant, of course, bigger and better dreams, perhaps for the central European Freud, too American an idea.

Some years ago a number of American colleagues met to discuss which of Moreno's ideas they thought had made its mark on them and they presented a list. I also tried to make a list, which ran to several pages and included the following. The importance of personal encounter; spontaneity and creativity; cultural conserves which inhibit spontaneity and creativity; tele; action precedes speech; speech is a later development and is not the royal route to the psyche; interactional learning; we cannot separate the body from the psyche; the importance of groups; a healthy model for our dealings with people rather than a sickness model; we are co-creators of our world and the cosmos; personal responsibility; the healer within.

I also remembered some of the key things he said that have stayed with me. First, that a truly therapeutic procedure cannot have less an objective than the whole of mankind. Second, his definition of group psychotherapy: one person the therapeutic agent of the other, one group the therapeutic agent of the other. Third, that psychodrama is the exploration of the subjective truth of the protagonist by methods of spontaneous dramatic improvisation. There were several more things I noted down about his creation psychodrama: that the catharsis of integration is best reached via action and interaction; that the catharsis of the actor augments the catharsis of the spectator; that every true second living through of an experience is the relief and release from the first; that when reality is too oppressive, we need to go beyond it, into the realm of surplus reality, into what might have or should have been; that our experiences are based upon our perception of these events and persons and that perceptions are subject to change.

There were six important subsections to interpersonal relationships that I learnt from him. First, that two healthy persons can have a healthy relationship, mutually productive and supportive. Second, that two otherwise healthy persons can have a disturbed relationship. Third, that one healthy and one sick person can have a healthy relationship, mutually satisfying and beneficial. Fourth, a healthy person and an unhealthy one can have a pathological relationship, which can be mutually destructive. Fifth, that two so-called sick persons can have a healthy relationship, one person as the therapeutic agent of the other. Sixth, that two disturbed individuals can have a disturbed relationship, in which they further contribute to the disturbance.

Moreno gave us practical tools with which to work: the psychodrama and its various techniques, action therapy in dramatic form; the sociometric test; the acquaintance test; the sociogram; the sociomatrix; the role diagram; the spontaneity test; spontaneity training (an apparent oxymoron); the role test; role training; role creating; surplus reality.

This was some of my list. No doubt there are many more that you can bring to mind. The list is for your augmenting. Perhaps the best way to evaluate a creative person's contribution is to consider what our life would be like if he had not been here in our time. What would we be doing in education, psychotherapy, social psychology and sociology, to mention but a few categories, if we did not have these riches that he left us?

This book will bring some of these ideas into further relief.

This book is dedicated to
Michael Watson
who died during the final stages of its production. Mike, a friend to many colleagues and an inspiration to his students, was a pioneer in the field of psychodrama in Great Britain. His warmth, humour, creativity and integrity will be much missed.

Zerka T. Moreno   Jacob Levy Moreno

Introduction

Paul Holmes and Michael Watson

> We shall not cease from exploration
> And the end of all our exploring
> Will be to arrive where we started
> And know the place for the first time.
>
> T.S. Eliot, *Little Gidding*

This book examines those key concepts which are identified with psycho-drama. Each author has taken a key Morenian concept and describes how it has inspired their clinical work as a psychodramatist. T.S. Eliot talks about starting at the end and how the end is often the beginning. We begin therefore with what Moreno has left us. None of Moreno's concepts was a finished product. He called such phenomena cultural conserves, advocat-ing that we should do away with those that stifled our spontaneity and creativity whilst using others as springboards towards creative and spontaneous activity.

Jacob Levy Moreno was born in Bucharest in 1889 and died in New York in 1974. He was a large man with a large vision, and a controversial figure in his lifetime. He left the world a rich and diverse legacy, which includes his creative views on philosophy and religion as well as the powerful and exciting methods of psychodrama and sociodrama. Each contributor to this book has approached a general concept in their own individual way and has left a glimpse of the colourful tapestry that was the man. Some have reflected his scientific and empirical interests, some his human concerns whilst others emphasise his philosophical, psychospiritual and cosmic aspects. All show his creativity and how it has grown through them in different ways. The range of styles and content in this book reflect Moreno's creative heritage; they show just how far he travelled across disciplines and demonstrate that he was often in the vanguard of philo-sophical and therapeutic developments in the early part of this century. The breadth and richness of psychodrama gives it a central place within the wider context of other schools of group psychotherapy, many of which share common roots in Moreno's work.

Dr Moreno's legacy is clearly linked to his own complex and divergent roots. He was the first of six children born to a mother who, at his birth, was just 15 years old. The family moved to Vienna in 1894, where Moreno remained until 1925. He studied philosophy and medicine at Vienna University from 1909–17 and his first appointments were as a director of a children's hospital and a superintendent of a resettlement community. In 1919 he became a general practitioner in Bad Voslau, a small town south of the city, where he used a form of family therapy in the community which was certainly a forerunner of later clinical work in this field. While in Vienna he was involved in the early developments in existential philosophy and a key figure in the artistic and dramatic life of the city. He experimented, both as a student and later, in four important areas which were to have a significant influence on his later work.

First, his informal playful encounters with children in the city parks helped him develop his ideas about play and dramatic re-enactment. Second, in Das Stegreiftheater or the Theatre of Spontaneity (which still exists in Vienna as a theatre of improvisation) he extended this work with a group of actors, challenging the preconceived ideas about theatre and breaking down the cultural conserves. His third area of experimentation was his work with the socially disadvantaged, such as groups of prostitutes, which laid the foundations for his later systematised group work. Last, his activities with the Daimon group, a loose-knit association of Viennese artists, thinkers and writers who were connected with the literary magazine of same name which Moreno edited, saw the flourishing of his free-thinking artistic spirit.

When he emigrated to the USA in 1925, Moreno began his more formal contributions to group psychotherapy and to psychodrama, sociometry and the encounter movement. He developed his theories during his initiatives in prisons, reform schools and hospitals. In 1932 he coined the term group psychotherapy and his influence was powerful in the early development of these therapies. In New York, in 1936, he founded the Beacon Hill Sanitarium in New York for the practice and teaching of psychodrama and this was followed in 1942 by institutes in New York City for the training of group psychotherapists and psychodramatists. He started influential journals in the field and founded the American Society of Group Psychotherapy & Psychodrama and the International Committee of Group Psychotherapy in 1951. He died in 1974 after a lifetime of pioneering work in the field of group psychotherapy (see Marineau 1989).

To make a beginning on his life's work seems a daunting task. He was not the most organised of theorists, as is indicated by some of the authors, and as a consequence the breadth of his vision and philosophy is not always recognised. Nor perhaps is his influence on the wider world of psychotherapy and the study of human interactions acknowledged, but his ideas undoubtedly inspired and informed the work of others, although the direct links may now be lost. We hope the reader will become, in the process of reading these chapters, awakened to the originality of Moreno's thinking.

In her Foreword to this book, Zerka T. Moreno, Moreno's professional and personal partner, comments on some of the reasons why his ideas have not found as wide an acceptance or acknowledgement as have those of his contemporaries. Blatner and Blatner (1988: 32–42) suggest other resistances to psychodrama and to Moreno's concepts and philosophy. Maybe the time has come for his ideas to be clearly identified as relevant and important to other schools of psychotherapy.

This book has been divided into three main Parts, each introduced by a commentary.

The first Part, 'Encounter as the principle of change', consists of three chapters which, through the style of their authors, convey both the spirit and form of psychodrama. The discussions of Moreno's philosophy, and of his concepts of creativity, spontaneity, locus, status nascendi and matrix, introduce readers to the core of the theory and practice of psychodrama.

The second Part, 'The locus and status nascendi of psychodrama', considers the place and time of the creation of psychodrama in the light of Moreno's own history. In Chapter 4, René Marineau, Moreno's biographer, describes the origins of the man and the method of group psychotherapy he created and gives the reader some historical background. The responses of Moreno to the influences of the time and place when he first began to mould his theories have a particular relevance to an understanding of psychodrama.

In Chapter 5, Moreno's son, Jonathan, considers the complex moral and ethical issues that arise from J.L. Moreno's concerns with both the treatment of individuals and groups and the artistic creativity of the theatre. The breadth of his ideas and interests, understandable in the context of his life in Vienna, resulted in a group method that straddles psychotherapy, education and the theatre, a position that, at times, presents psychodramatists with professional and clinical dilemmas.

The third Part, 'The matrix of psychodrama', considers the forms of modern psychodrama through the discussion of seven issues or concepts central to Moreno's work. The commentary considers the way in which these concepts reflect the nature of Moreno's psychology in terms of his own fields of academic study and the complex dynamics within his own psyche. It then lays out in more detail the rationale behind the ordering of the last seven chapters. They have been grouped into four clusters to help establish the relationships between the concepts under consideration and their relationship with other schools of psychotherapy.

The first of these clusters, which we have called 'The cognitive and conscious dimension', considers role theory (Chapter 6) and sociometry (Chapter 7).

The next two clusters concern the psychospiritual (or transpersonal) and the unconscious dimensions in psychodrama. Chapters 8 and 9 deal with Moreno's ideas about religion and spiritual life and his concept of the co-unconscious, an idea that has much in common with W.R. Bion's psychoanalytic theories of group processes. Chapter 10 discusses Moreno's concept of surplus reality, a challenging idea that is a principle feature of psychodrama which distinguishes it from other methods of psychotherapy.

We have called the final group of chapters 'The interpersonal dimension'. The first concept considered, role reversal, deals concretely with the process of 'changing places' with a significant other (Chapter 11) whilst the final chapter discusses tele, the mental and affective process that moulds our relationships with others (Chapter 12). We indicate in our commentary to Part III, that this way of mapping Moreno's ideas, i.e. into clusters, fails to adequately satisfy all the complex and rich nuances of Morenian theory. Indeed, the last two concepts – role reversal and tele – have features that could place them in more than one of the previous clusters. However, we felt that these could only be given full justice by indicating their emphasis on human interactions. But whereas role reversal has a more conscious dimension, tele undoubtedly involves unconscious processes.

And so we come to the beginning once again. Recent publications on psychodrama emphasise the use of psychodrama as a form of psychotherapy (Holmes 1992; Kellermann 1992; Kipper 1986). Whilst not wanting to undervalue the very important alignment of psychodrama to the profession of psychotherapy, a focus on clinical applications may risk the loss of some of the other significant contributions of Moreno. A process of integration with other therapeutic models, especially those associated with psychoanalysis, whilst enriching psychodrama, risks the loss of Moreno's emphasis on the importance of the transpersonal or psychospiritual aspects of our relationships and the philosophical concepts which are essential to understanding psychodrama.

We hope this book will introduce the central ideas of Moreno's psychology and its innovative practice to readers new to psychodrama in a way that will inspire them to be more creative in their work. We also trust that it will re-introduce the concepts to others already familiar with Moreno's work, in a way that both illuminates his psychology and challenges them to create a new fusion of ideas and action that will lead their work into more direct encounters with clients.

That Moreno was undoubtedly one of the most dynamic and courageous pioneers in the development of group psychotherapy, as well as an inspirational and original thinker, is evident in these pages written by some of his most inspired students.

REFERENCES

Blatner, A. and Blatner, A. (1988) *Foundations of Psychodrama: History, theory and practice*, New York: Springer.

Holmes, P. (1992) *The Inner World Outside: Object relations theory and psychodrama*, London: Tavistock/Routledge.

Kellermann, P.F. (1992) *Focus on Psychodrama: The therapeutic aspects of psychodrama*, London: Jessica Kingsley.

Kipper, D.A. (1986) *Psychotherapy Through Clinical Role-Playing*, New York: Brunner/Mazel.

Marineau, R.F. (1989) *Jacob Levy Moreno 1889–1974: Father of psychodrama, sociometry and group psychotherapy*, London: Tavistock/Routledge.

Part I

Encounter as the principle of change

Commentary

The first three chapters demonstrate the clinical excitement and thera-peutic power of psychodrama to create change and reflect on how the method entails more than the sum of its parts.

In the first chapter Ken Sprague takes the reader right to the heart of psychodrama through the discussion of the central tenets of Moreno's philosophy: time, space, reality and cosmos. These concepts challenge the reductionist model of some other psychotherapies (which see the cause of human distress as lying within the individual) and establish psychodrama's difference, and indeed potential for alienation, from the scientific, medical model, that underpins psychoanalysis and psychiatry.

In the second chapter, Marcia Karp takes two of the cornerstones of Moreno's theories, creativity and spontaneity (which together he believed to be the greatest of human resources), and shows passionately how they can inform the work of the psychodramatist. She gives examples of some of the ways the therapist can transform a group's experience of itself. Reflecting both the authenticity and inspirational qualities of psycho-drama, she guides the reader through moving accounts demonstrating how an appreciation and application of these concepts can transform a situation towards both problem solving and health.

In the third chapter Dalmiro Bustos considers and develops Moreno's ideas on the locus, matrix and status nascendi. These concepts refer to the place and time at which something originates and its final form. Their use in clinical practice allows for links to be made between the source of emotional problems and the methods that may bring about change. Some psychodramatists are perhaps not fully conversant with the potential of these ideas; they are, however, central to Moreno's metapsychology.

Moreno was a charismatic figure and there is a clear line of inheritance among the generation of directors trained by him. Two of the authors in this section, Dalmiro Bustos and Marcia Karp, worked with Moreno at Beacon. Each of these chapters has a directness which we hope will excite and instruct readers, both those who are new to psychodrama and those who are familiar with the method.

Chapter 1

Time, space, reality and the cosmos
The four universals of Moreno's philosophy

Commentary

The long tradition of folk tales that make sense of the world and hold a culture together find expression in our first chapter in which Ken Sprague breaks with academic tradition and uses his own creative technique of story-telling to introduce us to psychodrama and to the four fundamentals of Moreno's philosophy: time, space, reality and the cosmos.

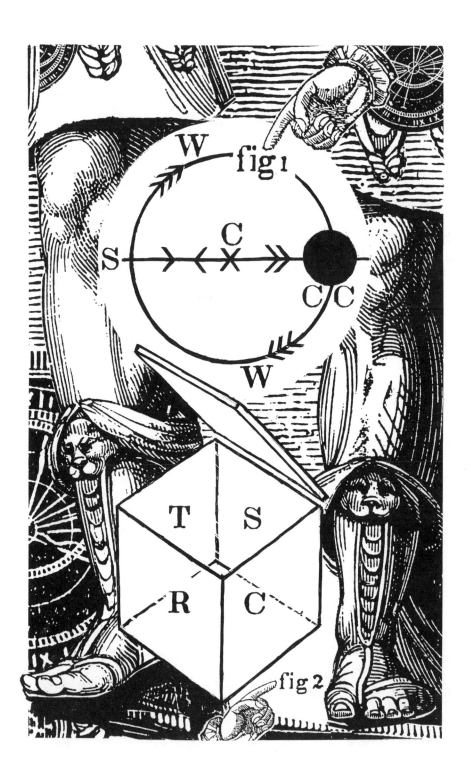

Stepping into the cosmos with our feet on the ground

Ken Sprague

Imagination is more important than knowledge.
> (Einstein 1932, quotation on poster
> of the Hebrew University of Jerusalem)

I am fascinated by the connection of psychodrama, books and story-telling. For me, every session opens an illustrated book of the protagonist's life.

Page after page, past, present and future of a group member's experience and dreams are re-created before our eyes. Things that didn't happen and perhaps should have happened are given life at last. Psychodrama is about what didn't happen as well as what did.

It all takes place in the time slot of the here and now. The group's energy flows to the stage in support of the protagonist. Each member waits, willingly available to be an auxiliary if called upon. The seeds of change are sown.

Stories and pictures have always caught my imagination. My hard-earned wages as a 13-year-old baker boy were spent within minutes of payment. I ran all the way to an antiquarian bookshop to buy bound but battered Saturday magazines. On one wondrous occasion the kindly bookseller let me have an *Arabian Nights, The Thousand and One Tales* printed in 1835, price threepence.

Before buying, I insisted the books be illustrated with black-and-white wood engravings. These were often crude apprentice work owing more to travellers' tales and the imagination of the artists than to their actual knowledge. (Some of these engravings are the basis of the montage illustrations in this book.)

Imagine my delight when, years later, Danny Yashinsky of the Toronto School of Story-telling gave me the following quotation:

> Besides the drama the thing that influenced me most was the tales of A Thousand and One Nights. To be perfectly honest with you, I really owe it to those Tales and to the tremendous world of Persia and how roles were played then on the reality level in the streets of Baghdad and

how it was told to us in such a wonderful fashion. And so if you want to become a role-player you ought to read that book again. It contains all we want to tell you tonight.

(Moreno 1948, unpublished transcript of a
psychodrama session in New York City)

Because of the importance of all this to me, this personal view of Moreno's philosophy is presented with stories and with comments. I want to tell what, for me, psychodrama's underlying philosophy is about, to show how it can be enjoyed and to suggest ways of discovering its relevance for us all as we approach the twenty-first century.

First story

Dr Moreno was walking on Columbus Circle in New York City. A policeman and a black man were having an argument. Moreno entered the situation and said, 'Excuse me, I'm a psychiatrist. Can I help?' Whereupon the two were each asked their side of the story. It ended with the black man being allowed to go on his way.

(Z. Moreno 1993, personal communication)

Moreno didn't pass by on the other side of the street thinking it was none of his business. He didn't dismiss the event as a case of a policeman doing his job. He didn't ease his conscience with the idea that the black man was, in all probability, a villain deserving retribution. He went over and got involved. He poked his nose in. Most importantly he took his professionalism beyond his doctor's office to show that psychodrama belongs in the street as well as in the clinic. The ongoing problem is that often we leave our skills in the therapy room and meanwhile the world proceeds to go horribly mad!

James Hillman looks at it from another angle:

Every time we try to deal with our outrage over the freeway, our misery over the office and the lighting and the crappy furniture, the crime in the streets, whatever – every time we try to deal with that by going to therapy with our rage and fear, we're depriving the political world of something.

(Hillman 1992: 5)

Surely Moreno anticipated this dilemma when he designed psychodrama as a life tool not just something for use in the clinic. He makes it explicit when he asks us to see ourselves operating responsibly in three dimensions – the personal, the social and the cosmic. There's nothing mystical about it, he's simply saying, keep our feet fair and square upon the ground, attempting to solve its problems even as we reach for the stars: it's all connected.

Second story

My partner, Marcia Karp (who was trained by Moreno), and myself attended the Eleventh International Congress of Group Psychotherapy in Montreal. On the second day we were walking in the Congress Plaza. It was early evening with a grey sky and a hint of rain to come.

Two elderly Chinese were doing Tai-chi, their movements emphasising the emptiness of the ugly concrete complex and its surrounding space. A young woman entered from the far corner of the Plaza and walked, head down, towards us. We had seen her in the Congress Hall earlier and knew that she was from one of the East European delegations. She caught sight of us, hesitated for a moment, and then veered away. Clearly something was wrong.

Marcia and I had been enjoying being together after a hectic day of plenary sessions, workshops and crowded meetings with friends old and new – the stuff of international congresses.

Marcia let go of my hand, went straight up to the young woman and said quietly, 'You look tearful; would you like a hug?' The two women held each other while the younger one cried. After a while she raised her head, looking somewhat embarrassed. Marcia said quickly, 'May I double you?' There was a grateful nod and Marcia stood alongside the young woman, adopted the same slightly stooped position, the same embarrassed expression and said, 'I can't stand being treated like a pauper. Nobody understands how I feel.'

The young woman gestured with her hand in a secretive behind-the-back movement and said, 'Yes, they are putting money in my hands as if it's a dark secret. I don't want their dollars.'

Marcia (as the double) said, 'I feel terrible. They make me feel cheap. How can I tell them that inside I feel richer than they are.'

'Yes, yes. How can I tell them of the richness of my own culture?' replied the young woman with energy.

We then heard the tale of coming from Eastern Europe (in itself no small task at that time) into the unhuman scale of the Palais de Congrès and opulence of the hotels used by the delegates. We heard of misunderstandings about money and of thinking that the expensive Congress fee (enormous by eastern European standards) included accommodation. Instead there were fees for everything: fees for breakfast and fees for coffee; fees for lunch, dinner, and for taxis to and from the proceedings. Our new friend had hardly eaten since arriving in Montreal.

All this at a congress entitled, 'Love and Hate – Toward Resolving Conflict in Groups, Families and Nations'.

Dr Moreno in New York and Marcia Karp in Montreal took the simple and direct action of poking their noses in.

There are three things that strike me about their two encounters:

HOW they did it. This I would call technique and personal style: both are important in psychodrama.
WHY they did it. This could be called theory – an understanding of which is essential for all practising the method.
THAT they did it. This I would call philosophy.

The philosophy of the 'encounter', the meeting of two people, is propelled by a spontaneous response to a situation and is open to the idea of an immediate creative exchange in the here and now.

The idea is of men and women as personal and social beings but also as 'cosmic' beings, that is as people needing to arrange their individual and collective behaviour in order that life can continue not just to survive but to survive with love. This is the goal that Moreno sought and the reason he developed psychodrama. It's an honouring of creation.

Betty Gallagher points out that 'poking one's nose in' is not a job for the faint-hearted, it takes courage. I agree, but it's more than courage. It needs a deep commitment to the craft of learning and understanding what's going on in the world around us. We must bring appropriate techniques into action, adding to and changing them if required. In other words, it means doing our homework, continually training spontaneity and developing creativity.

The following editor's note gets at the essence of my Montreal story: 'the importance of living one's truth in action; the validity of subjective reality; the premise of a here-and-now encounter between individuals (including client and therapist), and a deep egalitarianism' (Fox 1987: 3). The quotation is taken from *The Essential Moreno* edited by Jonathan Fox. It is a book which is, for me, a wonderful source of understanding. Chapter 1 on 'The four universals' is the best introduction to his philosophy that Moreno gave us. Often ahead of his time, when he set down the four universals in 1966, he was very much a man 'of' his own time. In the same year, Paul Abrecht, of the World Council of Churches, called for world economic justice and welfare provision. This was four years before Rachel Carson released *Silent Spring* (1965), an angry and challenging book demanding that we stop the destruction of our planet. This book was a great voice for the protection of our natural habitat; a demand that we love life.

Two years later Moreno delivered a paper at the University of Barcelona called 'Universal peace in our time'. The paper contained his famous statement that 'A truly therapeutic procedure can not have less an objective than the whole of mankind' (Moreno 1968: 175).

Moreno regarded this quotation as his best known opus. It forms the single opening sentence to *Who Shall Survive*, a title he coined to indicate that the fate of humankind may be imminently at stake. He was 'of his time' because the rest were catching up and being more specific about what was wrong.

As we approach the end of the century the industrial nations are crazily in pursuit of materialism while the other half of the world's people starve. Pollution of the shoreline and seas is greater than ever. Oil tanker disasters are almost commonplace and the leader writers still treat 'wild life' as something separate and not affecting our own life.

Professor Trevor Haywood calls it 'non-logic' in a brilliant video, *Managing for Absurdity*: 'Pollute and poison the world that is essential for our survival in order to manufacture artefacts that are not essential but provide transient pleasure or just marginally improve our convenience' (Haywood 1992). Journalist John Pilger reminds those young people who, to their credit worked so hard for Live Aid, just where real power lies:

> How many of us were aware during 1985 – the year of the Ethiopian famine and of 'Live Aid' – that the hungriest countries in Africa gave twice as much money to us in the West as we gave to them: billions of dollars just in interest payments.
>
> (Pilger 1991: 64)

Within the rich nations the gap between the haves and have-nots increasingly widens. Health care deteriorates, crime rises, drug abuse is at epidemic proportions; the arms trade is a 'growth' industry and people die by its products both overseas and at home. In Britain we have an ongoing war that has claimed more than three thousand English, Irish, Scottish and Welsh lives.

The politicians come out with the same threadbare ideas: more police, more guns and more military. A retiring military commander hands it back to the politicians saying the only solution will have to be a 'political one'. It's Tweedledum and Tweedledee, with death for both Tweedles.

New ideas, new dreams, a vision powered by spontaneity and creativity were never more relevant. Maybe psychodrama's underlying philosophy is an idea whose time has come? 'Man fears spontaneity, just like his ancestor in the jungle feared fire; he feared fire until he learned how to make it. Man will fear spontaneity until he will learn how to train it' (Moreno 1953: 47). I would like to update the last sentence of that quotation: 'Men and women will fear spontaneity and creativity until they learn how to re-train them.'

When we are small children, those life-giving qualities burst forth in all directions. It's only when the sausage machines of school, jobs and society get to work on us that those gifts of childhood go into retreat. They hide away and we end up fearing them.

Moreno saw his philosophy hidden away in dusty libraries. In the 1990s I see his ideas as relevant to our times and being reconsidered. The students enrolling for training in psychodrama all over the world may be the ones to give them life in the coming century. As new centurians they will face obstacles to creative change in human behaviour that are colossal. The Goliaths are bigger than ever and in the climate of current world reaction the Davids may be smaller.

There is, however, an important difference. The Davids now have Davidas alongside them, and often way out ahead. Women liberated! That, combined with our slingshot of spontaneity and creativity may yet give us the edge.

Third story

> In the 1960s when America was considering the bombing of China, Moreno proposed a psychodramatic encounter between President L.B. Johnson and China's Leader, Mao Tse-tung. He wanted it to be seen on television across the world.

The fact that it didn't happen does not mean that such encounters cannot happen. It's true, of course, that there are considerable obstacles. There is a somewhat understandable lack of interest, a feeling of 'I can't make any difference'.

This century has seen people's dreams and visions of the future smashed time and time again, promoting apathy and hopelessness. We get corrupted by our seeming powerlessness. Religious and social philosophies have become dull dogmas or oppressive scourges in the hands of priests and politicians. Helping people to dream again is no small undertaking.

Fourth story

> In 1912 when Freud asked the young Moreno what he was doing, he replied, 'Well, Dr Freud, I start where you leave off. You meet people in the artificial setting of your office; I meet them in the street and in their home, in their natural surroundings. You analyse their dreams; I try to give them the courage to dream again.'
>
> (J.L., Z. and J.D. Moreno 1964: 16)

Later in his life Moreno was a little less optimistic and well aware of the difficulties when he wrote:

> My philosophy has been misunderstood. It has been disregarded in many religious and scientific circles. This has not hindered me from continuing to develop techniques whereby my vision of what the world could be might be established in fact. It is curious that these techniques – sociometry, psychodrama, group therapy – created to implement an underlying philosophy of life have been almost universally accepted while the underlying philosophy has been relegated to the dark corners of library shelves or entirely pushed aside.
>
> (Moreno 1953)

Fifth story

A few years ago, trying to interest students in the underlying philosophy, I felt a bit isolated, stuck among wonderful techniques which would help patients, clients and students alike. It is clearly difficult to help individuals towards health while the collective body is so sick. The danger of training students, good at using the techniques but unable or unwilling to implement the underlying philosophical concepts the techniques were designed to bring about, has worried me for a long time. My attempts to interest people in the broader picture met with little success. A trusted colleague summed it up: 'I still don't accept that cosmic bullshit!' Then it hit me! Perhaps people could be interested in the ideas but was I presenting them in the wrong way?

The concepts should be 'shown' psychodramatically. It was time to take the advice suggested by my grandfather in the following story.

Sixth story

A man from Cornwall, interested in buying some horse harness from a dealer, said, 'You'll have to show me' (shades of Moreno) but the man from Devonshire, also interested in purchasing, said, 'You'll have to put it in my hand'.

It occurred to me that a philosophical model could be made, allowing people to 'see' the ideas, to play with them and discuss possible action for change.

THE HOLWELL BOX

There were many possibilities for constructing such a model – different shapes, sizes and materials. However there were four basics:

1 It must be big enough to be demonstrated in a group of 20–50 people.
2 It must be visually stimulating.
3 It must grow before people's eyes so that their imagination could be sparked and enactment and discussion promoted.
4 It must be transportable.

At the same time it must be possible to dismantle and rearrange the model so that people learn that just as they take a stand on important concepts they also constantly question the stand itself. They must take it in their hand, test it openly, otherwise dogma awaits us. The Holwell Box was my answer, born from these conditions.

THE FOUR UNIVERSALS – TIME, SPACE, REALITY, COSMOS

Seventh story

The first prototype was made at Riitta Vuorinens Institute in Finland. It consisted of a cardboard box given by the shop nextdoor. On the bottom we wrote SC (spontaneity and creativity). The remaining four sides we labelled T, S, R and C – Moreno's 'four universals' of time, space, reality and cosmos (See 'fig 2' in the montage illustration at the beginning of this chapter). The group divided into four smaller groups, taking time to choose with whom each person wanted to work.

After a few minutes of frenzied preparation, each group presented their view of one of the four universals. The presentations involved mime, dance, a tragic farce about reality and a discussion on cosmos. The latter took the form of the small group simply continuing their discussion preparation while the rest of us looked on. Each small group's work was extremely creative and served as a warm-up for the whole group. I drew Moreno's 'Canon of Creativity' diagram on to a large flipchart, intending to give a short lecture. However, the group was ready to go; the time for lecture or discussion was over; the group wanted action. We therefore made an action diagram, a big circle involving everyone. I had them move clockwise representing the field of rotating operations between spontaneity, creativity and cultural conserve. I asked them to chant in time to their movement and spontaneously they set the words 'warm-up' to the tune of a popular hymn. (Warm-up is the 'operational' expression of spontaneity.) I asked a young man in a grey jumper to pretend to go to sleep in the centre of the circle. He represented slumbering creativity (C).

If you look at the montage illustration at the beginning of this chapter, 'fig 1' is my own interpretation of Moreno's diagram from *Who Shall Survive* (Moreno 1953: 46).

The circle to which the finger points is our ring of moving people. A woman in a brightly coloured red dress not only volunteered to be 'Spontaneity' (S) but literally danced at the chance. She moved towards the circle centre ('C' in the illustration, representing creativity) and aroused him (S → C). The young man (C) opened his eyes and was responsive to dancing spontaneity (S ← C). Who wouldn't be! From their hilarious interaction the details of which can be imagined, a cultural conserve was born (S → C → CC). Cultural conserve (CC) is the end result of the creative act, including of course ourselves, or it can be a book, a painting, a loaf of good bread. All, given time, becomes worn, outdated or stale. Conversely, each also has the possibility of being the stimulus for new creativity.

This led us to explore the fact that cultural conserves are complex; they accumulate indefinitely and remain 'in cold storage'.

The group became a cultural conserve (CC) and froze, like statues in a museum's dusty storehouse. This caused some difficulty and head-scratching until the catalyst (S) 'Spontaneity', still dancing, came to revitalise them (CC → S → CC). Everyone was delighted at being reactivated. They were a sight for sore eyes; a group of friends who had together learned something of value and enjoyed themselves doing so.

Spontaneity does not operate in a vacuum, it moves towards creativity or towards conserves. The concept is fully explained in Moreno's tome *Who Shall Survive* (1953: 46) but I would urge you to activate it if you want people really to 'feel' that they understand it.

The philosophy of the spontaneity and creativity of every living person is, in my view, the basis of Moreno's ideas; that is why I made it the base of the Holwell Box. Moreno insists that the innate potential for spontaneous and creative action by individuals and groups represents untellable wealth. He builds upon this base a methodology of action that encourages us to release, develop and enlarge our own potential and the potential of others. In the process of reaching the limit of our creative potential the limit itself expands.

Joining our spontaneity and our creativity we can become our own gods. Each aspect needs the other in a creative relationship. If we fail to dovetail the two or get them in inadequate proportions, we can cause problems. My youth gave me hard lessons in that truism.

Eighth story

> Once there was a bullfight in the grand Roman arena at Nîmes in the South of France. The bull was large and the matador famous. I was eighteen with an English sense of fair play. The two together led me to jump into the ring in support of the bull. He was greatly outnumbered and cruelly wounded.
>
> My action was spontaneous but hardly creative. The bull did not speak English, was unimpressed by my assistance and active in urging me to leave the arena. The crowd agreed with the bull.
>
> I became a breathless example of spontaneous idiocy.

All psychodramatists need an ongoing commitment to learning. High on the learning list is the need to care for and develop our own spontaneous and creative gifts.

This applies to each of us and I suspect the greater our experience the more we need to polish and renew those gifts. Like spades and ploughshares, we should not allow them to rust. And yet, rust they do!

Ninth story

My partner and I were sitting in our dentist's waiting room. We both had appointments; mine was first.

Marcia was reading a magazine and another woman was turning the pages of an old colour supplement. Ironically enough, I was reading the chapter on spontaneity in my favourite book, *The Essential Moreno* (Fox 1987). The three of us were still and quiet. Four other occupants of the room were less so. A young mother was consoling a child beside her. The father was sitting slightly apart, pretending to read a car magazine while really anxiously watching a second child. She was alternately rolling on the floor or piling and demolishing toys in a corner of the room.

The child, aged about two and a half, selected three toys: a small cushion with a laughing face, a plastic doll and a large Welsh dragon. She carried this armful across the room and, full of confidence, arranged them on my lap. Her eyes tested me and she waited. I was flattered, put down my book and with exaggerated care looked at each of the toys. The cushion with the face was grotesque, the doll hard, cold and unhappy-making.

The dragon, in contrast, was soft, warm and the feel of it took me back to my own childhood and the little girl waiting at my knee. I made some friendly noises and replaced the dragon into my new friend's welcoming arms. At this point the mother said loudly, 'That man is reading his book.' The words halted the child and effectively excluded me. I felt robbed.

I wanted to say, the book in my hand is simply a lot of symbols on a page. In one sense it's quite dead, a cultural conserve, whereas the exchange with your daughter is pulsing with life. The book can be read some other time but there may be no other time for this encounter. Briefly, the child and I had been co-players. The mother's intervention had stopped the game and changed my role. If I had given voice to my feelings I would be engaged with the parents whereas the need of the moment was to stay in contact with the child.

The mother was acting out of concern or propriety or both. Perhaps she was also giving the message, 'Don't go with strangers.'

Suddenly it was my turn for the dentist's chair and I left the room. As the door closed behind me something wonderful happened. The small child took the toys once more and repeated her approach with my partner, Marcia. Once again the mother shouted, 'The lady is reading'. Both Marcia and the child were silenced by the maternal dictum and I suppose, and hope, the little girl took her wonder elsewhere.

In spite of her mother's censoring and our compliance, the girl's spontaneity remained intact and she came back for a second try. Her two-and-a-half-year-old spontaneous drive left all the adults far behind, their spontaneity and creativity corroding. But what of my own actions?

I regard myself as a spontaneous and creative man. There is some evidence to support that claim, yet, I watched as a delightful exchange was destroyed.

Why didn't I placate the parent quickly so that I could stay with the action? The dragon had a long, bright orange tongue. Jonathan Fox's book has a bright orange cover of the same brilliance. Being a paperback, it wobbles about like a tongue if held by its corner. The young child and I could both have held orange fire-tongued dragons in our hands. Fairyland and fantasy were ours for the taking. We both were robbed because my spontaneity, like spades and ploughshares, had become rusty. The parental dictum, 'They are reading their books', the assumed importance of adult behaviour over child's play and the decorum of the waiting room are all rust-makers. Each is in need of sand-blasting.

That illustration of the child in the dentist's waiting room has many connections for Morenian philosophy. I would like to consider three:

1 The primary importance of action.
2 The book as cultural conserve.
3 The role of the dreamer.

When the small girl courageously crossed the room, bearing toys, she used no words; her action was primary. Moreno called it the royal route to the psyche.

My response was important in developing the action she had begun. The way we both used eye contact, facial expression and, as trust was built, physical touch; each form of contact contributed. My vocal responses as the toys were given were acceptance noises, oohs and aahs rather than words.

By exercising sociometric choice the girl picked me to receive the toys. My book was no barrier to her action. Moreno would certainly have welcomed her initiative:

> From the point of view of a creative revolution, the book had become a symbol of a reactionary movement, not as much because of its contents but as *a form of creative behaviour*.
>
> Would God start the world by writing a book? Did He start the creation of the universe, billions of years ago, by writing the Genesis?
>
> (Moreno 1953: xvi)

Psychodrama is an action method growing from a system of theories that gives first place to creative action.

When the child held the dragon and I held the book that could have become a dragon, that was the moment of aborted creativity. In that second we lost the key of fantasy, the faculty of imagination. I gave up the role of dreamer. For me, and I believe for psychodrama, fantasy is not a road to escapism. Although in a given session fantasy may be used to escape from overwhelming sadness or stress, it is primarily a pathway towards reality. It is the dreamer's path.

When I started to work with Marcia Karp in 1973 I entered a psycho-dramatic dream.

Tenth story

There was a clear need for a permanent residential centre to establish the teaching and practice of the method in Britain. I had, two years previously, purchased a ruined hill farm in North Devon. The place was overgrown by trees and brambles. Wild creatures lived in rotting barns but it had the atmosphere of a forgotten Garden of Eden. It was the stuff of dreams and accordingly we dreamt.

Buildings with new purpose, colours and shapes arose in our imagination. Strange people and animals entered and acted out their lives and fantasies. Love was large within it all. Fantasy had become vision and vision became the process of visualising. We made drawings and little cardboard models but mostly we just built. My father and eldest son Sam helped.

Dream gradually became reality and vice versa.

It is important continually to link reality with fantasy so that we can participate in our own dreams. Even now, after twenty years, Holwell, the farm that grows people, remains, in part, a dream.

Our summer international workshop is an example. Sixty people from twenty-two different countries, using a mixture of languages, living and learning together; disagreeing and falling out, negotiating, trusting and loving. It all happens, it is all real but most important is the fantasy factor. What *can* happen? Will people dream again? What will each build, what will be built between them and what will they build when they return to their own lands?

THE BOX DEVELOPS

The second Holwell Box prototype was made in a Norwegian music school across the park from Edvard Munch's Museum. He was a painter who knew the effect of 'roles' on people and the Museum's conference hall with his great painting of the sun, cosmic in conception, would make a fantastic venue for psychodrama.

This time our box was more sophisticated – a lady's hat box. It had a tight-fitting lid and we had to cut a slot to get our fingers in to pull it off. The slot looked like a letter box so I had each member write their favourite technique on a piece of paper and 'post' it.

Role reversal, doubling, mirroring, warm-ups, cool-down ideas – the box was almost full – a philosophical model containing the techniques. For it to contain more (and there is more all the time, it's what this book is all about) the container must expand.

Someone produced a large knife from the kitchen. I cut the box apart and placed the base, spontaneity and creativity (SC) in the centre of the floor. The four sides, time, space, reality and cosmos (T, S, R, C) (see 'fig 2' on the montage illustration to this chapter) were taken to the four walls of the big room, leaving us with the slotted lid.

After discussion and humorous enactments, we labelled it 'Godhead' and hung it from a central-heating pipe high on the ceiling. It hung there, turning like a mobile, representing different things to different people. Most accepted 'Creation' as its name and the direct relationship to the label at our feet – our own creativity.

Eleventh story

A lady approached me at the Canadian Congress. She had been at the Norwegian music school session. She was enthusiastic for all we had learned and spoke of her own students' growing interest. I was delighted by her vibrancy but then she said what really caught her imagination had been 'the daring and dangerous way you opened the session'. Dangerous and daring? I had no such memory.

She continued, 'Yes, when you finished cutting the box apart, you threw the big knife and it stuck, quivering, in the floor – we were all riveted!'

There had in fact been no danger. I had stood in the centre of the big room with forty people sitting in a large circle around me. After cutting the box I dropped, rather than threw, the knife to the floor. In my youth I had worked in a circus and had been friends with the knife thrower. It was really a case of spontaneity meeting past experience. But it serves to remind us that a little show goes a long way! I think Dr Moreno would probably agree.

The box began to catch people's interest as a way of learning to see three-dimensionally, to think more broadly and to begin to act more in keeping with the unifying concepts of psychodrama. I do not wish to exaggerate: the box is simply a model; perhaps it can be a spur to making your own models and visual presentations.

BETTER BOX

The third prototype Holwell Box was made in the workshop of my village carpenter, Dave Cross. Village carpenters are people worth knowing! The assembled box is 1 foot square, brightly labelled and made of polished wood. The six pieces are held together with Velcro, Dave's idea. It has a separate stand which displays it on its corner where it can spin like the world and all the stars. It fits into a case and travels with me. Let us examine the four sides of the box and the 'four universals' in terms of therapeutic and educational procedures. We'll begin with time, space and reality.

TIME, SPACE AND REALITY

Twelfth story

Tess has Down's syndrome and at the time of this story was 18 years old. She rarely spoke, apart from one word, 'Naw!' That one word could be delivered in many ways, expressing mood, statement or question. Tess flailed her arms, hurting herself on table corners and school furniture. Anyone who got in the way could also receive a heavy blow. Although labelled violent, Tess was, for me, really incredibly frustrated. She was one of a group of young people with severe learning difficulties; an isolate taking little part in the group's activities.

We met as a 'life drama' class twice a week for two-hour sessions. In discussion the students had agreed on a four-week project on 'America'. Everyone, except Tess, wanted to become Dallas TV stars, gangster movie guys and dolls, or to visit 'diners' to eat hamburgers or hot dogs. New York meant a chance for the tall ones to be skyscrapers and the girl in a yellow jersey to be a New York taxi cab.

And so it was for several sessions. But then, my partner, Marcia, born in the Midwest, came to show her father's shoe store. I wanted the young people to see another America, one they didn't know about, one that would provide roles that would really challenge their imaginations.

We built the shop on the small-town market square. We emphasised the Revd Tom Wilson's sequence of scene-building – first there was space, then there were things in space, then there were people. One autistic youngster who declared himself a big-bang theorist objected to the 'Creation story'. This gave us the chance to slip in a mini-enactment of humankind re-inventing its own myths. Broaden our thinking and it's the same story. First, there was the big bang, then things evolved, then people. The classes are always conducted as a river of activity in which preconceived plans give way to the 'moment'.

The shop carpets were laid, the shelves stacked, and group members became farmers looking for working boots, housewives wanting sensible shoes and their daughters wanting anything but. Each role-player was encouraged to develop his or her own feeling for the part.

Daryl was different. He played Marcia's father, Jack, just as she had shown him – tall, upright, posing with his cigar. Jack didn't smoke the cigar. He posed with it, a symbol of the American businessman and also a reminder of exciting places that a small-town store owner would never visit – Bolivia, Havana and Brazil, birthplaces of cigars. We were all enjoying ourselves, none more so than Daryl.

I had taken Tess aside, my arm about her shoulders to stop her flailing arms from causing damage and hurt. After a while, her attention went to the stage area for the first time. She snuggled into me, enjoying the warmth of being held by teacher and returning it with her own affection. The tension left her body, a kind of 'oozing out' which told me that something was about to happen. The message was clearly communicated through body contact.

Suddenly, to everyone's amazement, Tess said in a loud voice, 'Light the cigar'.

Together we ran to the stage. Tess's hands, covered with sticking plasters from self-hurt, reached into her dress, produced an imaginary lighter, flicked it into flame and psychodramatically lit Jack's cigar.

It was a triumph. We cried and cheered.

That awakening could not have happened by sitting and talking. Tess didn't talk and couldn't sit for more than a few minutes. Her isolation kept her from contact, other than violent and largely accidental hitting.

TIME TRAVELLING

It could not have taken place without time, talked of not in the 1960s of Jack's actual shop but remade as a here-and-now 1960s. This concept of time allowed the past to be brought into the present and gave us all a glimpse of the future – a pointer of hope and change for Tess.

Looking at time in this way has important implications for personal, social and cultural behaviour. We can rehearse the future, try it on for size and not be punished for making mistakes.

CREATIVE SPACE

Space was the second essential, the filling of space with the shoe-shop details and character quirks of Jack's customers. Most therapy takes place in a space, a consulting room or hospital room which, apart from a chair or couch, is unrelated to the therapeutic process. The reforming of our space into a shop was imperative to what happened.

MANY-SIDED REALITY

Reality was more complex, a variety of perceptions that it was my job to bring together in a dramatic wholeness. Each role-player developed his or her own view of small-town America. They produced an aspect of American life they had never before considered; something demanding of their creativity. Marcia relived the reality of her youth again. I lived the reality of contacting the hidden Tess for the first time.

And Tess? Tess left the reality of her isolation, felt the reality of teacher's love and returned it. She entered the new reality of classroom activity and saw something that did not fit the reality of things she had seen. It raised the question within her, 'What's the point of having a cigar if you don't light it?' That led to her speaking and to her beautiful and hope-affirming action.

Let's look further at the question of creative space. Our local school of art is a large space, a concrete factory built at the top of a windswept hill. It is a mile and a half from the town centre and was purpose-built by economists with little knowledge of art or of artists. Architecturally they have turned a filing cabinet on its side and stuffed students into it. The classrooms are small and square with low ceilings. Windows face in any direction according to the room's position in a pile of rooms. It was not always so.

The old art school had studios with high ceilings and large north-facing windows. Rooms necessarily built on the south side were for storage, staff or offices. Most important of all, the school was set right on the quayside among the traffic, boats, ships, cranes, people and sea birds. The gulls could be fed from the windows. It was a place of creative learning, standing at the very heart of the town's daily creativity. The position that a learning space occupies within a community is of great importance.

At the back of the new art school and the technical college to which it is attached are two prefabricated huts for classes of young people with severe learning difficulties. The rooms are small and crowded with steel furniture, filing cabinets and sharp-cornered tables. The young people using these huts have many disabilities both mental and physical. It has taken some time for the huts to be fitted with ramps and only recently has some wheelchair access been arranged for the main college buildings.

The shed-like prefabrications were built to house a system designed to keep young disabled students apart from the college proper and out of the hair of the fast-moving society which the rest of the college serves. It does seem that society's understanding of human space and human scale is woefully inadequate. The rooms are suitable for teaching those able to absorb facts and may even be suitable for teaching people what to think. They most certainly are not suitable for teaching young people how to think, how to move or how spontaneously and creatively to express themselves. In working with young disabled people, stimulating environmental space is of prime importance. The rooms need to be less crowded and much more open; a changeable space in which mind, movement and emotions can be freed for action. Whatever the conditions, the psychodramatist has first to clear an area big enough for warm-up, enactment and sharing. The session can take place anywhere depending on the skill of the director and the willingness of his group, and I do mean anywhere – from the street or the football stadium to the clinic or classroom. Ideally, of course, the space will be specially constructed for action methods; it will have a stage area, a balcony, maybe theatre lights to help build up atmosphere and an audience area for those not involved in the action or waiting to be called upon to help. The reason for making this enactment area whether improvised or ideal is to give space for the group or individual member to work out a problem. The groundwork for my future understanding of the breadth of Moreno's space concept was laid in 1960. Although I did not appreciate it at the time, it brought together the four universals – time, space, reality and cosmos.

Thirteenth story

Radio and television networks told us that the world's first spaceman was orbiting Earth. Some people actually saw the ship just as satellites can nowadays be regularly seen passing across the heavens. As I looked for a sight of that first spacecraft, it occurred to me that it carried the Columbus of the twentieth century. A new era had been born and I felt that the young Russian cosmonaut on board, Major Uri Gagarin, was a man to meet and learn from. Fortunately, I had two partners who agreed – Ray Bernard and John Gorman. Humankind was at the point of important change. Our idea of space was being reassessed before our eyes.

Together with our friends, Dave Lambert (General Secretary), and Fred Hollingsworth (President of the Foundry Workers Union), we helped to bring Gagarin to England. At the union headquarters in Manchester he was given a gold medal which I had designed, and he was invested as an honorary member of the union. Major Uri, himself an ex-foundry worker, became the first, and, so far, only, space explorer member of a British trades union. It was the height of the Cold War, the visit took place against massive opposition from the giant of the British Establishment. A group of working-class Davids cut that Goliath down to size. They added a tiny victory to the struggle for peace on Earth.

Driving from Manchester airport to the headquarters of the Union, Gagarin was drenched by a torrential downpour. We had hired a Rolls Royce; it had been used by the Duke of Edinburgh in the previous month, was a brand new model and the only open-topped Rolls in Britain. A barbershop owner lent me a heap of hot towels and I went into the men's toilet with our interpreter and Uri to towel him dry. This was my one moment of intimate contact. I liked the man, and asked, somewhat naively, 'What did you feel up there?' Gagarin paused and said, 'A terrible beauty'. The first awe-inspiring sight of our blue planet was understandably beautiful. But terrible? I wondered. Gagarin caught my confusion and added, 'Who can I tell?' As he said so, a tear ran down the side of his nose. The first Columbus, the discoverer of America, had a crew with him on his journey into the unknown, albeit a mutinous one. But this second Columbus went alone, unknowing if he would ever return to Earth. Here was the bravest man I have ever met, yet his tear was as wet as mine.

Because of the euphoria of the moment and the success in actually getting this remarkable man to Manchester against all the odds, the full impact of his aloneness didn't hit me for years. His tender tear now brings home to me that human beings the world over are more alike than different.

My friend John Gorman recently (1993) wrote to me with a reminder that, when Gagarin arrived at London Airport, the government sent some underling with the rank of major to meet him, saying that protocol did not allow them to send anyone of greater importance as Gagarin was only a major. By the end of his visit, such was the volume of public acclaim that he was invited to tea with the Queen at Buckingham Palace.

CHANGING AND UNCHANGING

A fuller understanding of the changing concept of space and the unchanging need of humans for support and loving contact came fourteen years later when I read Dr Moreno's speech delivered to the Second International Psychodrama Congress:

> Yet, despite the fact that all therapies have noticeably neglected the element of space, the physicists, the astronomers and the astronauts have not. In the cosmic affluence of our time, space and physical communication through it have become enormously important categories in the mind of man, in his vision of life and of the universe as he plans to travel to the moon, the planets, and eventually the stars.
>
> (Moreno 1987: 5)

This wise overview is the reason a director has a group or a protagonist describe and concretise the space in which they make their investigation and their intervention. It is also the space where insight and catharsis are given life.

I have written of time, space and reality in terms of their formation within a psychodrama session but, as I have shown, Moreno asks us to work beyond the walls of the theatre. It's why I included the story of Gagarin.

We live in the time of incredible change – maybe of make or break for humankind. Everything is up for change, even to the extent of choosing what sex we will be. My stories, the Holwell Box, are simply small tools to help us think beyond the walls of our own heads and hearts as well as the therapy room.

COSMOS – THE FOURTH UNIVERSAL

The fourth universal is the cosmos, another side of the Holwell Box. Let us look more closely at how the philosophical idea works in practice. To quote A.S. Neill, writing in *A Dominie's Log*, first published in 1915: 'When our scholars discover that we are only human, then they like us, and they listen to us' (Neill 1986: 20).

Similarly, in a psychodrama session when we see the human reasons behind a person's feelings, thoughts and actions, we listen more carefully. We understand more clearly that people are the product of their experiences and, more particularly, of their relationships. Our lives make us what and how we are. Careful listening is one of the first tasks of a session. Psychodrama is an education and a therapy in and of, relationships.

The philosophy creatively applied through the techniques unites art and science. If we accept the concept of a continuous cosmic drama, we can also see that humankind is part of that drama. If, as Blake said, we see a world in a grain of sand, then it is also in a human cell. Wherever we are, the cosmic drama is all around us and we are part of it. When we enter a room or a space in which a psychodrama session is to be held, the drama is already there. It is hot or cold, light or dark, the rain drums at the window or the sun radiates from the skylight.

Fourteenth story

In Finland, a protagonist from the far north, estranged from his wife, felt loss and sadness for his brain-damaged son. As director I asked, 'What do you really want for your boy?' The man answered, 'Sunshine'. It was high summer and the sun beamed in through windows in an unused corner of the room. I had everyone quickly rearrange the whole place. The audience area was changed and the stage, or enactment area, put into full sunshine. Immediately the energy within the group lifted as people moved chairs and tables, jostling and interacting in their desire to give the protagonist his wish – sunshine for his son. The group feeling was good; the protagonist felt honoured. We had created a rich starting point simply by plugging ourselves into the ongoing cosmic performance, sunlight beaming into the room. Inside the room the man's moods and the mood of the group were accompanied by the changing mood of the weather outside. The sun came and went and at one point it began to rain just as the protagonist became tearful. There was darkness and light, coolness and warmth. We felt we were part of something bigger.

The high point came during the sharing. We sat in a circle as the daylight faded. Suddenly, the sun threw out its last light of the day. Magically, it fell upon the tired protagonist and the auxiliary who had played his cerebrally damaged son. It was a breathtakingly beautiful experience.

I'm not saying that psychodrama is magic. I am saying that magical things can happen when you connect into the cosmic drama. The director has to draw on cosmic phenomena for inspiration. If they are able to connect the session's personal drama with the universal drama, then sometimes the universal will get plugged into the personal.

When Dr Moreno asked us to see ourselves not just as individual or social beings but also as cosmic beings, he was looking far beyond the therapy-room walls. He was aiming beyond the streets, the fields and the mountains into the great cosmos itself. He was suggesting that we are part of the whole, an essential, though admittedly small, part of a great evolving system. What makes our smallness a little more significant is that we are creators. We have the ability to act and to think. With that ability goes responsibility, to ourselves, the world around us and to the heavens around our planet. That, it seems to me, is Moreno's holistic view – a view that is all the more urgent as we step into the cosmos with our probes and our spaceships. Moreno was somewhat ahead of the Green Movement.

My own view is that he was very much in contact with the ongoing evolution of cosmic thinking – Petra Kelly came after but St Francis came before. Moreno has an important place in that ongoing process.

THE GODHEAD

The greatest model of 'objectivity' man has ever conceived was the idea of the Godhead, a being who knows and feels with the universe because he created it, a being unlimited in his ability to penetrate all facets of the universe and still be entirely free of 'bias'.

(Moreno 1953: xli)

The Godhead is Dr Moreno's way of symbolically representing the source of creativity within the cosmos. In working with groups exploring Moreno's concepts by using the Holwell Box, the most contentious of the six sides is the Godhead. The 'Godhead' is the label for the sixth side or lid.

This contentiousness is precisely why it is important to my own teaching concept. The idea of difference, of discussion, agreement or agreed disagreement is essential for psychodrama's development and to the creation of practitioners who are non-judgemental beings. By this I mean people who see human variance and difficulty and accept, even as they help to change, such reality.

Moreno died in 1974. Life moves on and we must continually re-express his ideas in ways that are valid to the ever-increasing speed of change with which we live. That means constant testing of ideas and methods, our own above all. It also ultimately means learning to live together even without understanding one another!

I appreciate Moreno's view of Judaism and Marxism as great motivating forces of his younger days. I also agree with him that the former was religion without science and the latter science without religion. I would use the word 'spirit'. I believe that life has proven Moreno correct on both counts. I further endorse the creative way Moreno took the positive aspects of his youth and attempted to create a 'third way' forward.

HERE AND NOW

In an age and a culture so dedicated to materialism many find difficulty with a God concept and spend a great deal of time blaming religion and its running mate, politics, for 'failing'. My own observation is that the failure usually lies in the human use of ideas rather than in the ideas themselves. It's like blaming aeroplanes for dropping bombs or listening devices for destroying people's privacy. Men and women do those things, not ideas or the technology resulting from ideas.

Humans have looked for some guiding star or some model of an ideal or scientifically sound social system since the beginning of time. That long struggle has been full of contradictions. After the October Revolution in 1917 and the attempt to build a system which rejected religion and the idea of a Godhead, both were in fact re-created. A religious fervour inspired millions leading up to 1917 and continued long after the experiment had become thoroughly corrupt. The belief system of those struggling to create the 'New Man and Woman' blinded people to the corruption of their belief. It also made them blind to the behaviour of the new gods they had created. People constantly drew strength from their gods, not least from the god within themselves. These are important sources of energy that must constantly be checked to see that they haven't become false gods. In his early writings, *Dialogues of the Here and Now* and later in *The Words of the Father*, Moreno developed a new dimension, repeating it in the 'Preludes' to *Who Shall Survive?*

> A dimension which unconsciously was always there but which has never been properly spelled out, theoretically the dimension of the 'I' or God in the 'first' person (in contrast to the 'thou' God of the Christian, and to the 'he' God of the Mosaic tradition), the dimension of subjectivity, the dimension of the actor and creator, of spontaneity and creativity.

The dimension of subjectivity does not deprive the Godhead of the objectivity, neutrality and impartiality of the old model but makes the path free for the exercise of cosmic empathy, love and intimate participation, in other words, for the psychodrama of God.

(Moreno 1953: xl)

Personally I find no problem in accepting Moreno's subjectivity, neutrality and impartiality demand for psychodramatists even though I'm a lifelong partisan. His aim of empathy, love and participation is what, for me, partisanship is about.

Fifteenth story

Using the Holwell Box with a group in Sheffield, an older woman disagreed with my attempt to explain the Godhead. 'A long time ago, when my first child was born', she said, 'I reached down, felt her head breeching and knew it was the Godhead'. I remarked softly on being pleased that a girl could also be the Godhead, a position reserved in the period of which she spoke for the man child. The woman replied, 'Oh, her head wasn't about gender, it **was** the future, the child **is** the future.'

For me there is plenty of room in my concept for this older woman's poetic wisdom.

BACK TO THE FUTURE

An aspect of Moreno's philosophy of the encounter that I have not seen written about or heard much discussed is the ongoing process of self-encounter through psychodrama. Over and over again people taking part in psychodrama sessions encounter parts of themselves or 'other selves' of which they have previously been only partially aware and even wholly unaware. This happens not just to protagonists but to directors building relationships with protagonists. It can also happen to an auxiliary taking a seemingly unfamiliar role and finding a familiarity with some hidden aspect of the self.

Sixteenth story

My first child was born in 1952; we called her Janey. She was very beautiful and died two and a half years later.

Janey was buried on a bright summer's day on a hillside near Carlisle. Her mother and I entered a period of numbness asking ourselves over and over again the eternal question of bereaved parents, 'Why us?' As the pathetic little box was lowered into the ground it all seemed unreal.

It could not really be happening. The scene was a cardboard cut-out and the people actors in some kind of bizarre play. I felt the curtain would come down. We would applaud and all go home discussing the performance.

Then suddenly I was brought back to the reality of the little graveside by the words of my friend Walter Wallace. He spoke the cosmic truth of ongoing creation that, as our child was laid to rest another was already growing within my wife. His words brought awareness of my feet holding on to the earth and everything came into sharp focus. The trees at the cemetery's edge were framed by the colour of ripe corn moving in waves before the wind. Among the trees my neighbours stood dark, in suits and overalls. Some had come straight from the coal mine and railway yard their bicycles black against the corn. None came close, fearful of intruding on private family pain. I cannot recall their faces but will never forget the supportive touch of their hands as we left the graveyard. To this day the brown and gold of ripe corn is my favourite colour.

My wife retreated into a silent sorrow to be fuelled by other life tragedies that perhaps led to her own death from cancer at the age of forty-four.

My own way of coping was to become tougher, more macho, as seemed appropriate to a man working in the coal-mining industry. I never cried or spoke of our tragedy, threw myself into working-class politics and spent my spare time helping others found the Spastics Society.

Twenty years later I was a protagonist in a psychodrama session, my first. I felt doubtful about it, feeling that what went on inside me was my business!

My director was Doug Warner from Maryland. I was not particularly drawn to this pipe-smoking, rather aloof, man and yet, twenty-five years later, I feel as a brother to him. It's a brotherhood born out of his creative relationship to me in that one psychodrama session.

As the enactment reached its peak, Doug had the group come on to the stage and become the field of golden corn. It was corn become people and people become corn – total surplus reality. I had not gone back in time, time had come forward to us in that shining golden space.

My little girl, an Indian doctor in a beautiful flowing sari, touched my hand and walked away into the corn that closed around her. It was a wondrous second parting.

I was in a state of psychodramatic shock, heard little of the sharing but in the weeks that followed that encounter with my old self, important changes took place. My tough coping mechanism seemed inappropriate. I became softer, no longer afraid of my vulnerability.

My grief remained but its sad strikes became less frequent and even those I felt were shared with grieving parents throughout history and across the world. What had been a way of coping became a conscious, more tender way of seeing and a more creative way of getting on with my life.

The third self-encounter took place another twenty years on and is directly related to that psychodrama session directed by Doug Warner.

I had a massive haemorrhage and was found to have gut cancer. The operation was long, followed by nine days in an intensive care unit. It's a period lost to my conscious self except for one thing which I believe took place during the operation.

Seventeenth story

I was walking into a field of ripe corn. The colour of the swaying field was Arab Gold; I knew this from seeing the sun on the yellow-brown flank of a stallion in Baghdad. It was the days when Saddam was a darling of the English Establishment who were selling him weapons as hard as they could go. My mind saw everything clearly and also the meaning behind everything.

All was shining and crystal clear.

My little girl came towards me through the corn which moved in rhythm with her walking. She was exactly that little 2-year-old again and reached her arms towards me. Our fingers almost touched when a voice said in my right ear, 'Hang about, Ken, it's not time yet.' The words are mine but the voice was not. It was a voice from beyond me, perhaps the voice of collective wisdom of parents and lost children. My little girl stopped, a smile crossed her face and without sadness she turned and walked back to be lost again among the brilliance.

It was my third self-encounter and third parting from my daughter. It was a simple, almost matter-of-fact meeting and separation, utterly beautiful and totally without sorrow.

My mind tells me it was a dream or vision released by the anaesthetic; my feelings tell me it was a message that helped me leave the hospital and move towards recovery. In doing so I have changed again. I value every moment yet feel prepared to let go when the time comes. That last statement, 'when the time comes' seems inadequate. I want to decide the time and place; I want to be my own God. Dying, it seems to me, is a case of the right combination of reasons for death. Simply an ongoing life process.

Doug Warner introduced me to the old self that didn't know how to grieve, which, in turn, led to the birth of the vulnerable man – proud of vulnerability. The cancer fighter called on Doug Warner's psychodrama scene to avoid death, to turn it all into life-giving blood within and to get on with life.

Each encounter with an old but still living self seemed to give birth to a new more adequate self. Adequate to the changed circumstances and hopefully to future demands. It's what I call ongoing psychodramatic process.

CONCLUSION

As I write this chapter our media technology is being used to broadcast two main items.

The first is the cuckolding antics of Britain's future king and company. It's a sign of the times which leaves much to be desired, not least of the media makers. Psychodrama could help them all, commoners and kings!

The second item concerns the demise of the Soviet Union and is today headlined in my 'quality' newspaper, 'Marx's Ideas have Failed its People'. All my life I've heard one lot say that and the other lot say the same about Christian ideas. The truth is that great humanist ideas do not fail people: people fail great humanist ideas. Their greed, their frailty, their power seeking and stupidity get in the way. In fairness, even the best get tired and their dreams die. But the wonderful thing about people is that somewhere, someone always starts once more. They work for something better and begin to dream again.

Even now, in this dismal and vision-empty period, some have the courage to dream again. They include psychodramatists! It's an ongoing revolutionary process, an eternal continuum of creation.

Which brings me back to Dr Jacob Levy Moreno's philosophy. Isn't it a worthy guide to help us face current problems? Aren't they relevant ideas to carry with us into the new century, honing, broadening, changing and perfecting them as we go?

REFERENCES

Carson, R. (1965) *Silent Spring*, London: Penguin Books.
Fox, J. (ed.) (1987) *The Essential Moreno*, New York: Springer.
Haywood, T. (1992) *Managing for Absurdity*, Videotape issued by the University of Central England, Birmingham, or in book form (article in English) *Bibliotek-hagen Bendick Rugaas*, Oslo: Riksbibliotekt-Jenesten.
Hillman, J. (1992) *We've Had a Hundred Years of Psychotherapy and the World's Getting Worse*, San Francisco: Harper.
Moreno, J.L. (1941) *The Words of the Father*, New York: Beacon House.
—— (1953) *Who Shall Survive?*, New York: Beacon House.
—— (1968) 'Universal peace in our time', *Group Psychotherapy*, vol. 21, New York: Beacon House.
—— (1987) in J. Fox (ed.) *The Essential Moreno*, New York: Springer.
Moreno, J.L., Moreno, Z., Moreno, J.D. (1964) *The First Psychodramatic Family*, New York: Beacon House.
Neill, A.S. (1986) *A Dominie's Log*, London: Hogarth Press.
Pilger, J. (1991) *Distant Voices*, London: Vintage.

Chapter 2

Spontaneity and creativity

Commentary

For those who seek to understand human relationships, psychodrama, as a way of working psychotherapeutically, can be both attractive for its spontaneity and threatening in its direct expression. Indeed, its potential for excitement and drama and its belief in lessening rigidity, reducing poisonous pedagogy and toppling antique totems of belief may, in part, explain the caution expressed by some over the years.

The psychodrama director, perhaps more than any other group psychotherapist can become a sort of lightning conductor, tapping into the latent energy of the group. In this chapter Marcia Karp powerfully demonstrates how the forces of creativity and spontaneity can be harnessed to bring about change.

The river of freedom

Marcia Karp

The essence of discovery is that unlikely melange of cabbages and kings, of previously unrelated frames of reference or universes of discourse whose union will solve the previously insoluble problem.

(Koestler 1989)

INTRODUCTION

Many years ago I was walking up the spiral of paintings at the Guggenheim Museum in New York. I had the good fortune of walking behind a young child enthusing about the pictures in front of him. He stopped in front of a Kandinsky and shouted, 'Look at those elephants, Mom.' 'What elephants?' his mother asked. He moved up closer to the painting, looked carefully, shrugged his shoulders and moved on. The moment was an opportunity both gained and missed. For me, I was grateful to see the elephants; for him, he will never see them again. He learned that his discovery didn't exist; I learned that his discovery did.

This chapter is about learning and discovery through creativity and spontaneity. It is spontaneity that catapults creative people and creative methods into action. Psychodrama is just such a method whose various techniques, when wielded with an inspired hand, promote a mutual spontaneity between the user of the tools and its subjects. Spontaneity is catching. We become both affected and infected with this release of free-flowing energy produced first by the director and then the group.

J.L. Moreno, in presenting psychodrama to a group of Berkeley University students, formed an unforgettable identification with the students who were some sixty years younger than he. A student stood up and asked, 'Dr Moreno, what is the difference between you and Freud?' Moreno looked at the multitude of 1960s bearded faces in front of him. 'Freud had a close-cut beard, clipped by a barber; my beard was free flowing and spontaneous.' The students loved his cosmetic yet philosophical answer to a theoretical question. It spoke to them. The response was adequate for that moment, it created laughter and allowed others to enter equally into a playful and spontaneous moment. Moreno was excellent at warming up an audience of any size, small or large. He spoke from the moment. He spoke about what involved him that day or what he was contemplating. He gave the feeling that anything could happen. His authenticity hooked into those listening to him. He encountered them physically by sometimes shaking hands with members of the audience. This gave him a somatic sense of the person talking to him – whether the person was anxious or relaxed, ready or not ready for a profound encounter. With Moreno, the spontaneous warm-up was organic to the session. His talk to the audience, as the group began, was often poignant, funny, involving and was never the same. It was tailored to that group, that director and that moment.

One night, in the public theatre of psychodrama in New York, there was an obese woman who came up on the stage wanting to work on her relationship with her husband. She moved slowly and without motivation, seemingly trapped in a body of inactivity. The director asked her to run around the periphery of the wooden circular stage. She looked aghast. 'I haven't run in years!' She picked up her dress and began to run. She looked like a car lurching forward after years of disuse. She ran several laps and without prompting from the director stomped up onto the stage, faced an auxiliary playing her husband and said in a loud voice, 'I'm leaving you.' The session which followed was about her preparation to leave an abusive husband. Her physical movement of running gave rise to her emotional movement. She finally told her husband what she felt. Her 'stuckness' was in body and soul and once the body could move, the soul could be freed.

INNOVATIONS

There have been uncountable inspired moments of authenticity and spontaneity in psychodrama groups throughout the world. The innovative moments that stand out are varied and wondrous. How and why they happen is ponderable but that they happen is fact. I shall describe some of these moments and work backwards to their roots in Morenian theory. The moments that are personal to me are written to remind you of yours.

Moment one – the empty chair

One hundred Brazilians, Uruguayans and Paraguayans stood in a circle and faced an empty chair. For most, it was an ordinary May morning in Rio de Janeiro. For me, it was not. Several hours earlier I had been told that my husband had collapsed and been taken to hospital for emergency abdominal surgery, thousands of miles away from the spot where I stood on that May morning. At the time I did not know the outcome of that surgery: later I learned he survived it. The personal and the professional role conflict I felt was monumental. In that moment, the two roles gently melted together and joined in the very marrow of my existence. They had to join or I would have been too split to continue. I held on to one idea, of Carl Rogers, that what is most personal is most universal.

I was both eager and frightened to stand naked with my personal dilemma. But 'the moment fear enters your flesh, your chariot wheel plunges into earth', says the hero in *Mahabharata*, the Indian tale.

I stood in front of the group, alone and quiet. 'My husband was operated on earlier today. I am glad he is alive.' I placed a chair in the centre of the large room. The audience was invited to stand up and form a circle around the chair. 'Think of someone for whom you simply feel grateful that he or she is alive.' I began to feel braver, remembering that it is not important to be a hero but it is important to act heroically.

Within thirty seconds, heads were either bowed or focused on the chair and the profundity of silence was upon us. To my surprise, the first to speak was me. I spoke a few quiet sentences to Ken. The next to speak was a tearful Portuguese voice. She spoke to her daughter who had nearly died; a man spoke to his father who had survived a heart attack; a woman spoke to her sister dying of cancer, and on and on, people around the circle began to address the empty chair. Some people had their arms around each other, some were weeping, all were involved. I remembered a song written by a Chilean singer, Violetta Para, 'Gracias a la vidas' – 'Thank you for life'. As I began to sing the first few words everyone joined in and the song united us in an unforgettable way. As W.B. Yeats wrote, 'God guard me from the thoughts men think in the mind alone. He who sings a lasting song thinks in a marrow bone' (Yeats 1936).

The incongruity of 'Cabbages and Kings' strikes me most when remembering these moments in South America: incongruities such as that I was the expert who knew nothing; that there were huge cultural and language barriers and that there was great loss and great pain. If the essence of discovery is about previously unrelated frames of reference, we certainly had them. These factors contributed to resolutions in the experiential learning of a group.

Moment two – I deserve the shoes

The weather was hot as the director left for Finland. A friend had given her a pair of hand-made sandals that didn't suit. She put them in her hands as they said goodbye. Days later she was doing a workshop in the countryside of Finland and she tried them on. They were beautiful but way too big for her feet. She brought them to the group and determined that she would give them to someone else, but who best suited them? She placed the sandals in a circle of eager students and asked them each to think of a good reason why the sandals should belong to them. One by one, people tested their case as to why they deserved the sandals. Most of them tried on the sandals as they spoke. Self-esteem ran high.

One said, 'It isn't that I need them. They are already mine.' The group laughed at her cunning words. Another, a man, said 'I need more colour in my life, a new image. The shoes are a reminder with every step.' Another said she worked hard for the group and the group owed her the sandals. Another said, 'I am about to split up with my partner. It seems impossible. I need your support and if I could walk a path with you all around me, the distance wouldn't be such a lonely struggle.' She got the shoes.

A protagonist emerged from this exercise who was touched by the handicraft that went into making the sandals. It reminded him of his home region in Northern Finland. His issue was how to keep the primitiveness of his roots in city life.

The discovery in this group work was again an incongruity: playfulness and deservedness. Each person was able to play with their own deservedness in a safe and honourable way. Each person created their own reason to deserve 'the shoes in life' and used their own spontaneity to show it.

Moment three – a backwards psychodrama

There was an expectation of brilliance building up around the conference evaluation forms which were presented to group members at the end of each workshop to evaluate the workshop leader. As the director prepared her own presentation, the evaluation form seemed an intruder in her spontaneous plan of action. She decided to get the damn thing out of the way both for the group and for herself. She decided to run the workshop backwards. Since the evaluation form had come first, they would deal with it first.

Evaluation

'Imagine', the director said to a room full of conference hopefuls, 'that you've just been to a helpful and memorable workshop.' She placed an empty chair in front of the group. 'Please tell the director sitting in the chair why it was such a fine session.' The group burst forth with superlatives. 'You've worked in a profoundly universal way.' 'Humour was woven into pathos.' 'There was humility and greatness. It was ours.' 'Everyone was involved. Your voice was like a river touching each person in the room.' The evaluation went on for a long time. Each person was able to give their view of a great session. The group members had only just met each other. No workshop had taken place and yet each knew what would have made it good.

Processing

'Close your eyes', the director said next.

> Imagine you have just done the quintessential psychodrama. As protagonist you were finally able to work on an issue which has been lurking indeterminately for some years. It became crystallised in this session and you were able to shift some important blocks to new learning. Imagine what the session was about. See yourself in the session and visualise yourself making profound and new connections.

The group was silent. She placed twelve empty chairs in front of the group.

'If you are able to tell us the essence of what happened in your psychodrama, please come and sit in one of the chairs.' The disclosures that ensued were of monumental importance to each person who spoke. One woman resolved a long-standing rift between her sister and herself and briefly told how she was able to do it. One man said he finally confronted himself about surviving a war. During the war he had watched friend and foe die or become injured. In the session he owned responsibility for his participation. He mourned and he rejoiced in being alive. It became clear that these conference-goers, mostly advanced psychodramatists, when given the opportunity to do an internal psychodrama, grasped it with intelligence and worked hard at resolution.

Sharing

After each of the twelve sessions were processed, the director asked the group, 'Out of all that has been described, with whom do you most identify and why?' A tearful woman stood up and said that her sister and she also did not speak for years and on hearing one of the protagonists, she realised what she needed to do with her sister. Another war veteran came up and embraced the wartime protagonist and shared his thoughts and feelings as though he'd been with him for many hours. They met where their life experience joined. It was painfully touched off in a few key sentences from the protagonist. As is shown in full psychodrama sessions, when emotional content unites people, encounter is made on a profound and unforgettable level. The depth of encounter allowed two people to have protagonist-centred sessions during the workshop day.

Warm-up

After a resolution of the protagonists' work the sharing became the warm-up which ended the day's work.

> Place a chair in front of yourself. Identify which issues the protagonists worked on are your issues. Tell yourself how you will deal with those issues when you leave this room. See yourself clearly and talk directly to yourself about how to handle those issues.

This lasted several minutes while people warmed themselves up to the issues awaiting them as they went into a wider world. People took their time to integrate what had just taken place in a large group with what takes place in the reality of their own lives.

Slowly the people took leave of each other, the room and the director. How does one actually evaluate such an experience? One could argue that the director's warm-up was the evaluation form. The evaluation became the group warm-up, leading to imagined internal psychodrama sessions which produced enactments in reality.

The universe is infinite creativity

I have used the above example to show that even with a creative method like psychodrama, there are always innovations round the corner. The most creative gifts can become prisons if we treat them as frozen concepts. Moreno, for example, was always making up words to meet a given situation. He once asked a woman in the audience, 'Are you married, single or "mingled"?' He spoke of people connected to the greater cosmos as 'cosmonauts' and mentioned them easily together with astronauts. Another word Moreno used, along with neurosis and psychosis, was 'normosis'. He thought that the bulk of humanity was inflicted with 'normosis' or the struggle to be normal.

Creating novel moments in the psychodramatic method keeps the practitioner fresh and inspired. There is nothing worse for group members than to feel that this has all been done before, and better. The director can model finding his or her own level of comfort and interaction, much like a spring vine finds it way to the sun and growth. The vine grows differently every year depending on the conditions. So, too, the director changes in each moment, depending on the conditions. It gives participants a chance to feel change occurring in the very model they trust. It can lead one to feel that if change can occur in the model, perhaps it can occur in them.

In discussing the spontaneity and functions of the psychodrama director, Moreno talked about the director as (i) a producer; (ii) a chief therapist; and (iii) as a social analyst.

> As a producer he is an engineer of co-ordination and production. Unlike a playwright, he tries to find his audience and characters first, drawing from them the material for a plot. With their assistance, he turns out a production which meets the personal and collective needs of the characters as well as the audience at hand. His task is to make the subjects act on that spontaneous level which benefits their total equilibrium, to prompt the auxiliary egos.
>
> As social analyst he uses the auxiliary egos as extensions of himself

to draw information from the subjects on the stage to test them and carry influence to them.

(Moreno 1977: 252)

The director has the opportunity for many novel uses of the psycho-dramatic method. Each has its roots in surprise, spontaneity and unique-ness of response which are characteristic of the creative act. Some examples are presented here to illustrate these opportunities for infinite creativity. The first is the spontaneous emergence of more than one protagonist within a psychodrama session.

Multiple protagonists in psychodrama

In classical psychodrama one protagonist emerges from the group as a representative voice. The warm-up phase of psychodrama often builds a readiness in group members to look at their life as it is, as it was or as it could be. As the session unfolds, the action of that one protagonist can serve as a warm-up for others in the group. At certain moments, individuals become ready to express themselves through the process of watching and participating in someone else's emotions. In those moments, people are like ripe fruit ready to be picked; their emotions, ideas and thoughts are at the forefront. For me, there have been increasingly clear indications when it is appropriate for more than one person to participate as protagonist in the same psychodrama. These indications are (i) when the emotional pulse of the protagonist slows down and the pulse of a group member speeds up; therefore (ii) the act hunger of the group member is greater than that of the protagonist in a given scene; (iii) the protagonist is able to share his/her physical and emotional space with another person; (iv) when it is clear that the protagonist wants to express a particular feeling and can gain strength from hearing it expressed by someone else – it then re-activates the original protagonist; they spark each other off.

I shall discuss the first three of these points.

The emotional pulse of the protagonist slows down

Very nearly three out of four hospital births in the US are Caesarian. One of the reasons, it is postulated, is that if the baby dies the doctor may be involved in a legal suit. Since the baby's pulse rate drops before birth, doctors may take this as a warning sign that all may not be well and therefore unnaturally remove the baby by Caesarian section to make sure the pulse continues rather than stops. There is a parallel situation between director and protagonist. I think it is a natural development, prior to catharsis, that the emotional pulse may drop in the protagonist. Unsure directors may stop the scene because 'it isn't getting anywhere'. In fact, proceeding normally, it may be the lull before the storm. There are many ways to deal with the lull. Techniques can be used as the double, role reversal to produce counterspontaneity, interview, non-verbal expression, mirroring and many others can heighten or exaggerate the implicit feelings which can then be made explicit. Another intervention can be the use of an alternative protagonist just at the low-pulse point. The director must check out his/her perception to see if the group member is in fact about to give birth. The pregnancy in some participant observers is sometimes made clear by their crying, sitting on the edge of their chair, looking angry or, in one case, being asleep – complete denial often means just the opposite. The sleeping group member arose alert and ready to express himself, as do others when the time is ripe.

Act hunger of a group member is greater than the protagonist

If the labour pains of the group member are real, the person need only be brought onstage to face his/her own 'significant other' such as a family member or a concept, like death or fatherhood, for example. The true emotions which have been kept silent up until that moment are given their own timely birth. The original protagonist is still onstage, still part of the scene but the unspoken truth has begun. When the second protagonist is finished, role reversal may be indicated and also completed. If others in the audience are similarly warmed-up they may also ventilate what they are feeling, again with the original protagonist still onstage hearing their own particular version of a similar story.

The protagonist is able to share his or her emotional space

If the protagonist seems too stunned or overwhelmed by what is happening, it is wise to reduce rather than increase the number of protagonists. More often than not, the protagonist is encouraged by a sister or brother protagonist expressing similar emotions to their own, in a real-life situation, and spontaneously continues where the other left off. It is similar to the dovetailing that goes on in multiple doubling; however the concept is slightly different.

About the multiple double Moreno writes:

> The protagonist is on the stage with several doubles of himself, each portraying another part of the patient, one as he is now, another as he was five years ago, a third as he was when at three years of age he first heard his mother died, another how he may be at twenty years hence. The multiple representations of the patient are simultaneously present and act in sequence, one continuing where the other left off.

> The protagonist or patient in a psychodramatic production has as his

purpose to portray scenes and incidents from his own private world which for each person is unique.

(Moreno and Moreno 1975: 240)

Here, because each of the multiple protagonists is presenting his or her own feelings, not those of someone else, the details may in fact be different. I have found that the catharsis experienced by the second or third protagonist is as helpful a learning experience to each of them as if they had had their own full psychodrama. It assists the original protagonist by result not by design and gives permission.

In the New York ASGPP (American Association of Group Psychotherapy and Psychodrama) Conference in April 1981, I first demonstrated the use of multiple protagonists in a day-long training session. It was amazing to see how the primary protagonist could express deep feeling, then stop, listen to others' profound expression, and then easily slip back into her own uncompleted business. She seemed helped and continually sparked off by knowing and feeling that she was not alone in her struggle. As human beings we have a struggle to be the person we would like to be – to negotiate and navigate by continually recharting the route. How comforting it is to know that each of us is not alone in the vast sea.

Ways of unblocking spontaneity

Learning where the original flow of freedom becomes blocked is an excellent start in building new responses to old situations. The following are some examples of the ways in which spontaneity can be unblocked.

Russian Matrioshka dolls, which are dolls that fit one inside the other, can be used to focus on developmental blocks that prohibit spontaneous expression. As one doll is opened and taken off the stack of dolls, another is waiting to be opened. With the removal of each successive doll, a statement is made such as 'I can't show spontaneity because I won't show vulnerability.' When the next doll is removed the next statement might be, 'I won't show vulnerability because I might show need. If I show need, I might show hurt.' Tears and laughter become part of this exercise as the unexpected answers tumble forth.

The discovery of hidden agendas in each statement usually comes back to a point of stuckness in one's development. For example:

I show my neediness because I won't show my independence. I won't show my independence because I may lose support. I won't risk losing support because it would show my loneliness. I won't show my loneliness because I'd have to reveal my vulnerability.

In the above two examples, the quest leads back to the same spot – vulnerability – which may be a sticking point.

A psychodramatic exploration of the roots of the difficulty, vulnerability in this case, might release spontaneous expression which has become dammed up like old leaves in a stream. When the leaves are removed, the stream moves on in the direction of natural intention.

One participant found it helpful to connect with her shadow self. As she searched for what was blocking her spontaneous expression, removing each doll brought her nearer to her interior self. 'If I am spontaneous I show my vulnerability, I show fear; if I show fear I show need, and if I show need I may become spontaneous, and if I am spontaneous I will be annihilated.' Annihilation was a common block to spontaneity in this group. It led to a discussion of the need to draw on the light and dark sides of oneself for the fulfilment of spontaneity. But the fearful business of risking the dark and potentially destructive parts of ourselves seems to create intense fear of disappointment and therefore the self closes up or disappears. In the moment of fear, one is reminded of childhood attempts at spontaneity which were punished or not rewarded. The parental statement, 'I want, doesn't get' can be an example of this dampening effect.

We need to use both joyful and dark energies in spontaneous production. Another participant who connected with her shadow self later reflected:

> In psychotherapy, while it is important to touch and understand the personal/historical origins of one's own angst, it is also essential to accept and own one's 'shadow' for this provides life-giving energy towards creativity and wholeness and liberates us from the continuing need to blame others or 'life' for our insufficiencies. To live creatively, then, is to live with paradox – to embrace the two sides of oneself mirrored in Joy and Despair, Life and Death.
>
> (Elizabeth Ash 1989, unpublished manuscript)

A later use of this technique is to start with the largest doll already empty and go down in size with each revelation. For example, I will be spontaneous because I won't be annihilated. I won't be annihilated because I won't show fear; and so on, up the dolls as each is put together again.

The most common answers as to why 'I won't be spontaneous' were:

I won't belong.
I might be annihilated.
I might not be liked.
I might be a nuisance.
I might not be loved.
I don't trust myself.

Many people felt that the original message given by a parent figure was: 'Be careful not to react naturally because that will cause trouble.' The message later in life after entering therapy, becomes the opposite of that: 'Trouble exists because natural responses have been aborted. Be yourself.' It is interesting to note that the single most sought-after state for people asking for psychological help is 'to just be me'.

To 'just be me' takes courage and confidence. Courage and confidence can be trained in people, with the support of a group.

This curious conflict between being yourself in one situation and not being yourself in another situation restricts many people throughout their lives. Training for spontaneity, a seeming contradiction in terms, helps people reverse the negative dictum, 'Do not be you', to the positive one, 'Be you'. They learn both adequacy and appropriateness of a given response. Where spontaneity has been severely prohibited, the person may become anxious or hyperactive. He or she learns to do anything, just to be doing something. The opposite may also occur. The individual may close down entirely and be fearful of doing anything at all in case the response is externally judged as wrong. Both responses require loving encouragement back to a place of authenticity where the river of freedom, spontaneity and creativity, can flow again.

The train (Merlyn Pitzele 1989, in conversation)

The train sequence can be used as a warm-up or a session in itself. It evokes the stages of one's life, the people in it and core events.

The person is asked to imagine their life as a long train; people get on and off; events happen; there are losses and gains, and the journey goes on until the end.

Birth

Chairs are put on the stage for the first carriage in the train. This represents the beginning of life. The director asks, 'Who was there with you? Who got off the train? What events occurred in the first ride of life?' The protagonist reverses roles with each passenger on the train and talks about their relationship with the newborn, the role each played and events that occurred. Grandparents, special aunts and uncles or nannies might be crucial to this period of time.

One protagonist used this carriage to experience profound love for a nanny who was as much a mother as her mother.

Childhood

The train of life lurches and chugs as the protagonist observes the years go by. The director may ask, 'Who is still on the train and who gets off?' The protagonist might role-reverse with a grandparent who dies and gives a final message before departing, or role-reverses with a special teacher who sowed the seeds of change that can be remembered by kindling the teacher's action in reverse role.

The train stops at many stations throughout one's life, youth, adulthood, marriage and so on. Projecting into the future may be important. If death is a preoccupation and time has fixed one's vision, then it is an important event to 'ride through', imagining who will be there and what their reaction will be.

Spontaneity–creativity, twin concepts

The 'Innovations' section of this chapter has described various ways of releasing spontaneity. The finished product of a creative effort, named by Moreno a cultural conserve (Moreno and Moreno 1975: 268) such as a symphony, a book, or a song, has as its foundation a creative process. This process has links to the act, to the creator and to the spontaneity, which is the mulch or mixing ground of creative growth.

Spontaneity–creativity is often considered as a twin concept. One feeds the other and helps redefine a formal category of 'the present' into a more dynamic spontaneous–creative process called 'the moment'.

The duality of spontaneity–creativity is distinct from an impulsive or automatic spontaneity which neglects 'the deeper meaning of spontaneity, making it something uncontrollable and particularly characteristic for animal behaviour' (Moreno and Moreno 1975: 268).

What is it, then, to be spontaneous? Is it dangerous? Where do the innovations that become invented in a moment of inspiration have their roots?

In *Psychodrama*, vol. 3, Moreno and Moreno state: 'Spontaneity is the variable degree of satisfactory response an individual manifests in a situation of a variable degree of novelty. The root of this word is the Latin sua sponte meaning of free will' [or from within oneself] (Moreno and Moreno 1975: 270). It is interesting to note that in 1975 in the above book, psychodrama is listed in the glossary as:

> a term coined by Moreno. It means full psycho-realization. Under this term are included all the forms of dramatic production in which the participants, either actors or spectators, provide: (a) the source material, (b) the production and (c) are the immediate beneficiaries of the cathartic effect of the production. Every session is a co-operative, communal act: no part of the production is supplied or produced by outsiders. Psychodrama can be exploratory, preventive, diagnostic, educational, sociological and psychiatric in its application. Three principal forms are differentiated: (i) the totally spontaneous psychodrama, (ii) the planned psychodrama in which the group and auxiliary egos may or may not include the subject of the session in the planning, depending

on the need of the situation, and (iii) the rehearsed psychodrama in which a specific syndrome of a subject is worked out in detail, in dialogue, written and the parts assigned.

(Moreno and Moreno 1975: 270)

The totally spontaneous form is what is most used and taught today in 1993. One may ask why did this particular form became popular and not the others. I think that the core of Moreno's work was the release of spontaneity rather than the planning or the rehearsing of it.

Moreno and Moreno described the spontaneous psychodrama as:

at least consciously, fully unprepared; a conflict is presented around which members of the group can develop a session assisted by a director and his auxiliary egos. Although extemporaneous, the directorial unit [director and auxiliary egos, Ed.] is usually carefully organized and trained to handle the situations.

(Moreno and Moreno 1975: 269)

The next section of this chapter will continue to look at the roots of creativity and spontaneity as utilised in psychodrama.

ROOTS

'God was first a creator, an actor, a psychodramatist. He had to create the world before he had the time, the need, or the inclination, to analyze it' (Moreno 1953). The universe is infinite creativity. A child is a visible example of the creative act and the freshness with which the child enters each situation may be called spontaneity.

There were many more Michelangelos born than the one who painted the great paintings; many more Beethovens born than the one who wrote great symphonies, and many more Christs than the one who became Jesus of Nazareth. What they have in common is creativity and creative ideas. What separates them is the spontaneity which, in successful cases, enables the carrier to take full command of his resources, whereas the failures are at a loss with all their treasures. They suffer from deficiencies in their warm-up process. Creativity without spontaneity becomes lifeless.

(Moreno 1953: 40)

Creativity without spontaneity becomes lifeless

My husband Ken was lecturing to a group of local women amateur artists. As a warm-up to the event, we went to see their exhibition in a Barnstaple church hall. On entering the room you had the feeling that you'd been there before and would be again. These were 'token' paintings, that is to say each painting was a copy of what had been done before. For example, a rose-covered cottage, a token seascape, a token still-life – none very interesting or having a feeling of inspiration.

Ken then gave a talk about the importance of using stories as a basis for their paintings. A farmer's wife, who lived near us, asked if she could tell a story. Excitedly, she told us about the drunken sale of a pig. One night her husband had arranged to sell a pig. The buyer arrived and the two farmers began to chat and drink. After much drinking, at one o' clock in the morning, by moonlight, the two farmers tried to push the pig into the back of the buyer's car so that he could take the pig home. Both farmers, and their wives, laughed and shoved the pig into the back of the car. Margaret, the teller of the story, said she'd never forget the sight of squashing a pig into the back seat of a car by moonlight. What an idea for a painting! This idea became the basis for her new work and the spontaneity level entered her creation at last.

Spontaneity prepares the subject for free action. If the warm-up to an act is achieved and the person fails to complete the act, it is like being in labour forever without a birth. Anxiety occurs when the full state of readiness is aborted. When anxiety is high, spontaneity is low and when spontaneity is high, anxiety is low.

It is suggested by Paul Holmes that the presence of anxiety is the cause of a loss of spontaneity: 'it is increasing anxiety, associated with physiological changes needed for an adequate physical response to danger which reduces spontaneity and the ability to find creative solutions' (Holmes 1992: 143).

'Spontaneity is the state of production and is the engine that drives the creative act' (Moreno 1953: 334).

The creative act – four characteristics

In Morenian theory there are four characteristics (referred to as characters) in the creative act (Moreno 1977: 35). The first character is its spontaneity. The spontaneity prepares the subject for free action. The second character is a feeling of surprise, the unexpected aspect of the act. The third is breaking the existing reality in some way. And the fourth character of the creative act is acting *sui generis* or in a one-of-a-kind state. In order that the moment is sui generis, a change must take place in the situation, the change must give a feeling of novelty, and the perceived novelty involves activity from the subject, an act of warming-up to a spontaneous state (Moreno 1977: 104).

Margaret's story of the pig illustrates the four characterists of a creative act. The novelty of pushing a pig into the back seat of a car in the moonlight creates an excitement to impart the tale. Producing the story is allowing it to call out and be released from the person who experienced it. This raw immediacy forms a process that demands telling. When that must-tell phenomenon is allowed to unfold, spontaneous expression occurs. The feeling of surprise is evidenced throughout the story. No money for the sale was ever mentioned, for example. The manner of selling the pig, the drinking and the socialising were the key surprise elements. The actual sale of the pig happened at the end of the story. It broke existing reality because one's eyes see an illusion. It is hard to contemplate pig sales at this hour or in that light. It certainly was a one-of-a-kind state (fourth characteristic) as the business interreaction came as an aftermath of an evening's enjoyment. The sale of the pig was a small detail in the larger backdrop of acres of farmland, farmhouse, cars, tractors, all drenched in moonlight.

Brueghel's paintings of Flemish scenery have the same quality of spontaneity and surprise that break existing reality and create novelty. In *The Fall of Icarus* you see the foreground taken up with a farmer ploughing his field and in the very background of the painting is the small figure of Icarus falling from the sky. I like this painting enormously. It speaks of the most important subjects in life appearing as detail. In the novel work of Brueghel, his spontaneity allows him to take a huge subject – Icarus falling from the sky – and set it in perspective among the significant everyday acts of the Flemish peasants. Each act of theirs is as prominent as the subject of the painting. Similarly, the foreground of our spontaneity allows the backdrop of creativity to take its proper perspective. Creativity does not live unless spontaneity feeds it raw material. It catalyses and fuels the process. Icarus, as a subject, does not live in the Brueghel painting unless seen against the background of an ordinary Flemish farmer going about his daily activity. Greatness against the small gives the eye a glimpse of peasantry at its greatest and the grandiosity of Icarus at its smallest.

Psychodrama, it seems to me, is a production of small stories drenched in the magnificent light of spontaneity, moving towards creative resolution. The creative resolution comes only after the subject is freed for action and the action is novel. Breaking the script, throwing away the lines of the old, creating new boundaries through which behavioural change can occur is often the task of a person seeking help in therapy.

Forms of spontaneity

In *Psychodrama*, vol. 1 (1977: 89), Moreno talked about the forms of spontaneity as being creative, original, dramatic and having adequacy of response.

In the *creative* form of spontaneity there may be a new child, new works of art, social or technological inventions, or the creation of new social environments.

In the *original* form, a free flow of expression, for example, from the drawings or poems of children, adds to an original form without changing the essence. My young son Jackson, while playing and giggling one day, threw his head in the air and said, 'What would I ever do without myself?' He was delighted with his own presence and querying the impossibility of his own loss. Another configuration of his thought occurred when he was aged four and having a cuddle. The cuddle was pure and blissful for both Mum and son. He looked up and said, 'Oh Mum, how will I ever love anyone as much as you?' A dilemma of humankind spoken so freely and easily. My reply was, 'You'll love someone as much, but differently.' A creative act brought each of us into the world but our spontaneity expressed the state of our true selves at that moment.

The *dramatic* form has to do with the quality of response, newness in feelings, actions and in speaking.

The fourth form, *adequacy of response*, is about appropriateness of response to new situations. This form is the most diagnostic in the psychodramatic process. There may be three possible ways a person may react in meeting a novel situation: (i) no response; (ii) a new response to an old situation; (iii) a new or adequate response to a new situation. The inability to respond appropriately is of special interest to the psychodrama director.

Adequacy of response

Some roles in psychodrama render the protagonist speechless. The degree to which a relationship is pathological is often shown by the degree to which a person is able or unable to take on a particular role in opposition to their own. For example, in a difficult mother-and-daughter relationship the daughter may find it impossible to say anything in the role of the mother when playing it for the first time. This stuckness, or lack of response, in the role of the mother often manifests itself in expressions such as 'I don't know what she thinks or I don't know what she'd say.' The inconceivability seems an indicator of how entrenched the roles are and how the role boundaries are firmly set. In the original work done with children in Vienna, Moreno soon learned how easily children can fall in and out of role with parents and siblings. In pathological roles this is not the case. Particularly in abusive roles the protagonist should be protected from playing the role of the perpetrator. The protagonist's job is not to understand why the abuse happened but to concentrate on ventilating the feelings that have occurred because the abuse occurred (Karp 1992: 109). The same abusive reality may exist in the protagonist who cannot take on another's role. It is important to distinguish between the protagonist who cannot take on a role because it is abhorrent to them and a protagonist who cannot take a role because they simply can't understand or have never considered the other's point of view. The lack of a response in a psychodramatic role is discussed in the following example which utilises the principles of spontaneity.

A woman was working on the relationship between herself and her mother. Her mother was dying. The protagonist was unable to touch her for years. She could not give or receive a hug and wanted, after many years of analysis, to break these physical and emotional boundaries before her mother was dead and the possibility no longer existed. As we embark on the young woman's psychodramatic journey, let us review the principles of spontaneity. They involve the warming-up process, act hunger and catharsis, and an appropriate response to a new situation or a new response to an old situation (Moreno and Moreno 1948–77: 45).

The warm-up

The scene took place in the hospital room where her mother currently lived. It was a hospice and time was short; recovery was not expected. As the protagonist warmed herself up to meeting her mother she talked out loud, in a soliloquy, about her ambivalence. One part of her would be relieved if her mother died; another part of her felt stupid thinking this way and wanted to make amends before it was too late.

The more she spoke the more her fear in life became clear. It was that she would become like her own mother. She was afraid that the parts of her mother she detested were alive in her. Her warm-up to saying goodbye to a dying mother was the sneaking realisation that she may never be able to say goodbye. No wonder she would be unable to take the role of mother in the psychodrama. She simply didn't want it. Her warm-up began years before this particular session.

In describing the warming-up process, Moreno wrote in *Who Shall Survive?*:

> Bodily movements were found to follow one another in a certain order of succession according to which is the initiating starter. If the succession is interrupted the temporal order is spoiled and the state of feeling released is confused.
>
> (Moreno 1934: 334)

Each of us, when we begin to act or speak, has a series of bodily starters. Clearing the throat, frowning, clenching fists, piercing eyes or shuffling feet may be ways that we propel the body into action. These preliminaries to the warm-up process were studied by Moreno and seen as part of the evolution of expression.

Since the body must get itself going, the protagonist often has several starts. One warm-up may produce part of the process and when completed almost begs the next step. Numerous techniques help this process such as role reversal, self-presentation and exaggeration of resistance.

The protagonist in the above example began to pace the room when faced with having to talk to her dying mother. Her body was full of tension, hesitation and anxiety. She clenched her teeth and warmed up to expressing the hatred she had. As she approached her mother at the hospital she began to face her ambivalence. As she moved into the scene her anxiety rose – her spontaneity was blocked. Her body shook, her voice became quiet. As one does normally in psychodrama, I asked the protagonist to show us the role of her mother. She looked at me quizzically. Her mind was saying, 'What a strange request'. Her emotions were saying, 'No, I can't do this.' She began, in the role of her mother, but couldn't think of anything to say. Then she began a distant chatter about her illness, about the inadequacy of her daughter, etc. The inability of the protagonist to play the role soon revealed itself as not lack of insight but rather distaste at playing out the very behaviour she disliked. As herself, she spoke to her mother about how much she'd felt unloved throughout her childhood, how her mother wasn't the kind of mother she wanted and how, because her mother needed her now, she was expected to give love. She couldn't and she wouldn't.

Act hunger

The spontaneous expression of her anger and tears allowed the protagonist to participate in her real act hunger, that is, ventilating all the hurt that she felt towards her mother. As her anxiety mounted it had become evident that this was where her spontaneity was blocked. The act hunger to ventilate her real feelings took her to a birthday scene as a child where she felt abused and unloved.

Catharsis

The protagonist allowed these emotions to flow freely in a way that the child in the early trauma of her childhood was unable to do. She cleared herself of the core of dammed-up feeling. She could now participate in the relief of removing the block.

We then returned to the original scene in the hospital room. The protagonist was spent of her emotion and was now in a relaxed and free-flowing state. Using the principle that people are more spontaneous in another role, I asked her to reverse roles with her mother on the hospital bed. She did so and quite spontaneously held her arms out and said, 'I'm so sorry and now I'm dying.' She held her daughter and wept the tears of a lost childhood and motherhood. In the role of mother, the protagonist was free to choose a new response to an old situation. She had crossed the role boundaries and discovered spontaneously the response her mother wanted to give her which was physical closeness. It was impossible for the daughter to discover this in her own role but she was able to in the role of her mother. She then reversed roles and for the first time in years embraced her mother, something she'd wanted since she was a small child.

Act hunger

Another principle of spontaneity is act hunger or the action which the protagonist is hungry to complete.

The adequacy of response to a given situation needs to meet the act hunger. The desire for most people in psychodrama is to complete an act that has not been completed in life. The completion of this act may validate the protagonist's emotional experience and sense of active choice (Goldman and Morrison 1984).

Motivation is the key to behavioural change. Some protagonists need to do the session they want before they want to do the session they need. By this, I mean protagonists may decide the area of work they need is with, for example, their father. The session proceeds; the work may be adequate but the preconceived notion of what and how to work may have stopped a more natural warm-up to the real material. The session wanted, instead of needed, may have a somewhat stilted feel to it and often the director goes along with the protagonist rather than mutually co-operating. The difference is that of a bull being led by a chain rather than two horses riding together, unchained.

Completion of real act hunger is recognised by (i) the protagonist clearly indicating when the action is over – 'That's it', or 'I've done it'; (ii) the protagonist spontaneously utters a sense of surprise or novelty at being able to create a new response – 'I've never done that before', or 'I don't believe I did that'; (iii) clear relief in the body of the protagonist – 'I feel like the cat who's got the cream'; (iv) the group applauds, supports and congratulates the protagonist. The group can end it by their own surprise – 'I never thought you could really do it'.

The above are my observations. It is easy to recognise when the climax of expression is over. In act hunger, usually the level of spontaneity enables a creative result.

The level of spontaneity enables a creative result

Recently I worked with a protagonist who had been severely abused by an alcoholic father and emotionally abandoned by a domineering mother. In setting up the scene of her present bedroom she reversed roles with the most significant object in the room, her teddy bear. 'I've been with you thirty-two years. I've never betrayed you like they have. I will be with you during this next difficult period, as I always have been.' The protagonist looked rather shocked to think that this bit of worn fur was the most loyal and fiercely supportive member of her family. In later scenes, when she needed to trace the origins of her own drinking pattern, a fearful confrontation with her father was needed. She felt she hadn't the strength to stand up to him. 'Who could?' I asked her. She then took the role of her bear, bared her teeth at father and went to a scene where he beat her. In the role of the bear, she finally ventilated some of the rage pent up inside her and spoke of the gross indignity of her treatment by him. It was the first time a full-blown confrontation could occur and her hunger to act was completed. Her spontaneity in life had been blocked by her real fear and anxiety of further abuse. This new response to an old situation with her father was just what was needed to break through her role boundaries.

The phenomenon of spontaneity has effects in the body. The life energy that is created during the force of the spontaneous act can alter the mind/ body state. Spontaneity is the factor animating mental phenomena to appear fresh, new and flexible. This intense feeling of novelty seems to be the result of cognitive restructuring. The actor/thinker replaces known solutions with newly recognised behavioural possibilities. Spontaneity lies at the fountain of this transition. Leonard Laskow, a pioneering physician working on mind/body medicine, states that the physical body is a field of energy that has taken a particular form and by restructuring energy patterns through focused intention and imagery we can ameliorate or even cure (Laskow 1992: 189).

The relationship of spontaneity: creativity and how it fits into psychodrama directing

Spontaneity is the engine that drives the creative act. The process of psychodrama involves the movement from cultural conserves with stereo-typically prescribed roles to an increased role repertoire borne out of spontaneity. Protagonists develop greater role-taking skills and are released from their old frozen attitudes and roles, becoming more authentic and open. It seems reasonable to assume that as protagonists experiment with new roles in the psychodramatic situation, they begin to change feeling and thought in their new roles. Subjects report beginning to see their world differently and look at their own lives from a new perspective. Psycho-drama presents an array of novel situations which require the total attention of the protagonist and group members for the production of adequate responses. The opportunity for the emergence of spontaneity is maximised in creating new behaviour.

The lead person in creating new behaviour is the director. The director should be a model of spontaneity for group members to emulate. Just as the protagonist sets the role of the 'other' in the session, the director sets the role of 'the spontaneous group member'.

Though issues of transference are minimised rather than maximised in psychodrama, the role of good parent or bad parent exists for many directors with a particular group member. It may be a conscious effort for a director to play a good parent for a damaged protagonist. This necessitates responsibility and consistency on the part of the director. It is both dangerous and anti-therapeutic to have a damaged member let down yet again by an authority figure because of insensitivity or lack of therapeutic alertness. It may also be a conscious effort for the group member to thrust the director into a parent role. For whatever reason this may occur – to please, to irritate, to love or to hate – it is essential that the director continues to relate in a spontaneous way. Preconceived notions and calculation are soon felt and then copied. As soon as calculation is smelt, there are flames of avoidance and a raging fire of inauthenticity. The opposite is also true. If the emotional smoke is authentic, then spontaneity catches alight. The director may fail in his or her attempts to communicate with difficult group members in the early stages of the group. As a director, I have been told, 'Don't talk to me, don't touch me, don't look at me' and so on. The best I could do was to acknowledge the other's feelings and have mine equally respected. If the existence is respected in the group member, then so it must be in the director. Failure is momentary, it is the attempt that is most validated. As actress Mary Pickford said: 'This thing we call failure is not the falling down but the staying down.'

The director continually starts again. As Peter Kellermann aptly states:

> The psychodrama director is an ordinary person with an extraordinary, demanding job. He or she is not a magician but a reasonably spontaneous and creative individual, generally with more than an average amount of integrity. Being oneself with one's limitations, role repertoire and authenticity seems to be a basic requirement. It is therefore possible to function as a psychodrama director without acting omnipotent.
>
> (Kellermann 1992: 66)

The long training of the director helps him or her learn to guide the action through minefields and poppy fields, with the director always agile and ready to go where the protagonist leads. Adapted from a psychodrama director's processing checklist by Kellermann (1992: 168) I include a few of the many tasks in which the director uses his or her spontaneity. For those who do direct psychodrama, congratulate yourself on the enormous task undertaken by you each time you stand together and alone.

1 The director builds sufficient cohesion and constructive working group climate.
2 The director stimulates individual group members sufficiently and warms them up to action.
3 The director establishes a therapeutic alliance.

4 The director identifies non-verbal messages of the protagonist as well as the verbal.
5 The director identifies central issues in the enactment and helps the protagonist show the group what happened rather than talk about it.
6 The director uses psychodramatic techniques such as role reversal, doubling, mirroring and soliloquy adequately to move the action from the periphery of the problem to the core of the issue.
7 The core of the issue may involve a catharsis of emotion, insight catharsis, catharsis of laughter or catharsis of integration, which the director maximises appropriately.
8 The director shares from his or her own life history.

THE RIVER OF FREEDOM, SPONTANEITY AND CREATIVITY

It has been said, 'Don't push the river'. Doing what you love brings you all the other things that you think you want.

The freedom to fail is vital if you are going to succeed. So, let the river flow, do what you love and don't be afraid to fail.

One sunny day, a balloon seller handed a young girl a balloon with a long string. He looked her straight in the eye and said, 'Give it out and it comes back; you reap what you sow.'

REFERENCES

Goldman, E. and Morrison, D. (1984) *Psychodrama: Experience and process*, Dubuque, Iowa: Kendall Hunt.
Holmes, P. (1992) *The Inner World Outside*, London: Routledge.
Karp, M. (1992) 'Psychodrama and picallili', in P. Holmes and M. Karp (1992) *Psychodrama: Inspiration and Technique*, London: Routledge.
Kellermann, P.F. (1992) *Focus on Psychodrama*, London: Jessica Kingsley.
Koestler, A. (1989) *The Act of Creation*, London: Arkana.
Laskow, L. (1992) *Healing with Love*, San Francisco: Harper.
Moreno, J.L. (1934) *Who Shall Survive?*, 1st edn, New York: Beacon House.
—— (1953) *Who Shall Survive?*, 2nd edn, New York: Beacon House.
—— (1977) *Psychodrama*, vol. 1, 4th edn, New York: Beacon House.
Moreno, J.L. and Moreno Z.T. (1948–77) *Psychodrama*, vol. 1, 4th edn, New York: Beacon House.
—— J.L. and Moreno, Z.T. (1975) *Psychodrama*, vol. 3, New York: Beacon House.
Yeats, W.B. (1936) *Prayer for Old Age*, Collected Poems, London: Macmillan.

Chapter 3

Locus, matrix, status nascendi and the concept of clusters

Commentary

An individual's psychological make-up, or psyche, can be understood both in terms of its locus and status nascendi (the place and moment of birth) and its present structure, which Moreno called the matrix, considered in part to be clusters of psychological roles within the mind.

Dalmiro Bustos takes these concepts, which are underappreciated parts of Morenian theory, and shows how he has developed them into key elements that guide his work. Later in this book we will consider psychodrama itself in the terms used in this chapter. These aspects of Moreno's metapsychology explain what many psychodramatists have observed, but never quite conceptually understood, while they are directing a session. By making the theory clear, Bustos has given psychodramatists information that they can apply consciously in their work with clients. His clinical example shows the humanity of the method and how it can transform a previously blocked-off life. It also provides a moving link between the histories of the old and the new worlds.

Wings and roots

Dalmiro M. Bustos

> In a philosophy of the moment, there are three factors to be emphasised:
> the Locus, the Status Nascendi and the Matrix. These represent three
> views of the same process. There is no 'thing' without its locus, no locus
> without its status nascendi, no status nascendi without its matrix. The
> locus of a flower, for instance, is in the bed where it is growing. Its
> status nascendi is that of a growing thing as it springs from the seed.
> Its matrix is the fertilised seed itself. Every human act or performance
> has a primary action-pattern, a status nascendi.
>
> (Moreno and Moreno 1977: 58)

Here, Moreno offers some features for a rational approach to a comprehensive perspective of reality. If these are valid for all human acts or
performances, can we apply them to understand the psychodramatic
method? He goes on to say,

> This principle can be applied to the origins of the human organism: the
> locus is the placenta in the mother's womb, the status nascendi is the
> time of conception. The matrix is the fertilised egg from which the
> embryo develops.

I started my career as a clinical psychiatrist, working for five years, from
1957 to 1962 as a resident in psychiatric hospitals in the USA. After those
important experiences, I studied and practised psychoanalysis both individually and with groups. Freud, Klein and Bion were my guides. In 1964
I met J.L. Moreno during a psychodrama congress in Paris. I had attended
the Sixth Psychotherapy Congress in London, where an aloof Anna Freud
was the brilliant star. Mysterious and distant, she was the symbol of the
unconscious kingdom. I had been invited by a friend to attend the
psychodrama congress where Moreno was in the splendour of his prime
and I saw him directing a session with Zerka Moreno and Anne Ancelin
Schutzenberger as auxiliary egos. Imagine my shock on finding that
Moreno was not aloof at all, but stood with his arms open to plethoric
emotion. I turned to my friend and whispered, 'I wouldn't like to be
treated by this clown.'

Imagining an alliance was indeed prophetic, for not long after that encounter I started my training at Moreno's Institute in New York. There I gradually started to incorporate a new way of watching reality. This was fundamental to me and radically changed my direction. Zerka and J.L. Moreno gave me permission to be spontaneous. I have learned the pleasure of being myself, even with my multiple defects. I have learned to treat my patients from an existential position of encounter, not because it is less responsible and serious, but on the contrary, because from this position I have seen much more and increased my contact with life. Of course there have also been moments of anguish. It seems that anguish and spontaneity are two phases of the same process.

Taking up this stance of living in a continuous recreation of my universe, without totems, is like jumping off the trapeze without a safety net: one has to be ready for anything. Sometimes I watch with envy those people who can live with closed dogmas, but the envy soon disappears (though sometimes not soon enough) and I feel the relief of instability. Having taken the position of living and thinking in faithful union with myself, I keep rediscovering Moreno. His techniques and formulations are my roots, which are nourished in the fertile soil of the Morenian psychodrama. But being faithful to my teachers is also about having my own wings and flying without betraying my roots. I know Moreno wished that I would use my wings. I once asked him, whilst playing his role in a psychodrama, about this. He replied, 'If you keep my lineaments in a dogmatic way you would be betraying me. I told you to "be yourself" and not try to be me.'

MORENO'S THEORY

It took me very little time to incorporate dramatic techniques into my work. Soon after starting my training, I was ready to dramatise small scenes and practise reversing roles. I came closer to my patients, showing and sharing my feelings with them. But it was difficult for me to comprehend theory. Accustomed to the clear systematisation of psycho-analysis, it was difficult for me to get inside the chaos with which Moreno presented his thoughts. He contradicted himself thousands of times and left people free to order their own spontaneity. He did not give us a completed doctrine.

Marineau (1989) says that Moreno spent the time travelling and teaching psychodrama that he could have dedicated to systematising his theories. In some ways I think this is true, but I also feel that the process of systematisation was opposed to his thinking, which was not methodological or structured. He only achieved a methodological, structured theory in *Who Shall Survive?* (Moreno 1934/1953) in relation to sociometry. The truth is that it is our turn, his disciples, to reorganise his work creatively without betraying the roots.

During the years, whilst practising and teaching psychodrama, I have found difficulties in communicating the method in ways other than the active, experiential way. The best way to learn psychodrama is by doing it, in the roles of protagonist, director, auxiliary ego and group member. The emotional factor is the guiding star. Contrary to psychoanalysis which exalts the rational, emotion takes a central place for psychodramatists. When submerged in the dark, psychodramatists feel their way whilst psychoanalysts think their way.

To confuse thinking with rationalisation is erroneous, just as it is to confuse emotionality with emotional instability. I have therefore tried in my search through my Morenian roots to find something that allowed me to order in a rational way the theory of the psychodramatic method. First, it is clear why Moreno did not develop this himself. Psychodrama was designed to function as a therapeutic act: that is, it was therapy reduced to only one session or at least to a sequence of only two or three. Moreno never thought of it as a method to apply in a long psychotherapeutic process. It was the first time that a therapeutic approach allowed for a beginning, middle and end in a reduced time. Psychoanalysis proposed daily sessions until the pressures of real life made it impracticable. It is impossible to demonstrate a psychoanalytic session in public because it was not designed to fit into such a format. It is possible to speak, write and think about psychoanalysis, but it cannot be shown. Many times during a psychoanalytic session, nothing apparently significant occurs: it has to be understood from the process. Psychodrama allows comprehension independent of a process within it. It may or may not be described. But when we apply psychodrama as a method within individual treatment (*psychodrama à deux*) or in a group, we need a different methodological framework. Many people turn to psychoanalysis when confronted with the problem of a seeming lack of a theoretical basis.

Before continuing, we must emphasise the specific use of the word 'matrix'. It comes from the Latin *mater* meaning mother, the greatest nutrient, nurse, the earth. 'Matrix' was also used in Latin as the word for the uterus or womb. But Moreno uses the words in a creative way (sometimes a capricious way). What he strictly defines as locus (the bed where it grows, or placenta in the mother's womb) would be a matrix, generally speaking. This is confusing. If we respect Moreno's sense, we see that the term 'locus' determines the place where *something* was born. Status nascendi is then the temporal dimension, the moment in which it occurs. So, the term matrix designates that *something* in its maximum specificity.

If we continue with the concept of matrix as the fertilised egg or the germinating seed, we see that it contains the elements of genetic information which will determine in the future whether it will be a plant or a baby. It is something specific and not repeatable. It is to this aspect of the *something* that Moreno is referring. The term locus is a conditioning factor but not the determining factor *per se*. It is not specific, but it has a great influence on the final character of that something. The soil in which a seed is planted can be more or less fertile, the placenta can provide good or poor nutrition. These conditions can determine whether a rose is more beautiful and full of colour, with strong or weak petals, but they cannot transform a rose into a violet or a daisy. Neither can a male baby be transformed into a female baby or vice versa. The moment or status nascendi is a temporal dimension, without a form except for the space wherein it occurs. It also plays a conditioning role: a plant that germinates at the right moment when the soil offers maximum fertility is different from the plant which germinates at the wrong moment when the environmental factors are not favourable.

THE LOCUS, STATUS NASCENDI AND MATRIX OF PSYCHODRAMA

Let us now look at the psychodramatic method. A patient comes for a consultation about a specific complaint. This is equivalent to that 'something': a flower or a baby. It is the 'what' that we now have to investigate. Now we consider the following:

1 A clear, specific determination about what is wrong and what has to be put right.
2 An investigation of the locus or group of conditioning factors where this something was created.
3 An investigation of the specific determining response that the person made to the stimuli that were present, i.e. the matrix.
4 An investigation of the specific moment when this response emerged, i.e. the status nascendi.

The session

Let us consider a specific psychodrama session. We have a protagonist with a certain complaint whom we shall call Betty. She complains of being unable to relate to men. When she is with a lover, she feels totally weak and accepting of anything they say or do. Her complaint is acted on the stage with auxiliary egos during a group session. She shows a scene in which she ends up giving up everything she has to follow a man who mistreats her. We now have the task for the first part of the psychodrama, to investigate in action 'what' is going to be the focus of the session. Through the technique of concretisation, she chooses an auxiliary ego who will represent this particular behaviour. We shall keep this auxiliary on stage all the time. Betty says that this behaviour is a constant pattern regardless of the characteristics of any one lover. She calls this behaviour the 'pleasant martyr'. In role reversal with the pleasant martyr, she informs us that she was born to please people. She is asked at this point when she was created by Betty and what was she created for. She recalls a scene from her early childhood. She is 4 years old, it was 1945, and she is with her two older sisters and parents as they are emigrating to Argentina.

Nobody has explained to her why they have moved from Germany. She doesn't understand Spanish. When asked what she is feeling, she replies, 'Fear', and bends over. She says that we should speak in low voices. I ask her who 'we' are. She replies, 'All of us, including you.' The lack of discrimination between reality and the psychodrama shows the degree of involvement. We were all there.

She says, 'Don't let my father listen to us. If so, he will kill HER.' Very carefully, she picks the auxiliary ego to play her father's role. Once he is on the stage, I ask her to reverse roles with him. I feel she might not be able to reverse roles with him because of her great fear. But she does and rapidly changes her expression and body posture. In the role of her father, she says he has been a sergeant in the Nazi army. He has decided to leave Germany after being wounded. He has managed to escape from hospital, but feels he is a coward. He says, 'Men are born to stand for their ideals and be ready to kill or die.' I ask him, 'What about women?' He replies, 'They are frail and need protection. They cannot think for themselves.' The scene continues between father, mother and the three sisters.

At one point, the eldest sister, played by Betty in role reversal, starts to cry and shouts accusingly at her father that he is torturing the whole family. Next moment, in the role of father, she turns towards her mother and beats her. I am surprised. Betty's sister shouts and her mother is punished? Betty as her father says:

> I have to keep them all under control, this country is full of Jews. If my family start saying what they shouldn't, we'll all be in severe danger. I'll punish their mother for anything they do. Guilt is the best rope.

Up to this point we have investigated the locus, the combination of social and familial conditions surrounding the protagonist. The main question now is how is she going to react to the situation? What type of response will she make that will be specific and to a certain degree chosen by her? This response constitutes the matrix. Our focus in psychodrama should be to investigate the locus in order to operate on the matrix. Often therapies waste too much time working on the series of circumstances, often tragic, which condition the patient's maturing process, instead of going directly to the instance in which the response operated. Since it is her response, she can change it. Betty could have denied the whole situation, or learned to run away or perhaps become a Nazi herself. The particular response we make to stimuli is ours and depends on various factors. As Moreno pointed out:

The area ranging between hereditary influences and tele operations is dominated by the S factor. The S factor is thus the soil out of which later the spontaneous, creative matrix of personality grows. This personality can be defined as a functionof G (Genes), S (Spontaneity), T (Tele) and E (Environment).

(Moreno and Moreno 1977)

Betty is faced in psychodrama with her response to the situation and confronts the auxiliary playing the part of the 'pleasant martyr': 'If I hadn't have used you, the situation would have been worse, much worse.' I ask her to show me how this little 'pleasant martyr' solved the situation. The pleasant martyr replies: 'I smile with pain, I accept the punishment he was giving my mother as if it was the natural thing to do, then he will stop.' In the role of father this is accepted and he says: 'She is the only one who makes me feel guilty and since I can't stand the feeling, she controls me.'

So she wins by being the loser. She then replies: 'If I don't do this, I would feel so much anger that I would kill him.' I tell her she could do that now and give her the space to experiment with new ways of handling her aggression. She has a strong aggressive catharsis but afterwards says: 'I don't want to kill you, I need you.' She then embraces the father tenderly. I ask her what she is going to do with the 'pleasant martyr' now?

This is the moment for re-matrixisation: she created this pattern of behaviour so she can change it if she now understands why she behaves in this way. She can re-create her life and thus be born again. She helps the auxiliary playing the role of 'pleasant martyr' to rise and says: 'Now you are free. The question is not to be the martyr in order to control them, or otherwise you would kill them. You are not happy doing that, so get up and start trying to bounce.'

The catharsis is necessary prior to the re-matrixisation, otherwise the amount of tension interferes with the re-establishment of spontaneity. She had developed a fixed pattern of behaviour defensively which was therefore connected with anxiety instead of spontaneity. By focusing on her response, she takes an adult and affirmative responsibility for her behaviour as a first step towards positive change.

THE CONCEPT OF CLUSTERS

So far, I have described the theory of the method of psychodrama, hoping it will help psychodramatists to conduct a session. But another of my concerns when practising and teaching psychodrama is, can we understand human suffering in a systematic way, without having to resort to classical formulations about psychopathology? Those concepts are widely accepted in our culture. Terms such as neurosis, psychosis, hysteria, etc. are part of our day-to-day language as well as being diagnostic categories in psychiatric and psychological classifications. Moreno always felt strongly against using the ideology underlying psychiatric formulations and instead offered a new way of looking at human suffering which was more sympathetic and based on health rather than on pathology. Within his theoretical formulations we can find some concepts, which, if properly developed, could help us to complete his theoretical work without betraying its essence.

The concept of 'clusters' (see Figure 1) is one such formulation of Moreno's that I found which could lead us forward in this way. He says: 'Roles are not isolated, they tend to form in clusters. There is a transfer of S from unenacted roles to the presently enacted ones. This influence is called Cluster Effect' (Moreno and Moreno 1977). Again in his book *Who Shall Survive*, he says when referring to his role diagram: 'It portrays the clusters of roles of individuals and the interaction between these roles' (Moreno 1934). This means that roles *intercommunicate*: they have the capacity for experimental exchange. A pattern of behaviour acquired in the father's role can be applied to others of a similar dynamic in which the exercise of authority dominates, e.g. the role of boss or the role of professor.

What are the essential dynamics of a human being? To answer this question we must observe the first evolutionary experiences. In its matrix of identity, which is totally undifferentiated, the baby finds himself completely defenceless. Its survival depends totally on its mother or the responsible adult who takes care of it and feeds it. This dependence is total and the baby's actions are related to the ingestion of food. Defecation is involuntary, as the baby does not have any active control over it until later. These are the roles that Moreno called *psychosomatic*. I rather think that these can be called functions of the role of the baby, for they do not completely conform to the concept of a role, which is a psychosocial unit of behaviour and presupposes a two-way process with rules governing its action. Therefore, from my point of view, psychosomatic roles should be seen as protoroles or inherent functions of the role of the baby and not strictly speaking roles in their own right.

The three main clusters	
Cluster one	To incorporate passively and to depend
Cluster two	To look for what we want, to achieve autonomy
Cluster three	To share, compete and rival

Figure 1 The main clusters

Cluster one

Let us go back to the role of the child in its early stages. It is dependent, passive, incorporative. If these experiences occur with more spontaneity than anxiety, then their capacity for adult acceptance of the dependence will be positive. Culturally, the word dependence is in some way denigrated: there is much cultural pressure to be autonomous, self-sufficient and not needing anyone. Our culture exalts an autonomous figure that is very close to loneliness. But we know that to be able to love as an adult, we have to learn to depend spontaneously and maturely on the loved person. Not only under these circumstances is it necessary to assume dependence. Life, sooner or later, confronts us with losses and frustrations. No-one lives in a state of constant success and triumph. Losing hurts. It is there, when it is necessary to accept being passive and dependent, that we can allow ourselves to be cared for and held until the pain passes.

The spontaneous anticipation of this holding makes it possible to take risks to love and we then feel stronger. If these first experiences generate anxiety instead, which is linked to abandonment and loneliness, then they add to the natural pain that is present in any change, frustration or loss. The denied anxiety leads to an avoidance of the search for consolation and holding. I call this experience cluster one, which unifies functionally those roles where the dynamic is passive–dependent–incorporative. This would include the roles of son, daughter, pupil, patient, etc. In these roles there is a spectrum of necessary and inherent dependence.

Symmetric and asymmetric bonds within clusters

At this point it is important to mention that the possible bonds between roles can be symmetric or asymmetric. Symmetric roles are those where the complementary roles have the same hierarchy and equivalent respons-ibilities. They are recognised because the bond has a proper name, e.g. siblings, lovers, companions, friends. They are essentially symmetric as the same rules are applied to both roles in the interaction. Asymmetric roles do not have a proper name and have to be nominated by the two people in the interaction, e.g. parent–child, teacher–pupil, therapist–patient, boss–employee. Different responsibilities and hierarchies mark these roles. They are relationships in which the power is clearly handled by one of the two in the bond.

It was significant to state this here so that the dependence bond could be understood. In the dependent relationship, there are two parts: the one that feeds, takes care and has the responsibility and power. The other one is the one that is fed, cared for, is passive and dependent. Besides such specific roles, the capacity for dependence is a necessary function in other roles, e.g. husband–wife, where one periodically takes the holding function depending on circumstances. If this doesn't occur, then the interactional dynamic fails.

Cluster two

If we advance through the developmental process, we know that the child passes from total dependence to a more autonomous awareness. He or she takes food in through his or her mouth, he or she learns to control his or her sphincter muscles, he or she walks and achieves his or her own aims. The predominant figure during this growing stage is sometimes the father, who can be linked to activity and the outside world. Although this is culturally and not naturally determined, it is usual that the child has the experience of the mother as the first holding figure. It is her face that the child first learns to discriminate, which is linked to the first stage. Afterwards appears the other figure, the father, which coincides with the acquisition of an active, autonomous position. This dynamic defines cluster two and conditions the performance of active roles which involve work, self-confidence, the capacity to achieve, the exercise of power. They are also asymmetric, but presuppose a prevalence of autonomy and activity.

Cluster three

Clusters one and two, in adult life stay as circumstantial alternatives and exist as potentials. The potency of these alternatives can be masked because the roles more exercised are the symmetric ones, corresponding to cluster three. The prototype of these roles is the fraternal relationship. A brother, sister, friend, companion, colleague acts as the model for these symmetric bonds. No-one takes care or is officially responsible. One has to learn to compete, to rival, to share. But the cluster-three role knows as much or as little as we ourselves know. Such roles put limits, take care of possessions, attack or defend themselves from aggression. Within this field we learn to take care of ourselves more carefully. Therefore these are the three essential dynamics.

To have adequate access to each one could be the answer for that unstable equilibrium called maturity. But life always leaves scars as it passes. This is when the usefulness of these concepts can help us to understand the dynamics of patients. We should seek the wounds in the different clusters. Which are the preserved roles? Which are the roles most affected? Which are the functions that need re-training and repairing?

CLUSTERS IN BETTY'S SESSION

Let us return to the case of Betty. Her complaint was that she couldn't love or devote herself to anyone. She felt humiliated before men and recaptured her power through guilt. Autonomy was impossible within the loving bond to which she submitted. Her father, a factor in the locus, never allowed an independent and strong person to get near him and his capacity for role-modelling being active and autonomous was very low. Cluster two was the first one to be repaired. Betty slowly began to give assertive responses. The myth that 'aggression destroys' which took her into the role of martyr, gave way to a more open display of assertiveness. The aggressive catharsis necessary for this to happen took several months of therapy. In her daily life she was able to begin to set limits for aggressors.

The matrix that generated the martyr as an adaptive response was open to being relearned. My role as the therapist was clearly in cluster two. I was the father who allowed her to rebel without submitting to demands. She could be aggressive, learn to measure her aggression, handle it and use it more appropriately. This enabled her to accept commanding roles in her profession. But her relationship as part of a couple did not improve. During one session, an important point emerged for the first time. Betty stated that when she is alone she feels anxious. Instead of asking herself what must she do she gets in touch with what she wants to do and the anxiety rises.

Betty in one-to-one sessions

This session was an individual one without auxiliary egos. I asked her to close her eyes and to be that anxiety. When she asked, 'What do I want?', she again bent down, but this time covered her head. She said that she felt a 'sour emptiness' which was like that of a baby that is not fed. She only felt hunger, cold, lack of protection; there were no warm feelings. She had become a baby of 3 or 4 months old and the year is 1941. Her scene was set up without actual memories; she only had the bodily sensations to go on. It is crucial to remember that the sense memory contains the most primitive registrations of the human being. Before having affective and intellectual faculties, the human being lives in a world of sensations.

Only later do the affective and intellectual representations appear. Betty said she was 3 months old and only had these bodily sensations. I asked her who took care of her and she answered that her mother was somewhere around and picked up a cushion to represent her mother. I asked her to role-reverse. As her mother, the first thing she did was to ask for some gloves. I did not have any in my office so I told her so. 'Then it is impossible to play the role', she replied. So I got two pieces of cloth and she put them on as gloves. Since the age of 17, Hanna (the mother) has not taken off her gloves, even to sleep. For a short while her husband forbade her to use them, but during the war, while he was at the battlefront, she returned to using them. She told me it was a matter of hygiene. Betty told me, in the role of mother, that when she was an adolescent her father sexually abused her. Since that time she has used gloves so as not to feel dirty. She continued to say: 'Thanks be to God that I have three daughters whom I never touch directly because all contact skin to skin is dirty. I took good care of them, but I never caressed them, that was unnecessary.'

She was then able to watch the scene using the mirror technique. She saw herself as a baby, her mother, the gloves and her rapist grandfather. She began to get in touch with her aggression. She took hold of one of the batakas that I have in my office and sprang forward towards the grandfather, letting out both her own and her mother's aggression together. Afterwards, she symbolically destroyed the gloves, looked at her mother (represented by a cushion) and cried. She embraced her and said: 'How much I needed the contact with your body.'

(It had become very important for her to be touched by another woman. Betty had had homosexual contacts to try and recapture these absent sensations. But it wasn't sufficient to recover the sensations to confirm her existence. She cut off the recognition of what she needed, especially contact with others.) At that moment, she took hold of the baby (represented by a cushion) and caressed it. I returned Betty to her own role and noticed that as the baby she was tense. Gently, I caressed her head and she held me crying: 'I want to be looked after.'

We investigated cluster one and I conducted myself principally from the role of mother. Betty had recovered a healthy aggression, autonomy and a capacity for being alone without fragmenting. Later, when she had recovered, we made a review of what she needed for emotional health and being cared for. She was only able to recover the possibility of good relationships after recovering the functions of cluster three.

Follow-up session

During a group session, one group member called Celia was a protagonist and cried for the first time. Her wounds were in cluster one and prevented her from 'loosening up'. Betty made a critical comment and called her a tearful person who can't share. We then enacted a scene with Celia's eldest sister. She was the fragile one, the one who cried, the sickly one. She was protected by everyone. This made Betty jealous. Emma (her sister) was born during peacetime, when crying was possible. Again the story was told through the role of the mother. When Betty was born, during the war, Hanna (the mother) felt it would have been better if Betty had been a boy. Although she detested boys, war was the time for men. Her disappointment was great, but her husband's was greater: he did not want to see her for several days. From her own role, Betty said: 'I never want to be with my sisters because they always have rights that I haven't. I will pretend that I don't care being with them.' (She simulated disdain preferring her own company.) (This was her matrix.)

Her attitude of being superior to her companions made her unpleasant to be with, which contrasted with the role of 'pleasant martyr' seen earlier. This created difficult bonds where she appeared cold and distant when what she really wanted was contact. In the role of the possible man in her life, Betty understood her responsibility for what happens to her and without feeling guilty she corrected these inadequate responses. From then on, Betty owned her life. She had created her responses, so now she could fight to change them.

Wounds in cluster one are very common in our culture. The Rambo syndrome, not needing anyone, includes men and women. Sometime ago, a doctor who had just suffered a heart attack, came to consult me saying:

> My life has been a constant training to avoid needing someone. Instead I have been trained to attend to others needs, to answer the urgent needs of my patients, my wife and my children. My mother overprotected me and my father divorced her when I was 3. So as not to be a foolish kid, I had to invent 'the steel man' for myself. But the pain of impotence and the need for feelings and caring, infiltrated my heart and trying to recover them nearly cost me my life.'

The truth always finds a way to express itself and when our behaviour creates a barrier, it can become lodged in our body from where it tries to get noticed.

Personally, understanding the concept of three clusters has illuminated me considerably and helped me make things clearer for my students. Some years ago I experimented with another model. Through sociometric testing I tried to understand personality dynamics using positive, negative and neutral signs. But it wasn't sufficient. I then used my 'wings' to develop a sociometric reading of psychodynamics based on a modification of the perceptual test. I still use it in my study groups but the concept of clusters is far more useful. But there is scope for further evolution. My aim is to open a reflective space where I present the essential issues without any preconceptions about their future elaboration.

EPILOGUE

Psychodrama is a rich and inexhaustible resource. It offers a world of dangerous adventures and some peaceful moments. Some psychodramatists leave the profession and turn to other techniques. I have been dedicated to teaching psychodrama for many years and I have observed that many who stop practising do so because their personal style needs a more rational instrument. To direct psychodrama you need a strong capacity to give adequate answers quickly to stimuli and not everyone has this capacity. During moments of personal crisis I have found it very difficult to access my spontaneity. In those moments I use words more and I am more able to control my emotions than when I am using psychodrama.

During periods of social conflict, sociodrama allowed me to help others as well as myself. My son was a soldier in the sad Malvinas War (The Falklands Conflict). Two governments, each wrapped in their own paranoia, foolishly sent many men to their deaths. Together with my wife, also a psychodramatist, we gathered other parents and through sociodrama we created a locus of anti-craziness in the middle of chaos. We were 700 people sharing our anguish and carrying out activities to support our children. At the same time, without knowing it, my friends Marcia Karp and Ken Sprague were using sociodrama to work with families of English soldiers. Moreno's great discovery was being used to create bridges of peace between two countries, whilst their governments were hurtling towards death and destruction. Moreno would have been very proud. He believed in the potential greatness of humans and created an instrument capable of achieving it.

While studying Moreno's work, I always tried not to fall into the trap of disqualifying him because of his grandiosity. I understood that to categorise him as paranoiac and megalomaniac was a misunderstanding of his invitation to an 'Encounter of Gods'. He did say, 'I am God.' But he also invited us to be Gods while reading his works. An 'Encounter of Geniuses', where the genius of one didn't hinder the other. Only if one is in contact with one's own genius, daring to use one's wings, is one then ready to read and understand Moreno. Each one of his ideas is ripe for new developments. The roots offer us rich nutrient to transform them with our wings and to take them to places not yet reached.

I see my own life as a continuous pact between my roots and my wings. When I wish to be tranquil, resting with security and a sense of permanence, my wings are soon agitating to be off again. Then a struggle starts that sometimes finds resolution, sometimes it does not. When this happens I feel strangled until I can find a way out. I identify more with my wings, but I love all my roots: my parents, my brothers and sisters, my teachers. Psychoanalysis was an opening onto a fascinating world. Klein and object relations theory gave me answers to some of my questions. Klein gave me something solid to cling to in the internal world. Moreno fought with these people, but those were his wings not mine.

To end I would like to tell you something more about our friend Betty. She was able to return to her native Germany, where she stayed for two months. She stopped punishing herself as the only means of resolving her guilt, her conflict with her parents and with others. She prayed in a concentration camp, she took flowers to the abandoned graves of her grandparents. She cried a lot and with that crying washed away some of the wounds. She returned to Argentina and is trying to live together with her partner. They want to adopt a child. When she returned to the group, she approached Celia, the group member whom she called 'tearful person'. She embraced her and cried in her arms. Celia is a Jew.

REFERENCES

Marineau, R.F. (1989) *Jacob Levy Moreno 1889–1974*, London: Routledge.
Moreno, J.L. (1934/1953) *Who Shall Survive?*, New York: Beacon House.
Moreno, J.L. and Moreno, Z.T. (1977) *Psychodrama*, vol. 1, 4th edn, New York: Beacon House.

Part II

The locus and status nascendi of psychodrama

Commentary

The two chapters in this section place Moreno and his creation psychodrama within an historical and philosophical context.

René Marineau describes Moreno's early years in Bucharest and Vienna, seeing his work as a response to his personal and cultural experiences, whilst Jonathan Moreno (Jacob and Zerka Moreno's son) considers psychodrama both from his position as a professor of medical ethics and as a psychodramatist. René Marineau in Chapter 4 deals with the Morenian concepts of encounter and creativity and shows how Moreno lived his early life through these two concepts and how they developed within the particular context of his family and the two cultures of Bucharest and Vienna. Jonathan Moreno also deals with the concept of encounter in Chapter 5 and discusses how his father took a different course to that of Freud. Both these chapters deal with where psychodrama had its birth and the moment of its creation when many strands came together for the man. We get an understanding of how Jacob Moreno responded to these forces around him and how he was able to fashion them into his creation, psychodrama.

Chapter 4

Bucharest and Vienna

Commentary

In this chapter, René Marineau considers the locus and status nascendi of psychodrama through his discussion of Moreno's origins in Europe. He points out how Moreno's use of metaphors initially formed a large part of his literal thinking, but later became more differentiated and symbolic. This apparently concrete use of language is perhaps one of the major reasons why Moreno's ideas were subsequently spurned by some of his contemporaries.

Marineau puts this tendency firmly in the context of Moreno's development within his family and culture, which influenced all his youthful fancies. It is in his earliest writings that Marineau sees the development of some of Moreno's key concepts: that life should be based on action, cosmic relationships and the power of surplus reality. These writings also reveal how the duality of revolt and creation in Moreno ran through his life. He was a social revolutionary in action and writing, seeing theatre as devoting itself to getting rid of cultural conserves, and constantly fostering creativity and facilitating encounters in many different spheres. This is why his ideas can still generate new interest and wide appeal: they can reach out to parts of the reader that might otherwise be dormant or disinterested.

The cradles of Moreno's contributions

René F. Marineau

At the beginning was action

At the beginning was the relationship.

These two sayings, the first by Moreno (1975: 25), the second by Buber (1969: 38), are the best illustrations to sum up the origins and meanings of Moreno's heritage. All his life he worked tirelessly to implement a way of life that would enhance creativity through action, and foster encounter through meetings – two realities directly linked to doing and relating. He was a living model of a cosmic person, showing the way by developing methods and techniques that were scientifically sound and helpful to mankind.

The two main thrusts of Moreno's philosophy are the concepts of *creativity* and *encounter*, which are both complementary and intertwined in his behaviour, his writings and in the therapeutic methods he developed. They can be considered as the basis of all his psychological ideas, and the cornerstone of his scientific and professional legacies.

In order to understand both these concepts, and the further development of Moreno himself, a rapid historical overview is needed which we will consider from two perspectives: the first has to do with his early internalised values and attitudes in Bucharest, especially in relation to his parents and his religious mentor, Bejerano; while the second deals with his later personal and professional development in Vienna.

BUCHAREST AND MORENO: HIS EARLY DEVELOPMENT

Moreno was born in Bucharest in 1889 (Marineau 1989). His parents were both very creative in their own right, action-orientated and intuitive. When one looks at what could be called Moreno's psychological process of internalisation, namely his identification with figures from birth, one has to begin in Bucharest, and assess the influences of his father and mother.

Moreno Nissim Levy, the father, was an intriguing figure: an active citizen, a failed businessman and an absent father figure who was going to be even more idealised by his eldest son because of his distance and remoteness from the family. This Turkish-born man married with little enthusiasm, worked most of the time away from the family home, but retained his authority over the children. A businessman who repeatedly failed in various financial ventures, he remained a citizen involved in the community, travelling the 'world', helping friends and neighbours. Even though he was, by traditional standards, a poor role model as a father and husband, he succeeded in influencing his eldest son in the areas of imagination, self-taught education and the primacy of action. In fact, he became an almost mythical figure for the young Jacob, who later transformed his own name to incorporate his father's surname as his new family name, the former Jacob Levy becoming Jacob Levy Moreno. The ability of this young child to transform a real, but unsatisfying relationship, into a more acceptable imaginary one, was going to remain a trademark of Moreno throughout his entire life. To be creative is to develop the ability to transform historical truth into a more acceptable poetic or psychodramatic one, and to find in daily life, even though boring or difficult, a 'surplus of reality'.

The young Jacob's relationship with his mother Paulina Iancu was equally important to him. This very young mother was a warm and cheerful woman, who was also active in the Sephardic community. She was well educated for her time, multilingual and refined. She was going to be much more at ease, unlike her husband, when the family moved to Vienna. Her eldest son Jacob, or Jacques as she used to call him, was her favourite child becoming her right arm, replacing her missing husband. Her son responded, while a young child, to his new role with spontaneity and dedication: we have numerous anecdotes in which Jacob plays God, or takes the lead in children's games. Even though later on he was going to shy away from the responsibilities of fatherhood at first, in the family, he took his role seriously. Spontaneity and imagination were the roots for his creativity, and responsibilities elevated him to the level of God.

Rearing the family in Bucharest was not easy. The family had to deal with a difficult economic crisis, a situation made even more difficult because of the father's repeated financial failures and absences. Nevertheless, the young Jacob Levy was a happy child. In addition to his parents, he was also influenced by the Rabbi Bejerano, an impressive figure in the Jewish community. This man was the director of the school at that time, and the young Moreno was so impressed by his knowledge of the language of religion that he became a quasi-physical double for his image of God. In the imagination of the young child, two figures dominated his imagination and play: the figure of God, (represented by his own father and the Rabbi Bejerano) and the person of Jesus, introduced to Moreno by his mother from her former education at a Catholic school. At an early age, the young Moreno experienced meaningful encounters with God and Jesus, in reality, in imagination and in play, in what might be called a 'normal megalomania' that persisted throughout his life. In a way, he could genuinely say I – God, or I – Jesus. During his adolescence, he would even profess to being Jesus returning to Earth.

In summary, one could say that before leaving Bucharest, the young Moreno had internalised, through his relationship with his father, mother and the Rabbi, most of the creative attitudes and values that were to become so much part of him. The seeds for creativity (which requires imagination, boldness and action) and, in a lesser way, encounter were planted.

Before going any further, a comment is in order. Moreno liked to think and talk in metaphors which were grounded in reality. When he compared himself to God, even called himself a God, one has to remember that this was for him, at first, very real. It is only later on that he himself was able to consider them as images, and not reality. When he was a child, in the period that he called his normal megalomania, he saw himself as God, Jesus, a prophet. While an adolescent, he was still pondering the real meaning of these images. Later, he learned to see them as a way of talking about himself, even though it is uncertain at times as to the real meaning of the words that he used and the action that he took.

When he came to the United States, he chose to abandon the religious metaphoric vocabulary that helps us to understand his philosophy. He moved into the world of psychiatry and deprived his students of a full understanding of his philosophy. One of my aims here, is to fill the gaps in order to show the unity of his contribution. To do so I will have to restore the words that he used to describe himself; the images of himself as God and as a prophet, both as a creator and co-creator of the universe.

When the Levy family left Bucharest for Vienna in 1895 or 1896, the young Jacob was already playing games in which he took the role of God. He had a very ambivalent relationship with his father and displayed much attachment to his mother. Already one could see the type of religious perspective, in a very broad sense, that he was going to display later in a search for a cosmic person. On the other hand, in his later works, we notice very few other traces of the cultural environment from Romania, besides children's songs and games. Still, it would be dangerous to overlook the tremendous influence that these first few years played in his later development, especially in the areas of philosophy, religion and education, which are at the root of his spontaneity, imagination, creativity, role reversal, doubling and encounter. If we consider this early period in terms of methods and techniques of psychodrama, we can see Moreno's early ability to role-reverse and double (with God).

VIENNA AND MORENO: THE CREATIVE UNFOLDING

The family moved to Vienna when Jacob Levy Moreno was 6 or 7. The young child rapidly adjusted to his new surroundings. Vienna was a city that he came to enjoy even though, like his father, he always felt like a refugee among long-established Viennese families. In that sense, Moreno was never to become a true Viennese like those described by Hofmannsthal in *Rosenkavalier* who 'talk with ease and grace, artful in role taking and smooth in their gesture and general approach to life'.

Although he was going to display much of these abilities later in life ('the proper manner that makes all the difference between a true Viennese and the others' (Schorske 1985)), he would often display his rougher and more stubborn side in certain circumstances, rather than display those more cultivated origins. However, being open, clever and involved, the young Moreno was to become, on the whole, a well-adapted schoolchild.

It is important, having said that, to acknowledge the influence that Vienna did have on Moreno, and to follow this through his development, as this shows his integration into the environment in which he grew up. As indicated earlier, the two main pillars from which Moreno's legacy can be examined are his concepts of creativity and encounter. If we examine his early writings and activities with and for people, we can find most of his subsequent methods and techniques. With this in mind, let us review the surroundings in which Moreno grew up and some of the anecdotes about his time in Vienna.

Moreno liked to play the role of God, and through identification to be God. We see that in his children's games (when he sat enthroned above his brothers, sisters and friends), and later, when he told stories to young children while climbing up trees. In every situation he occupied the place of honour. Moreno's need to be seen and recognised was going to form part of his ongoing ambivalence about being God among lesser Gods, yet striving to make everyone equal. This was evident in his search for anonymity and constant striving for fame. It was also going to have an impact, as we shall see, on his way of seeing the psychodramatic stage.

Moreno went to school in the second district of Vienna, a mainly Jewish area. As a young boy, he was exposed to Austrian culture and learned the religious and cultural basis of the Austro-Hungarian heritage. He lived in a city where history was on every corner, and creativity was not only an idea, but a daily reality. People like Mahler, Klimt, Schnitzler, Altenberg and Freud were active in bringing new ideas and developments to the city. Compared to Berlin, Paris or New York, Vienna was a small and provincial metropolis, which nevertheless holds a very special place in the history of the twentieth century and is remembered as being the cradle of many revolutions: political, social, economic, religious, artistic and medical.

It was in the midst of this new sociopolitical context that Moreno grew up. He witnessed, for example, the fall of the Austro-Hungarian Empire, the emergence of communism, the surge of Nazism and the development of socialism in Vienna. However, Moreno was never active in politics. His own values were carved and tested in an environment of pluralism, ideological opposites and contradictions. His own political philosophy was to reflect the view of a man that was above political parties and sectarianism. Being God, or a prophet, made him look at politics and religion from a distance. However, he was to be both a champion of individualism, 'We are all Gods' and communism, 'We all need to share our wealth and support encounters'. It is no surprise that he both advocated anonymity and yet fought for personal recognition. When he decided to leave Vienna in 1925, we can therefore understand why he hesitated, even agonised, between Russia and the United States. From a religious and political perspective, he claimed a kind of universal territory for himself. The locus nascendi (a basic concept in Moreno's philosophy) of this cosmic person would have to be somewhere on a ship which was either Spanish, Greek, Turkish or Romanian. This claim allowed him later to be able to say that a director of psychodrama or sociodrama is above and beyond the members of a group. Even Moreno's roots in the Jewish community were often minimised, except in time of crisis. However, deep down, one can see his attachment to the members of his community through his writings about his close friend and double, Chaim Kellmer. These facts show us that Moreno was and was not a real Viennese, an active militant Jew or an involved citizen. In his own way, he was passionately a part of the cultural and social tissue of Vienna, while his religious upbringing and values made him sensitive first of all to the suffering of people. As we will see, this was very clear when he stood in front of a statue of Jesus during his adolescence.

The idea of **creativity** is everywhere in Viennese tradition and can be explained in a variety of ways, ranging from the ethnic variety of the Austro-Hungarian Empire, the role of the Jewish community, or the geographic situation of Austria on the Danube, to Vienna's position between Eastern and Western traditions or its educational system. Austria is a land of contradictions and it is hard to put into words the essence of this culture which is part of a world-wide re-evaluation of ideas, and yet is so different from other countries. Perhaps, the best definition comes again from Hofmannsthal when he says that for someone to be a true Viennese they must have the 'manner', a mixture of savoir-vivre, politeness, cultural knowledge and time for long discussion (Schorske 1985: 8).

Moreno's first experience of education was quite traditional and typically Viennese. However, as an adolescent, he went through a period of revolt and quit school altogether to pursue his own learning in his own way. His adolescence was a time of rebellion that can be interpreted both as a time of confrontation with and distancing from a dysfunctional family (which ended in his parents' separation), and as a re-evaluation of the society in which he lived and which appeared to him as artificial and false.

This period of revolt can be seen in some of Moreno's early writings. It is truly in the stream of Expressionism, a movement that was then developing in Austria and Germany. In one imaginary monologue, Moreno is talking to God:

> Why did you create the universe in the first place? You could have saved us all from life. . . .
>
> Why did you not start with me? And why did you finally create me? I don't feel good. I don't like myself. I have to eat. But the best food goes out the rear end. I have to walk, but I may slip and fall. I have to grow old, become sick and die. Why? You must have created me when you were sick and old, when your energy had been spent.
>
> Why did you split me in half? I know that I am an imperfect and unworthy being. When you saw that I was incomplete you tore me to pieces and brought forth another being, a woman. I was inferior enough, but she was still more inferior.
>
> This was the beginning of endless misery and futility, the chain of birth and death. . . .
>
> (Moreno, in Marineau 1989: 22)

THE VISION IN CHEMNITZ

This kind of writing is not unusual for an adolescent. However, it was followed, in the case of Moreno, by a mystic experience that was going to change the course of his life. While in Chemnitz, he had a vision in front of the statue of Jesus:

> Standing there in front of the statue, I knew that I had to make a decision, one which would determine the future course of my life. I believe that all men have to make such a decision in their youth. This was the moment of my decision. The question was, how would I choose: was my identity the universe, or was it with the particular family or clan from which I had sprung? I decided for the universe, not because my family was inferior to any other family, but because I wanted to live on behalf of the larger setting to which every member of my family belonged and to which I wanted them to return. . . .
>
> From that time on there was a new surplus of meaning in everything I did, and in everything which was done around me. There was an excess of feeling, of joy, of depression, of love or of anger. It was the way lovers feel in their first excitement at finding one another. The sun, the stars, the sky, the trees seemed bigger. Colours seemed brighter. All events seemed more dynamic to me than they seemed to other people. If a child was born, if a man died, if a fire broke out, if a stranger came in the door, it all seemed so deeply significant, bursting with riddles and questions, and a challenge to my most interior sense of values.
>
> (Moreno, in Marineau 1989: 23)

Moreno never looked back. He made further choices accordingly, including his choice of valuing his relationship with a greater cosmos more than his being a student, an Austrian or a Jew. He embraced a much larger life based on action which sprang from his religious–philosophical choices. The above description is interesting in many ways. From a psychodramatic standpoint, we could see an early definition of surplus reality, and the future commitment of a director as a universal leader.

MORENO AND THE EXPRESSIONIST MOVEMENT

In addition, this text, written around 1904–5, shows us a Moreno quite in tune with the period in which he lived in Vienna. His values resemble much that was to be typical of this new philosophical, literary and artistic movement called Expressionism. Looking at Moreno's development, one has to acknowledge that he was part of this movement. Moreno's early writings, including *Invitation to a Meeting* (1914) and *The Words of the Fathers* (1920), as we will see, are very much in line with this philosophy.

Expressionism was not a School: it had no leader or theoretician. Many of its protagonists did not know each other. Expressionism was born before the First World War, but in fact developed during and immediately after that war. It can be defined as a deep call from the soul and the heart. In order to save the world, poets, philosophers and artists called upon the younger generation to get rid of the old-fashioned (to 'kill the fathers'), and to manifest their creative genius, their moral purity in the development of a new world order. In order to shake up and destroy the 'bourgeois' society which was responsible for the failing social and political organisations, youth needed to express violence and despair, and get rid of both the institutions and their protagonists ('the fathers'). It was even necessary to change the means of expression such as language and art. Ultimately, one would find new emotional qualities and expression in daily experiences. 'Let's destroy and rebuild from new perspectives' was one motto of the movement.

Obviously, Moreno's early writings show signs of the dual movement: revolt and mending, his revolt against God being followed by an act of faith in the Creation. By rebelling against the wealth and arrogance of the rich and encountering with the poor, these deprived souls were then elevated to the level of gods.

This duality of revolt–creation was later to find expression in Moreno's life, especially when he wrote *The Words of the Father* (1920). Nowhere is this as obvious as in this book, a religious and philosophical essay which he wrote with his girlfriend Marianne. If one reads it as an expression of Moreno's philosophy, one recognises that a new world order is possible if each individual:

1 Restores his primary capacity to create (using his spontaneity and his imaginative potential),
2 believes in his own capacity, thus acknowledging his being God,
3 takes responsibility for becoming a cosmic co-creator of the universe,
4 recognises that everyone is equally God,
  and
5 acknowledges that the future of mankind resides in the meaningful encounter of all Gods.

(Moreno 1920)

Moreno wrote this philosophical–religious essay while he was living quite happily with his muse, Marianne: this good relationship allowed him to be creative. This essay, first published in the journal *Daimon*, shows a Moreno that went full circle: the 'prophet' who used to wear a green mantle while at university speaks creatively because he experiences himself as a complete person (he and his female partner being 'one'). This was not possible when he was alone and unhappy. He showed here that while an adolescent he was 'split in half' and could only revolt, but when he became a 'whole and unified' person (especially through a significant love relationship) he could 'father' the universe. Creativity and encounter were intertwined for Moreno, and very concrete. When later he met his future wife, Zerka, he would again acknowledge that in order to be creative, he needed to encounter this other half that allowed him to breathe, move, talk (Moreno in Marineau 1989: 104). The importance of a muse in Moreno's life was to be a persistent factor in the manifestation of his creative genius.

To summarise, let us say that Moreno's self-development made him associate with ideas of the Expressionist movement, and that these ideas found a concrete manifestation in his relationships and writings. In both, Moreno made it explicit that more than the 'end product', it was the process of creation and the nature of the relationship that counted (Moreno 1985: 1). It is interesting to note that among the contributors of the journal, *Daimon*, that Moreno created with a group in 1918, we find many writers and artists directly associated with the Expressionist movement: Franz Werfel, Oskar Kokoschka, Georg Kaiser, Albert Ehrenstein, Heinrich Mann. In fact, the content of this journal was such that it could be considered as a vehicle for the movement. All his life, Moreno would show his dual nature, the revolutionary and the creator, a split shown also by some of his contemporaries and colleagues, such as the Viennese painter Egon Schiele, the playwright August Strindberg and the architect Walter Gropius.

FROM PHILOSOPHY TO ACTION

Moreno, the adolescent who ran nude in the streets of Vienna, also chose to dedicate his life to his fellow citizens, and in the first instance to the children of Vienna. The story is well known.

As a young man, he liked to go to the park, to gather children around him, to tell stories and play games. What was obvious, was his attempt to restore creativity in the children by suggesting games that prompted spontaneity, and re-evaluation of traditional educational values. He brought revolution to the Gardens of Vienna by fostering creativity and encounters with and among children. As in other areas of his life, Moreno played multiple roles with children. He re-enacted his pleasure in being a child and a godlike child by climbing to the top of trees; he relished the special place that children gave him in reality and dreams; he acted as a guide in the children's challenge of the roles of authority.

All these roles were to be part of Moreno the psychodramatist. Later, he enjoyed directing the protagonist, identifying with them, role-reversing, mirroring and doubling for them, in order to challenge their cultural and personal conserves, yet remaining the one vehicle for their journey.

In an experience that was the forerunner of group therapy, he also worked with prostitutes and assisted them in finding their own way, being helpful to one another. This became a kind of self-help group, which was made possible by the homogeneity of the participants. This experience can be seen as a forerunner of a well-functioning organisation based on sociometric choice and true encounters. However, we have to remember that at the same time Alfred Adler was active in developing career choices for adolescents and Wilhelm Reich was focusing on the use of body work in psychotherapy. Moreno was part of a larger environment where experimentation was very popular.

With some friends, including Andreas Petö, Moreno also founded a house for refugees. Here again, he showed his concern for his fellows (he, too, was once a refugee), but now in a context where this house was more than a roof over the heads of needy people. He did it with fellow students, in an atmosphere of dedication and joy, community spirit and creativity; in short, a kind of Beacon before its time. This house was a place, but it also reflected a philosophy: the religion of encounter.

The young Moreno also liked to re-enact courtroom trials in which he took many roles, including that of the judge, and in which he was able to predict the verdict. Moreno, who brought the concept of role to psychiatry, followed here his original path of action by experimenting through role reversal, doubling, soliloquy, mirroring and using dramatic representation of the essence of the conflict as a diagnostic and predictive tool. He was to do the same later while training his students, and even while being an expert journalist forecasting the winner of boxing matches in America. He enjoyed great success. Here, we see for Moreno the importance of action that was to become fundamental to psychodrama (Marineau 1989: 116–18, 130–6).

AXIODRAMA, SOCIODRAMA AND PSYCHODRAMA

Moreno was also very involved with revolutionising society. He came to believe that this would best be done through theatre. In order to achieve fundamental changes, theatre had to devote itself to doing away with cultural conserves, which were seen as the finished product of a creative effort, like a play, a book or a symphony. He used two ways – action and writing – and he hoped that through spontaneous theatre this barrier to creativity would be lifted. So Moreno experienced successively with methods which would become known as axiodrama, sociodrama and psychodrama.

Axiodrama is drama based on the exploration of social ethical values. The best-known example took place around 1911. In this a spectator in a theatre confronted an actor playing the role of Zarathustra by going onto the stage and forcing the actor to talk about himself rather than a role written by someone else. The ultimate aim of this axiodrama, whose protocol was later published in the *Daimon* (Marineau 1989: 45–6), was to force everyone – the actor, the director, the writer and even the spectator – to let out their true 'self', rather than to hide behind a mask or a role. Axiodrama was an exorcism for social coerciveness and a plea for a real meeting of people without their masks.

This is what the young Moreno meant by doing away with cultural conserves. Alone or with his friends, he undertook quite a few of these bold confrontations, hoping to create enough of a stir to shake the establishment in the theatre, the school or the church. While Moreno understood the impact of confrontation, he had not yet mastered the importance and subtlety of the process of the warm-up, which would become the strength of his psychodramatic techniques. He would discover only gradually and through repeated failures the necessity to prepare the audiences, the groups and the protagonists for changes and to be aware of the need for proper timing (Marineau 1989: 45).

Sociodrama, a psychodramatic treatment of social problems, was soon to follow. During his medical studies, Moreno mediated between professors and students. While working in a children's clinic during the war, he helped groups of refugees in Mitterndorf to cope with problems that resulted from differences in religion and social origins. In 1921, on All Fools' Day, Moreno made an attempt to address the rebuilding of, in the immediate post-war period, the social tissue of Vienna. Taking the role of the King's jester, Moreno invited everyone, from diplomats and politicians to ordinary citizens to come up on stage and make suggestions for the future of society. The play flopped because of the failure to warm up the audience. But the idea was planted.

In these various experiences, one can see the emergence of sociodrama based on sociometric observations and the use of techniques such as role reversal. Sociodrama would re-emerge later on when he had Germans and Jews, Blacks and Whites explore ways to resolve their problems and tensions.

Then came the Stegreiftheater, which was the forerunner of the theatre of psychodrama. By 1922 Moreno learned, through repeated failures, that it was better to start in a small way with a group of individuals rather than with a bigger crowd. He knew much more about the importance of the warm-up. So he rented a space, and with a group of actors started performances based on improvisation.

The rest is well known. An actress Anna Hollering, known as Barbara, found solutions to her problems by acting them out on the stage. Many links can be made between the production of the impromptu theatre and psychodrama: the use of a stage, the role of catharsis in exploring a problem, (real or imaginary) on a safe therapeutic stage, the presence of ego-auxiliaries, the importance of spontaneity in representing an issue through diverse techniques like the 'living newspaper', and work with couples as protagonists. Impromptu theatre had led to the birth of therapeutic theatre. All of this was going to find its way into a small book that pointed to the future of psychodrama, namely *The Theatre of Spontaneity* (Moreno 1924).

When, around 1909, Moreno entered the medical school of the university of Vienna, it was only to fulfil his need to become a doctor so that he could establish himself as professionally competent. At the same time, he pursued a parallel 'university' of learning; as a storyteller in the Viennese Gardens, as a co-therapist with prostitutes in the city underworld, as a social worker with fellow friends in a house for refugees and as a director of a new kind of theatre. Moreno's tools for learning were never conventional or institutional. He used his creative intelligence to gather information and to profit from experience.

When Moreno was hired as a medical doctor (before his graduation because of the tremendous need for doctors during the war), he discovered and applied sociometry with refugees from the Tyrol. Here, too, his genius was at work: he found solutions through action. Later as a qualified medical doctor in Bad Voslau, he experimented with what today is called individual psychodrama: a depressed German count experienced acting-in of his depression and suicidal fantasies and made a good recovery. The young doctor, Moreno, played the role of the director. He used his nurse assistant as an auxiliary, the patient as the protagonist and experimented with various psychodramatic techniques (Marineau 1989: 68).

THE PSYCHODRAMATIC STAGE

The psychodramatic stage was a very important issue for Moreno's future development and during his life he experimented with two types. The

Viennese stage was developed around 1924 and presented that year at the International Conference for New Theatre Techniques in Vienna. This stage was circular, multilevel and had no balcony and was situated in a building reminiscent of a church or synagogue. People were seated in the building in a way that made it possible for them to move up and down on the stage, which occupied the totality of the surface under the roof. The rational to this design meant that everyone could occupy centre stage at a certain time (meaning they were then the protagonist), or the lower level at other times, which meant being more on the sideline, either as audience or auxiliary egos. This stage reflected a philosophy in which everyone was equal and a participant. There was no audience and no role was assigned before entering the theatre. In this model, Moreno acknowledged that we are all gods deserving, in turn, the leading role before leaving it to someone else. What takes place inside the theatre implies warm-up, action and sharing for everyone. This form of the stage is truly democratic.

The second type of stage, known as the *Beacon stage*, is situated in front of the audience. It has three levels plus a balcony. This model brings us back to the time of the young Moreno in his house in Bucharest or Vienna, who was not only playing God, but also being God when he broke his right arm falling from the top of chairs piled on a table. This model also reminds us of Moreno telling stories to the children in the Garden of Vienna, seeing himself at the top of the tree with the children scattered below. Moreno's first real life theatre in his childhood was a representation of a universe with a god (an authority) above. He was to reproduce this theatre in Beacon, using the balcony to play roles associated with authority, defiance, control, etc. This second model has the advantage of facilitating the confrontation with fearful, domineering or paternalistic figures from above (real or internalised) which prevent the protagonist from taking a meaningful, equal and significant place in his or her environment.

These two stages are radically different, even though they have many similarities. It seems to me that the Beacon model is more traditional and reflects a philosophy less egalitarian than the Viennese model. The more mature theatre of Moreno, which he exhibited in Vienna in 1924 was truly democratic and anonymous: everyone found a place inside, people rotating from one level to another, hence implying that we are all gods, no-one being higher than anyone else. This model never really materialised for Moreno, a fact that suggests interesting questions about his deep commitment to equal status among people and/or his perception of the therapeutic process (Marineau 1989: 82–4).

The two therapeutic stages have their own validity, but also reflect Moreno's early contradictions. Are we all gods and equal (the I–thou position), or are there gods that are above other gods? It is ironical that the real circular stage (the Viennese model) is now widely used in psychoanalytic psychodrama, while the more traditional one (the Beacon model) is associated with classical Morenian psychodramatists.

I could continue to describe Moreno's interests while he lived in Austria, but his life was so rich with experimentation and creation that one would have to follow him through his entire journey. Therefore, I shall discuss only two further points to show how this man of action was constantly open to new ideas and realities, and that he sometimes forgot the danger of not completely mastering the tools he used.

A CONSTANT QUEST FOR INNOVATION

While working as a family doctor in Bad Voslau, Moreno was one of the first professionals to petition for the inclusion of an X-ray machine in his office. One has to remember that Röntgen only discovered X-rays in 1895, and that the practical applications of his discovery only became possible in the early 1920s (with the problems of radiation not being overcome until a considerable time after that). Moreno, in spite of his lack of training, bought an X-ray machine and used it in his office, thus bringing innovation to the small town of Bad Voslau. He got into trouble with the Austrian Health Commission who questioned his competence to use such a dangerous machine, but he went ahead, and invested time and money because he believed that a doctor should be in the vanguard of science. This dangerous, but innovative device is a metaphor of his therapeutic work with people. Moreno was always ahead of his time and was not always attentive to the danger of innovations. Here, he is in good company with his fellow Viennese colleagues, Freud and Reich.

Moreno also worked around 1923 on a device for recording and reproducing sound. It is not clear the exact role that he played in 'inventing' this sound-recording machine but we do know that it caused controversy with the brother of his girlfriend. It was this device that brought fame to him in America, and was the cause of his immigration to the United States. That he played a minor or major role in developing a sound-recording machine is not the issue here, even though it becomes an important ethical issue in Moreno's paternity syndrome. I wish mainly to acknowledge the fact that once again he was interested and involved in developing a new tool for communication: this in itself exemplified his constant interest and quest for creating new methods and techniques in the arena of mankind (Marineau 1989: 95).

CONCLUSIONS

When we look at Moreno's involvement in the medical arena, the theatre and literary scene, we are struck by his constant need to foster creativity and to facilitate encounters. We also become aware of his own contradictions that made him hesitate and sometimes change his way of acting with and for people. However, it seems to me that throughout, two prevailing concepts emerge: creativity and encounter.

Even though he may not always have been a good protagonist of his own philosophy, Moreno's legacy resides in the presence and interaction between these two concepts that were reality for him. We need to be creative at all times. We need to restore in ourselves, through spontaneity and use of imagination, our creative capacity to reflect our inner genius, and to adapt with maturity to any given situation. We then become Creator. If we all do this the cosmos is then filled with creators which makes humanity much better, as long as we are equally attentive to one another's view. Everyone then feels co-responsible for the existence of the cosmos.

The ideas, 'We are all co-responsible Gods' and 'We all need to meet in meaningful ways' are pervasive throughout Moreno's actions and words spoken in Bucharest and Vienna. And so were most of his methods and techniques that he was later to refine. If Moreno was and still remains such an impressive figure, it was then, and still is, because of his unique ability to conserve his spontaneity, probably the most important ingredient for real creativity and encounter among people.

When Moreno finally left Vienna, it was by no means because the city was not a land of creativity, but because he found himself in difficulties, in his personal life and in his professional pursuits. In addition, Vienna was a land of much experimentation, a land of so many gods, that it was difficult for Moreno to create his own place. He decided to go elsewhere. He brought with him his discoveries, the tools that still make Moreno a genius today, a creator and a guide for so many therapists and patients alike.

REFERENCES

Buber, M. (1969) *Je et Tu*, Paris: Aubier.

Marineau, R.F. (1989) *Jacob Levy Moreno 1889–1974: Father of psychodrama, sociometry and group psychotherapy*, London: Routledge. (Moreno's biographical details are taken from this biography.)

Moreno, J.L. (1914) *Einladung zu einer Begegnung (Invitation to a Meeting)*, Vienna: Anzengruber Verlag.

—— (1920) *Das Testament des Vaters* (*The Words of the Father*), Berlin: Gustav Kiepenheuer Verlag.

—— (1924) *Das Stegreiftheater* (*The Theatre of Spontaneity*), Berlin: Gustav Kiepenheuer Verlag.

—— (1946/1985) *Psychodrama*, vol. 1, Ambler, Pa./Beacon, NY: Beacon House.

—— (1975) *Psychothérapie de groupe et psychodrame*, Paris: CEPL.

Schorske, C.E. (1985) *Fin-de-siècle Vienna*, Cambridge: Cambridge University Press.

Chapter 5

Of morals, ethics and encounters

Commentary

Moreno's bringing together of theatre and therapy resulted in clinical tensions, which are discussed here by his son. Therapy seeks to make connections. People's minds are often dramatically lacking in an inner 'population' when disturbance first brings them forward to seek help. The psychodramatist and protagonist play out a real drama in a session in which the patient's symptoms, behaviour and feelings reveal the hidden corners of the past.

This process also occurs in other more verbal therapies, but in psychodrama the healing and the drama are interwoven. The enactment provides revelation, consolation and confirmation of our humanity. This link between drama and enactment was first noticed by Moreno in the Augarten in Vienna, when he was conducting his play experiments with the children.

Moreno's concept of the encounter is another view of the I–Thou relationship. Jonathan Moreno explores why his father took up a different position to that of Freud. In the present re-evaluation of reality and equality in therapy, Moreno's non-hierarchical position, stressing therapy be 'face to face', can be seen as having won a wider acceptance. For example, it is interesting to note that the importance of reality and equality in therapy are now considered worthy of comment by psychoanalysts, a position Moreno espoused in the 1920s. Moreno saw encounter rather than transference as the principle of cure, and his emphasis on action and relation rather than words was a direct refutation of psychoanalysis.

Psychodramatic moral philosophy and ethics

Jonathan D. Moreno

INTRODUCTION: MORALITY AND ETHICS

In the writings and psychotherapeutic work of J.L. Moreno and his followers there is an implicit moral philosophy. This moral philosophy, by which I mean a general orientation towards the good, is bound up with the ideas and outlook of Moreno's formative years in the early twentieth century. This was a time marked by spasmodic political and social revolutions and the introduction into Europe of 'total wars' that did not spare innocent populations. It was also a time of exceptional creativity that broke new ground in the arts and theoretical sciences, especially mathematics and physics. Vienna, where J.L. Moreno attended medical school and lived most of his early life, was at the epicentre of these developments (Janik and Toulmin 1973; Marineau 1989).

When psychodrama emerged, most moral philosophy was a highly abstract study, closely tied to metaphysics. In our own time, there is a more concrete concern about ethical conduct in the professions, suggesting a return to Aristotle's classic understanding of moral virtue as closely tied to practical action, without which claims to personal morality are hollow. When academic philosophers use the term ethics, they refer either to the study of morality, or the study of the standards of moral conduct of specific professional groups, such as health care professionals. Thus morality is, as the word suggests, a *quality*, whereas ethics is a standard of behaviour that is justified according to a moral theory. Therefore behind discussions about ethics in these senses there is a continuing need for a normative theory that can provide a basis for discussions of ethical standards (Kellermann 1992).

In this chapter I will attempt to suggest some moral dimensions of psychodrama theory and also to sketch some ethical issues in psychodrama therapy that are of a practical nature. The founder of psychodrama recognised these latter more concrete ethical concerns, but they were not a preoccupation at that time. The philosophical goals of psychodrama during Moreno's lifetime established a different moral agenda than that which would be required by the standards of professional ethics of our own day. To some extent this reflects the fact that the philosophical morality of psychodrama as a social movement has had to undergo the difficult transformation into the professional ethics of psychodrama as a psychotherapy, a transformation that some will find unfortunate. Yet, I believe that the aims of psychodrama therapy cannot be fully understood without an appreciation of its underlying moral philosophy.

One cautionary note: I have not in this chapter attempted to provide systematic linkages between the ensuing discussion of psychodrama as a moral philosophy and practical problems of ethics in psychodrama. Thus there is an undeniable conceptual break between the two parts of my presentation. It would be desirable from an aesthetic standpoint to identify some connections between psychodramatic moral philosophy and the ethical norms that are to govern the practice of psychodrama therapy. One possibility is that the idea of interpersonal mutuality can do this job.[1] Perhaps I will be able to pursue this question in detail some day, or others will. In the present chapter, the discussion of psychodrama as a moral philosophy proceeds against the background of my reading, experiencing, and thinking about my father's ideas. The discussion of ethical issues in psychodrama therapy is rooted in my professional perspective as a professor of ethics in the biomedical and behavioural sciences.

PART ONE: THE COSMIC DILEMMA

J.L. Moreno is not usually associated with darker thoughts about the human condition, especially as compared to, say, Freud. However, as a child, Moreno seems to have engaged in the same sorts of morbid reflection that many of us can recall in our own childhood, attempting to come to terms with our own mortality before we even have a glimmering idea of what life itself is about. Typical of these childhood reveries, as well, was Moreno's vacillation between nihilism and megalomania:

> Am I only a corpse that will rot and turn into meaningless dust? Or is this consciousness that I now feel extending into the cosmos the most real thing there is, indeed, all that there is? In other words, am I nothing or am I God?

> (Moreno 1941)

For Freud, these alternatives were manifestations of the same fundamental psychical structure, dynamically expressed as the principles of *eros* and *thanatos*, with the latter ultimately prevailing (Gay 1988).[2] For temperamental as well as philosophical reasons, Moreno could not accept such an outcome. Moreover, the logic with which he attacked the problem was different from that of Freud. For instead of looking inwards for a reductive explanation of this dynamic, he looked outwards towards its implications for his conduct in the world. In this sense he behaved more consistently with his medical training and the classical philosophers than did Freud, for in his existential paradox he sought a prescription for action rather than for more study. Moreno's solution was that if he had the choice between meaninglessness and universality, between (in other words) being nothing and being God, then of course he would choose being God!

Strategies towards universality

Several comments are pertinent to this cosmic dilemma and Moreno's personal solution.

First, from a psychiatric standpoint one can understand Moreno's subsequent identification with his patients, who also struggled with the absurdity of existence. In his view, one difference between the mental patient who acts out a psychotic delusion and the 'normal' person is that the former is, for one reason or another, unable to ignore the cosmic paradox; but the result is a terrible loneliness and despair, a result that comes with being an isolate for having pursued the problem of existential absurdity to a socially unacceptable extreme. In this respect Moreno foresaw R.D. Laing's brilliant evocations of mental illness from the 'inside' (Laing 1965).

Second, some would argue that Moreno has a view of mankind as finally 'good', while Freud's treatment of eros and thanatos is more subtle; and it could be added that both are reductionistic in their account of human nature, but that Moreno's reductionism is more simplistic.[3] (In this regard, I remember him telling me that, unlike Freud, as he understood Freud, he believed that platonic love is possible.) To address the latter point first, it is not clear that reductionism to monism is 'more' reductionistic than to dualism, only that the hypothesised target items are structurally different. Further, as I suggested above, I do not see Moreno as pursuing a post-Kantian psychology of mental structures as did Freud. By this I mean that Freud inferred from patterns found in psychoanalysis characteristic sorts of mental activity (e.g. repression and sublimation). He then hypothesised entities (e.g. id, ego, superego) that could account for these mental activities. Moreno was quite uninterested in such speculation, regarding it as abstract and unnecessarily detached from human affairs. If Freud was a part of the platonic tradition in his concern with abstract entities, Moreno was an Aristotelian in his concern with functional processes. In this respect he was indeed closer to the behaviourists, but his behaviourism was akin to that of George Herbert Mead and John Dewey (who served on one of his editorial boards), rather than that of John Watson or B.F. Skinner.

Third, in this period Moreno was also among those who anticipated later-twentieth-century French existentialism, with its emphasis upon the unavoidable nature of choice and individual responsibility, a matter to which I will return. Not usually noted, however, is the similarity of Moreno's existentialist strategy in his personal crisis with that of another physician–philosopher, the American William James (1842–1910). As a young man James suffered from the depressive disorder commonly identified in the nineteenth century as 'neurasthenia', which was also manifested somatically in various aches and pains. Coming upon a catatonic mental patient in a Berlin asylum, James felt himself facing his own potential nothingness. Treating the problem as one of freedom of the will, James determined to adopt the view that his choice was free so long as he *determined* it to be free (Myers 1986). Much like Moreno forty years later, James asserted his own will as the way out of the crisis. From another point of view their decisions might seem self-indulgent, but to James and Moreno theirs were exercises in freedom and affirmations of their personal significance in a vast and ambiguous universe.

Fourth, from a logical point of view, the existential problem that Moreno and others have framed as a choice between insignificance and universality appears to commit the fallacy known as the false dilemma, for surely there is a vast middle ground between these extremes. Having established a false dilemma, we appear to be driven to one unsatisfactory conclusion or the other (meaninglessness or universality), while the more reasonable possibility (that our moral status as beings is somewhere in between) gets ruled out in advance by the way the problem has been set up.

Without speaking for others who have addressed themselves to the fundamental existential problem (expressed in personal terms as 'Why do I exist at all?' or in more general terms by Martin Heidegger (1889–1976) as 'Why is there something rather than nothing?'), I believe that at least in Moreno's case there was a specific rationale for his extreme approach and his radical 'solution'. Like other Viennese intellectuals of the day, Moreno was acquainted with Einstein's early efforts in relativity theory; Einstein was a lecturer at the University while Moreno was a student. In order to formulate his theses, Einstein engaged in the *Gedankenexperiment*, or 'thought experiment'. His method called for the assignment of extreme values to variables in his physical formulae, values that could not be achieved in reality, like perfect vacuums or ideal gases, then following the implications of the result. A salient difference is that Moreno's experiments took place in action rather than only in thought: he took the role of God. Whether Einstein's thought experiments actually inspired Moreno or not, his method was similar: let us see what would happen if we gave individual existence either null or total value. The implications of the former are familiar, in light of which some might choose suicide or depravity. On the other hand, since there is no independent basis or criterion for choosing universality or nothingness, why not select universality?

The strategy I have been describing starts with the ontological question ('What is the status of my own existence?'), exercises the will to believe one alternative ('I am universal'), and issues in a certain moral significance ('If I am universal then I am God, responsible for all beings'). Another strategy achieves the same result, but starts with the question: 'For whom am I morally responsible?' Shall I say only those emotionally or physically closest to me, those related to me by blood, or by marriage, or those on the same street or in the same town or nation? Anywhere one draws the line must be arbitrary. Therefore either I am responsible for nothing or I am responsible for everything. In this approach the moral question is primary, the 'ontological' question (having to do with one's existential status), is derivative.

What is striking is that one can move back and forth between the idea of universality and that of responsibility. I believe that Moreno was intrigued by the 'dialectical' relation between the two, much as Freud was taken by that between eros and thanatos. Moreno's insight was closely bound up with his conviction that, as humankind's conception of the godhead evolved, it came to have greater universality and moral responsibility, from the distant and warlike 'He' God of the Biblical Hebrews to the loving and intimate 'Thou' God of the early Christians. According to this theology, now comes the 'I' God who is personally universal and responsible, both ontologically and morally inclusive. Because the 'I' God is me, and because from my point of view the entire universe is contained 'in my head', I cannot escape responsibility for the whole of the universe (Moreno 1941).

Moral responsibility: the protagonist and role reversal

The dialogue between ontological universality and moral responsibility is embodied concretely in the 'protagonist', literally 'one who undergoes the test' (Greek: *agon*). In the ancient theatre that so influenced Moreno, Oedipus is of course the most famous protagonist. This opens up the question, about what does the protagonist 'agonise'? In the most general sense, what is the nature of the test? I believe one can answer this question in psychodramatic moral philosophy in terms of the nexus of universality–responsibility, that this nexus provides the background of the struggle. The tale of Oedipus provides a convenient and familiar example; it also provides an interesting contrast to the psychoanalytic interpretation of the story's ultimate significance.

Oedipus's crisis, prompted by his *hubris* or arrogance, propelled him into questioning his moral responsibility for the world in which he lived, a world in which he committed patricide and incest. As soon as that question was raised Oedipus also necessarily confronted his true ontological status in such a world: from a man of heroic, nearly divine proportions at the beginning of the play to a fallen god, a 'tragic hero' at the end. In the psychodramatic view, the deeper significance of the play is not the unconscious libidinal impulses acted out in Oedipus's relations with his mother and father, for this was only the dynamic that propelled him towards his fate; rather, of deeper significance is the stage upon which Oedipus is destined to live out the rest of his days, that which is defined by the framework of universality and responsibility.

Let us take this account a step further. The Oedipus story is fascinating and powerful even for those of us who cannot (consciously) identify with his dark passions, drives of which he himself was once unaware. In spite of what psychoanalysis would regard as his rather successful repression, we identify with Oedipus as one who is thrust suddenly into an inescapable web of ontological and moral doubt. Oedipus suffers as we do. His catharsis is a projection of our own. So universal and morally compelling is his situation that we cannot resist role-reversing with him. We may only *sympathise* with his horrific discoveries, but we surely and irresistibly *empathise* with his existential situation. The distinction is significant, for patricide and incest do not for most of us excite immediate empathy, but the agony of ontological and moral doubt is instantly recognisable. It is, in a word, the human condition. We spontaneously reverse roles with Oedipus because his struggle or *agon* is ours.

I have finally used that familiar term in psychodramatic theory – spontaneity. What is the relevance of spontaneity and its conceptual sibling creativity in my account? Clearly, the ultimate test that we and Oedipus face is the occasion for the most spontaneity and creativity that can be mustered. Moreno liked to note an etymological link between *spon*taneity and re*spon*sibility. Linguistically he was wrong, but his error nevertheless provides some insight into his implicit moral philosophy linking the two. Oedipus's situation is one for which he bears moral responsibility, one so harrowing and final that it calls upon the utmost in spontaneous and creative response.

Sociometric morality I: the encounter and the double

All this sets the stage for Oedipus's last calamity: his spontaneous response to his tragedy is to pluck out his eyes and permanently remove himself from human contact. In so doing he symbolises the ultimate in sociometric disconnection: first, Oepidus is blind and therefore literally unable to 'encounter' in the way of the sighted, for he cannot gaze into the eyes of another; and second, Oedipus is an isolate, an abomination to the society of others. Both points deserve elaboration.

The standard interpretation of Oedipus's physical blindness at the end of the play contrasts it with his figurative blindness to his actual situation at the beginning of the play. As if to drive the point home, only an old blind 'seer' is able to forecast Oedipus's downfall. A psychodramatic account of Oedipus's blindness as a metaphor emphasises not only its epistemological significance, but its significance for the encounter as well. Recall Moreno's famous motto in his *Invitation to an Encounter*:

And when you are near I will tear your eyes out
and place them instead of mine,
and you will tear my eyes out
and will place them instead of yours,
then I will look at you with your eyes . . .
and you will look at me with mine.

(Moreno 1914)

Both at the beginning and at the end of the play, Oedipus is incapable of authentic encounters. He is incapable at the beginning because he is blind to his situation, and therefore he is 'living a lie'. He is incapable of authentic encounters at the end not only in the rather trivial sense that he is blind to the gaze of others, but more profoundly because he has become aware of the bankruptcy of his personal identity, of all that he valued in himself, and therefore he is fated to be alone. Finally, because both forms of blindness may render complete encounters impossible (that is, Oedipus is either figuratively or literally isolated), Oedipus himself cannot role-reverse with another.

Sociometrically, Oedipus is at first a 'star', and at the end is an isolate. In the beginning Oedipus is adored by his people and his family, truly the sociometric centre of the Theban city-state, and it is universally recipro-cated. At the end Oedipus is cut off from everyone, despicable in the sight of others and himself determined to stay out of their sight, as they (and he) are forever out of his own sight. But Oedipus's sociometric position as the star was a false one because it depended on a false set of assumptions about who he was. In reality, Oedipus was always an isolate because the 'true' Oedipus, the father-killer who slept with his mother, was not the one who was chosen by all.

Role reversal is a symmetric act, requiring the protagonist to participate. But our protagonist Oedipus is literally and figuratively isolated at the end of the play. He cannot engage in role reversal with us. But isolates can still have doubles, for doubling is asymmetric. All that is required is that the double be able to empathise (in psychodramatic terms, be 'telic') with the protagonist. In fact, the isolate is the easiest sociometric role to double because each of us understands that position so well and fears it the most. Since doubling does not presuppose the reciprocity of role reversal it is a 'nobler' act. It demands more spontaneity and creativity on the part of the other, at least in its first moments, than does role reversal. Looking after the poor and infirm, as Jesus is said to have done, might be just such a noble act. Thus, in the Christian tradition Jesus is able to double for those who are indifferent towards him, and even for those who reject him.

Sociometric morality II: interpersonal choice

Sociometric choice is both the symbol and the occasion for the emergence of the individual as a social creature. When that choice is mutual the idea of moral responsibility is concretised. Consider, for example, the relationships of Jesus and his original group of followers. In psychodramatic terms they chose one another for the roles of saviour and disciples. The drama of the Crucifixion story necessarily unfolded according to the logic of their relationship: as the saviour only Jesus fully understood the significance of their mutual responsibility, and he sacrificed all for them while they betrayed him. The full moral significance of sociometric choice as mutual responsibility is clarified in light of this example of failed mutuality (J.D. Moreno 1990).

The patterns that emerge from sociometric choices are also concrete expressions of universality. These patterns are paths of connectedness through which telic sensitivity instantaneously travels, affirming that each individual's place in the matrix is both discrete and comprehensive. Appropriately, the sociogram resembles constellations in the night sky, each unit both separate and an essential part of its context. In his fanciful tale of 'Johnny Psychodramatist', based loosely on the American fable of a boy who plants apple seeds wherever he goes, Johnny as a child drew lines between the people in his neighborhood, with different colours depending on the way they felt about each other. The result resembled a map. After a lifetime of drawing lines from one to another, Johnny was taken to heaven where, in accordance with his unshakable habit, he drew a map of God and his angels as well. When their surprising feelings were exposed on this map they all began to laugh.

> Johnny was frightened because he thought that punishment would result from his deeds. But as he looked up, he saw to his astonishment that every figure on his heavenly map had turned into a star, and as he looked, farther and farther, more and more stars took their places, millions and millions of them, on the heavenly firmament. And from star to star sprang the lines, in all the colors he had ever envisioned, until they became what they were from the beginning of time, the starry skies of the universe. Every star was the picture of a man he had known when he was on earth, and their emotions were written in the lines that ran between them. The map he had drawn as a boy was now hinged to the skies above.
>
> (Moreno 1987)

A note about Nietzschean irony in Moreno's philosophy

I believe that Friedrich Nietzsche's (1844–1900) writings may have had a considerable impact on Moreno's thinking as a young man. Certainly they were well known enough at the time he was engaged in his early philosophising, even though the implications of *Also Sprach Zarathustra* (Nietzsche n.d.) and Nietzsche's other writings were more obscure than they are today, following a generation of scholarly analysis. That allegorical work, so central to Nietzsche's thinking, describes a (western) world that has stumbled upon modernity, a world in which the old values, and perhaps the very idea of moral value itself, are at hazard. Hence, a revolution in the human relation to God and all values took place while most were at best dimly aware of it. Nietzsche can be viewed as one standing in the distance on the horizon, wildly shouting and waving his arms, trying to call our attention to the full meaning of modernity, while the rest of us go about our business as though the old rituals are not now empty husks. There is enough in Moreno's handling of the God question to suggest Nietzsche's influence, which clarifies initial puzzlement about Moreno's approach to the God question.

In particular, Moreno's identification of himself with God can be understood in terms of Nietzschean irony. Again, ours is a world in which 'God is dead' in the sense that pre-modern values no longer have the gravity they once did. Following Copernicus even gravity does not have its same value, nor directions in space, for in a Copernican universe 'up' and 'down' make no objective sense. The 'direction' provided by morality has also withered. Yet in a world such as this belief becomes even more important, for there is no abolute moral authority to impose constraints upon us. Without such an authority we are literally lost, directionless, doomed to float in a moral and cosmic void without a compass.

Unless, of course, we provide that compass for ourselves. But how, under the circumstances can this be done? Only by executing a kind of psychological trick (a 'will to power'): we must vigorously insist upon and defend certain 'truths', even while we know we might be wrong about them. In the modern era that is the best we can do, and it is enough. But perhaps we are not mature enough, strong enough, to see things as they are and take this ironic attitude. In that case it awaits a 'higher race', an 'over-man', to embrace the reality, to 'love our destiny'.

Moreno's identification of himself with the Godhead may be understood in this ironic spirit. In the ironic sense needed to preserve meaning and value in the modern world, any of us may say 'I am God'. If in the twentieth century it seems there is no God we can still 'will' God to be. Unlike Nietzsche, Moreno does not believe it takes a superman to do this, but that in principle all of us have the spontaneity and creativity to do it. Perhaps, by training the spontaneity and creativity implicit in each of us,

Moreno thought that the psychodrama could produce the Nietzschean superman.

PART TWO: ETHICS AND 'ACTION METHODS'

As a group psychotherapy, psychodrama has in common with other group modalities a number of elements that raise ethical concerns. I have addressed these more general issues elsewhere (J.D. Moreno 1991). Perhaps most fundamental among these is the question whether any psychotherapy can in practice give content to the ethical doctrine of 'informed consent': can psychotherapists disclose the risks and benefits of a proposed therapeutic intervention to a patient or client, as compared to the risks and benefits of other interventions, or to none at all? Although I believe this question poses a signficant moral challenge to the profession of psychotherapy, I will not pursue it here. Rather, in the remainder of this chapter I want to consider two aspects of psychodrama work in particular that create special ethical problems for the practitioner: psycho-drama as an 'action method' and the 'open' psychodrama session.

As noted at the outset of this chapter, ethical concerns have become prominent in the health care professions. It is useful to distinguish between traditional and emerging ethical issues. An example of the former is sexual contact with clients, which is by consensus regarded as a grievous ethical violation. By contrast, emerging ethical issues usually have to do with more novel health care 'technologies', from genetic engineering to psychodrama therapy, and carry with them questions that are not easily managed in traditional terms.

While not new in the history of psychotherapy, action methods like psychodrama are new in the history of health care. They are also a departure from traditional western physician–patient relations, in which the latter is literally the passive partner. Classical psychoanalysis replicates the physician–patient relation more closely than do the action psycho-therapies, which involve a variety of interactional situations between therapist and client. Thus, in addition to talking to the therapist, which resembles reporting one's medical history, in these other psychotherapies there is also enactment. In classical psychoanalysis the potential ethical problems are roughly the same sorts as those of medical practice, including inappropriate sexual advances and violations of confidentiality. But with action methods, and especially with the addition of the group, these issues are complicated further.

Psychodramatic shock

Psychodramatists frequently observe the sheer power of enactment. Explained in psychodramatic theory by the idea of the 'warm-up', as compared to 'talk therapy' alone, engagement in overt bodily activity vastly increases the protagonist's affective involvement in the subject matter. Several kinds of inadvertent harm can accompany the otherwise advantageous nature of enactment for psychotherapy: unresolved psychodramatic shock, physical harm to the protagonist or others and accidently revealed confidences or secrets.

Psychodramatic shock occurs when a protagonist's warm-up suddenly sharply increases or peaks, and remains there for some period of time during the scene. Unlike the usual more gradual warm-up that resembles a gradual curve, this vastly accelerated form often occurs as a surprise to the protagonist him- or herself as well as to the director and group members. The slightest feature of the enactment may trigger an unconscious image fraught with emotionality, often one associated with a painful childhood event. Behaviour resembling hysteria can result, including weeping, trembling, and shocking changes in the protagonist's voice and carriage. Even a language unspoken for many years and seemingly forgotten may re-emerge. In one memorable case, a man brought up in Louisiana enacted a scene in which, as a little boy, he came upon his drunken and abusive father in their living room. Weeping hysterically prior to a furious outburst, he slipped back into the voice of a small child wailing fluently in his native Acadian or 'Cajun', a language he had not spoken in decades. The protagonist may 'come out' of this unforeseen role momentarily and remark on his or her surprise at what is happening, as occurred in this case, but then return to it with little prompting.

The skilful psychodrama therapist will utilise the therapeutic advantages of such incidents, and the catharsis that follows may be quite extraordinary. However, the seering nature of this experience requires more than the usual care in reintegrating the protagonist, both intra- and interpersonally. Failure to accomplish adequate closure is indicated by the protagonist's feeling that he or she has been 'left hanging' and has been exposed to something he or she has not resolved, even in a short-term sense. It is important for the director to recognise this phenomenon even if he or she is uncertain how to accomplish resolution, for often the group can be called upon to provide a comforting 'womb' in which to encircle and cradle the protagonist, providing at least a physical minimum of comfort and reassurance. Psychodramatic shock and its sequelae provide an excellent example of the therapeutic power of the method as well as the importance of well-trained practitioners.

Psychodramatic shock and other deep warm-ups may also expose the protagonist and other group members to the danger of physical harm, as violence may accompany the reactive phase. At such times the director's first obligation is to protect everyone from injury, including the protagonist, suspending the action if necessary to do so. Hesitation in this respect, however well intended, is simply a failure of the director's professional responsibility and judgement. Often risks are taken when the director feels an obligation to help a protagonist complete a catharsis even though the physical arrangements are inappropriate, such as permitting an auxiliary ego to be wrestled to the ground on a hard floor and without the protection that can be afforded by several sturdy and experienced co-therapists. Admirable as directorial motives may be in such circumstances, they should not be permitted to 'trump' his or her better judgement.

A different sort of harm that can accompany warming up occurs when the protagonist blurts out secrets or confidences that could prove embarrassing or even personally or professionally damaging, either to the protagonist or to someone else who may not even be a member of the group. In one case a protagonist working on her anger towards her therapist, who was not present, portrayed what seemed to be a bungled job. Although the director had reached an agreement that the therapist's actual name would not be used, in her warmed-up condition the protagonist used it anyway. At such times it is important to stop the action and remind everyone that they are co-therapists with the moral responsibility to maintain confidentiality. Later, before the session is ended, it is highly advisable to revisit the issue and perhaps even to ask group members to engage in a role reversal with the protagonist and with any other individual who might be harmed by the information. In this way the moral point may be reinforced. In such situations it is most important for the director to establish an atmosphere in which transgressions from the norm of confidentiality will be regarded as intolerable by one's fellow group members. To do that the issue must be addressed directly, perhaps more than once, with an attitude of utmost seriousness.

The 'open' psychodrama session

The open session is an interesting example of the way that ethical concerns in psychodrama have changed, along with the understanding of what psychodrama itself is. For if psychodrama is essentially *theatre*, then some things will be permissible that would not be if it is essentially *therapy*. For decades, Moreno and his colleagues conducted psychodrama sessions that were open to the public, for a modest admission fee. Members of the audience, mostly strangers to one another, were warmed up to very complex psychodramas, and the protagonist and other actors emerged from the group. These sessions, held mostly in New York City, attracted a large following and helped make psychodrama a well-known medium, especially among intellectuals.

When one attended an open session, was one paying for entertainment, therapy or education? Clearly, all three elements were present, and arguably so was a fourth: social reform along the lines of sociometric theory. The problem with assessing the ethics of the open session is precisely that it is difficult to know which category it falls into. If it is therapy, then there are obvious and probably intractable problems of confidentiality (not to mention extraordinary legal risks), in which case one would have to conclude that it is unethical to conduct psychodrama sessions open to the public. If it is theatre or education then the standard of confidentiality does not apply, at least not nearly so stringently, and one would not reach this conclusion.

My own impression is that the open session is often, if not always, implicitly presented as an opportunity for psychotherapy. This would be true in those cases in which the director's goal is obviously to reveal deep emotional content, and I think it is hard to defend such an objective from ethical concerns, in spite of the benefits that might accrue to some indviduals. On the other hand, if the director obviously seeks to limit the exploration to more superficial subject matter, then I think one could argue persuasively that the aim of the open session is educational or theatrical. One way to do this, and to accomplish the social-reform aims as well, is to conduct the session as a sociodrama, so that the action does not dwell upon the details of individual lives.

The ethical challenges of open psychodrama sessions have become more apparent in recent years for at least two reasons: first, psychodrama has gradually become more identified as a therapy than as a form of theatre; second, our society generally has become more aware of ethical issues in health care, such as confidentiality. As one who years ago witnessed hundreds of open sessions and conducted a number of them, I can testify that such questions were hardly in the forefront.

To be sure, Moreno explicitly recognised the problem of maintaining confidentiality in group work. In his *Code of Ethics for Group Psychotherapy*, Moreno asserts that the Hippocratic obligation to keep matters of professional practice secret extends in group psychotherapy to all group members. He also raises a salient rhetorical question about preventing 'leaks' when group members are electronically linked to one another, as in closed-circuit television (Moreno 1962). Perspicuous as he was in raising the latter concern so much in advance of others, his reference to the Hippocratic tradition is dubious, since the oath in its various versions is meant to be part of a socialisation process of professionals, not patients. Promises among non-professionals to keep secrets must be based rather on a sense of human decency or, perhaps, prudence (considering the fear that one's own privacy is also at hazard), but bringing them under the rubric of professional codes seems to me to be a confusion.

There is, however, a further dimension of the open session that is not precisely captured in the categories of entertainment, therapy or education, and this is perhaps its most important quality. This dimension is exemplified in the 'sociodrama' and might be considered as a 'sociotherapy.' The goal of sociodrama is not to provide psychotherapy to any individual, but rather to foster the wellbeing of the group, usually by enhancing its cohesion and potential for co-operative activity. Group members play social roles such as 'teacher', 'policeman', 'bureaucrat' or 'politician' rather than individual roles, and the enactments are based initially on protocols familiar to members of the culture, then modified by the group based on concerns that emerge from the group. In this way a heightened sense of social solidarity often results.

In the open session, a sociodrama has the virtue of including all in the action, at least symbolically, through their membership in the culture that is host to the social roles being enacted. Emotional material that usually individuates group members is transformed into content that energises and enlivens the shared story. The salutary result is that social solidarity is enhanced while individual self-disclosure in this inherently 'leaky' environment is minimised.

Considering the ethical profile of sociodrama, one that is benign for the individual but a powerful agent of change for the group, the open setting for this method is not subject to the same objections as that for classical psychodrama. Indeed, often without calling it sociodrama or even being aware of its conceptual origins, sociodrama has become a routine element of conflict resolution, personnel training and education. Perhaps it is time for the psychodrama community to reclaim the sociodrama in all its richness in the open setting, wherein an ethically sound mix of entertainment, education and social therapy can be accomplished.

CONCLUSION

In this chapter I have attempted preliminary explorations that ranged over a great deal of territory, from psychodrama as a moral philosophy to ethical issues about and within psychodrama. Earlier I argued that psychodramatic moral philosophy turns on the nexus of universality and responsibility. I have also suggested that the ambiguities inherent in the nature of psychodrama (especially whether it is theatre or therapy), raise interesting and important ethical questions, as does the inherent power of psychodrama therapy itself. These and other questions will surely be discussed more as psychodrama continues to establish itself as a precious and unique medium of human expression.

NOTES

1 The editors of this volume, particularly Marcia Karp, suggested this to me.
2 I recognise that my interpretation of this dualism in Freud is by no means universally agreed. My view derives from the drift of his work in the last decade.
3 I owe these points to Kellermann, personal correspondence, September 16, 1992.

REFERENCES

Gay, P. (1988) *Freud: A Life for Our Time*, New York: Norton.

Janik, A. and Toulmin, S. (1973) *Wittgenstein's Vienna*, New York: Simon & Schuster.

Kellermann, P.F. (1992) *Focus on Psychodrama*, London: Jessica Kingsley.

Laing, R.F. (1965) *The Divided Self: An existential study in insanity and madness*, Baltimore: Penguin Books.

Marineau, R. (1989) *Jacob Levy Moreno, 1889–1974*, London: Tavistock/Routledge.

Moreno, J.D. (1990) 'Das Phänomen messianischer Anerkennung und seine Beziehung zur soziometrischen Wahl', *Bausteine zur Gruppenpsychotherapie* 3: 675–72.

—— (1991) 'Group psychotherapy in bioethical perspective', *Journal of Group Psychotherapy, Psychodrama and Sociometry* 44(2): 60–70.

Moreno, J.L. (1941) *The Words of the Father*, New York: Beacon House.

—— (1946) 'Einladung zu einer Begegnung' (1914), *Psychodrama*, vol. 1, New York: Beacon House.

—— (1962) *Code of Ethics for Group Psychotherapy and Psychodrama*, Psychodrama and Group Psychotherapy Monographs, no. 31, New York: Beacon House.

—— (1987) 'The story of Johnny Psychodramatist', in J. Fox (ed.) *The Essential Moreno*, New York: Springer.

Myers, G. (1986) *William James: His life and thought*, New Haven: Yale University Press.

Nietzsche, F. (n.d.) *Thus Spoke Zarathustra*, New York: Modern Library.

Part III

The matrix of psychodrama

Commentary

The source for the duality that exists in the discussion of Morenian psychology can be traced to his early experiences. He studied both philosophy and medicine at Vienna University and there is a tension running through all his writings that reflect these two interests which can also be found in the chapters in this book. We believe that this polarity is reflected in much of his legacy and that it has been underestimated by many of his followers. Once it is appreciated his psychology and indeed his writings as a whole become clearer and yield their understanding more easily.

The chapters in this book indicate the divergence of positions that exist within the psychodrama world, the richness and range of Moreno's ideas relating directly to the creative tensions that exist between, for example, the scientific and the metaphysical; the theatrical and the clinical; the personal and the public; and the written word and the spontaneous moment. In any one chapter, the reader can see the presence of both poles, indicating that there is no pre-eminence of any one position and that these tensions between various potential positions add vigour to psychodrama. This situation reflects Moreno's view of himself and the world. On the one hand he was involved in attempts to measure and compute factors involved in human relationships (the results of this area of interest are described in Chapter 7 on sociometry and sociodynamics), whilst on the other hand his concerns with the cosmic nature of man involved an awareness of life that was immeasurable. These ideas are central to the chapters on Moreno's philosophy, religion and the spirit and the co-unconscious.

Rowan and Dryden, in their introduction to the book *Innovative Therapy in Britain* (1988) have a diagram in which the various schools of psychotherapy are plotted in what they call the 'therapeutic space', which they consider to have two dimensions. The first relates to the degree of consideration that the therapy gives to conscious or to unconscious processes. The second dimension addresses a psychospiritual continuum, which stretches from those therapies having a principal concern with intrapsychic phenomena, to those therapies with significant emphasis on

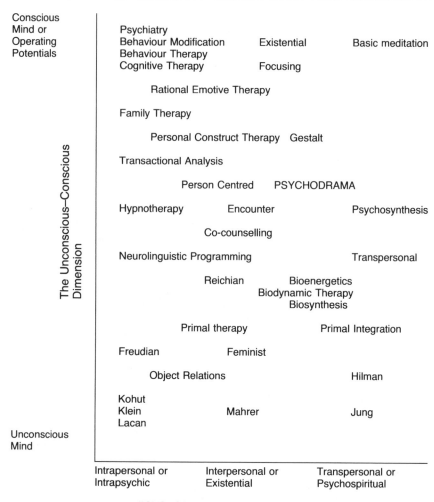

Figure 1 The position of psychodrama, plotted in a therapeutic space

Figure 1 The position of psychodrama, plotted in a therapeutic space
Source: based on Rowan and Dryden 1988

transpersonal or spiritual issues. In the middle of this axis are those therapies which deal with the relationships of the self to others. In Figure 1 (which is an adaptation of theirs) psychodrama appears in the centre, surrounded by thirty-two other schools within psychotherapy. The reality is that the different concepts in psychodrama pull it towards all four corners of this graph (see Figure 2), making it a multidimensional, multifaceted method of psychotherapy.

It is possible to conceive of Moreno's concepts as falling into clusters within which certain ideas predominate. Chapters 6 to 12 in this book have

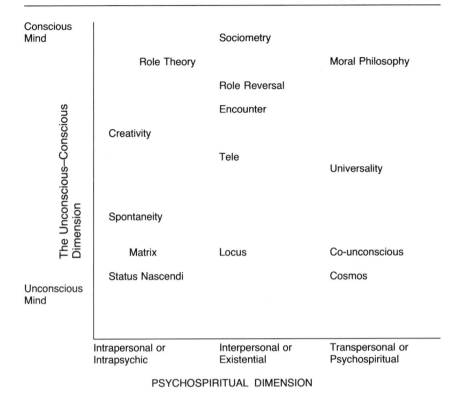

PSYCHOSPIRITUAL DIMENSION

Figure 2 The distribution of Moreno's concepts within a therapeutic space

been organised into four parts that reflect how the different concepts can be clustered or grouped together.

The first cluster (the cognitive and conscious dimension) consists of Chapter 6 on role theory and Chapter 7 on sociometry and sociodynamics, approaches which consider an individual's relationships in a more conscious or cognitive manner. In this respect the method of psychodrama has associations with treatments such as cognitive and behavioural therapy and the modern techniques of family therapy.

The next cluster (Chapters 8 and 9 on the transpersonal and psycho-spiritual dimension) considers Moreno's ideas on religion, spirit and the cosmos as well as his concept of the co-unconscious. Clearly Ken Sprague's chapter (Chapter 1), placed in this book in the introductory section, could also have been placed here. These ideas, while acknowledging the signific-ance of the individual, reflect Moreno's concerns with the psychospiritual realm and unconscious processes in groups and society and have associa-tions with the theories associated with psychosynthesis (Assagioli 1965), Bion's views on group dynamics (Bion 1961) and with the work of Jung.

The third of our clusters (the personal and unconscious dimension) is so termed as Morenian concepts also focus on the psychic processes that occur in individuals (whilst also acknowledging that we live and work in groups). In this book, this cluster contains only Chapter 10; however, the concepts of locus, matrix and status nascendi (discussed by Dalmiro Bustos in Chapter 3) link developmental concerns in the individual with the logic for treatment methods. In this respect there are clear similarities with the developmental models of the Freudians and Kleinians and the psychological theories and treatment methods associated with object relations theory (see Holmes 1992). We would also place the concepts of spontaneity and creativity (already considered in Chapter 2 by Marcia Karp) in this group as they are powerful forces (or resources) which, in the right circumstances, rise up within us.

The final two chapters, on role reversal (Chapter 11) and tele (Chapter 12), stress the interpersonal elements of both assessment and treatment, and acknowledge both conscious and unconscious processes in a way that is not dissimilar to encounter groups and gestalt therapy.

We must stress once more that such groupings, whilst aiding the mapping of Moreno's ideas, fail to encompass the richness and variety of psychodrama as a powerful and integrated therapeutic method.

REFERENCES

Assagioli, R. (1965) *Psychoanalysis: A manual of principles and techniques*, Wellingborough, Northamptonshire: Thorsons Publishing Group.
Bion, W.R. (1961) *Experiences in Groups*, London: Tavistock.
Holmes, P. (1992) *The Inner World Outside: Object relations theory and psychodrama*, London: Routledge.
Rowan, J. and Dryden, W. (1988) *Innovative Therapy in Britain*, Milton Keynes: Open University Press.

The cognitive and conscious dimension

Chapter 6

Relationships and roles

Commentary

Relationships are the central theme of Max Clayton's chapter. Through many years of clinical experience, he has made role theory an integral part of his work as a teacher and clinician. In sessions he labels aspects of the individual that are neither mystical nor bewildering. Morenian psychology has sometimes been criticised for inconsistency and complexity. This chapter clearly sets out the essentials of role theory in a way that makes it accessible to the non-psychodramatist.

Role theory and its application in clinical practice

Max Clayton

INTRODUCTION

I have applied role theory in a wide range of situations since 1971 and taught it throughout Australia and New Zealand. Therefore my own experience and emphases are reflected in the material presented in this chapter. A large number of professional people in different fields have developed a knowledge of role theory and role analysis and a significant number of reports and papers have presented analyses of individuals and groups based on role theory. Some of this work is included in this chapter. The particular type of role theory presented in this chapter and the concept of role and role relations is that developed by J.L. Moreno (see the relevant sections of *Psychodrama*, vol. 1 (1946) or any of his major writings). The method of categorising and charting roles has been developed in Australia and New Zealand and is in our view consistent with Moreno's role theory. The historical development of role theory and the differences between the role theory developed by Moreno and that of other role theorists have been discussed elsewhere (for example, Moreno 1978: 688–92; Biddle and Thomas 1966: 3–19) and these subjects are outside the scope of this writing. Here, the emphasis is placed on the application of role theory such that human beings develop a deeper feeling and appreciation of one another. The point of view taken is that role theory may be applied so that incisive analysis is infused with feeling and so contributes to the development of a humane culture.

DEVELOPING KNOWLEDGE OF ROLE THEORY

Personal knowledge of role theory develops as a result of a number of factors. High on the list is constant involvement in many different situations and with a wide range of people. The picturing of one's own social relations as well as those of others and reflection on these pictures is needed. The development of role descriptions, frequent guessing about the nature and quality of role relations and the checking of one's conclusions with others results in the development of abilities such as role analyst, systems analyst and personality theorist, and eventually in the development of a new identity.

Creating written descriptions of individual roles and role systems and complete descriptions of the social and cultural atom of individuals have been of considerable assistance in the learning of role theory. Entering into a supervisory process with a teacher or trainer has assisted in the integration of role theory into clinical practice.

The reading of literature in conjunction with the completion of written work and supervision opens up new perspectives. Jacob Moreno's written discussions of the role concept and of role relations continue to open up fresh perspectives for many readers. These include sections on role theory in *Who Shall Survive* (Moreno 1978: 75–9, 533–7) and *Psychodrama*, vol. 1 (Moreno 1964: 153–76, 328–47). The monograph 'Psychodramatic shock therapy' (Moreno 1939) contains several social atom diagrams. The monograph 'Psychodramatic treatment of psychoses' (Moreno 1940, 1945) discusses the development of the cultural atom in mental patients. The use of role theory in clinical practice is highlighted in the chapter on Psychodrama in the book *Experiential Psychotherapies in Australia* (Clayton and Clayton 1980) and in several journal article papers including 'The use of the cultural atom to record personality change in individual psychotherapy' (Clayton 1982) and 'Psychodrama with the hysteric' (Clayton 1973). The application of role theory in role training is described in detail in *Enhancing Life and Relationships: A role training manual* (Clayton 1992). A large number of papers and theses discuss the role systems of a wide range of people and include 'The cultural atom as a dynamic concept' (Di Lollo 1987), 'The suicidally depressed person and psychodrama' (Hurst 1992), 'Magister Ludi, the master of play: a role profile of the playwright (Batten 1992), 'Using psychodrama in individual counselling and psychotherapy' (Fowler 1992), and 'The role structure of a patient' (Crawford 1984).

Reading of literature which discusses role theory from a different point of view will bring a larger perspective to the subject. George Herbert Mead's book *Mind, Self and Society* (1934) emphasises the process of taking the role of the other and incorporating that role into the self. *Role Theory: Concepts and research* (Biddle and Thomas 1966) presents material on the nature and history of role theory and a wide range of other subjects such as role structures, role enactment and role conflict and its resolution.

USAGE OF TERMS

The term role theory refers to the body of knowledge associated with the interactive functioning of human beings. Its focus is on the functioning form of human behaviour as it emerges in response to other people or objects in specific times and places. It is systemic in its nature taking into account individuals and their relationships.

The term role description refers to one of the basic elements in the analysis of a role system. Role description is the identification of a significant segment of human functioning in a meaningful and enlivening way. A number of role descriptions may be made in such a way as to portray the nature of much larger segments of human living and these provide some of the raw data for a larger role analysis.

The term role analysis refers to the consideration of a role system in terms of whether it is achieving its purpose or not and what is required to cause the role system to function adequately. Role analysis focuses at times on the different elements of a single role in terms of their congruence or incongruence with one another and sometimes on the relation between different roles or between one role system or another. The purpose of role analysis is to make sense of systems of roles enacted by individuals or groups of individuals or of role relationships between groups or between cultures and on the basis of such analysis to plan means whereby roles may be developed further so that the aims of individuals and groups can be achieved.

The term role analysis is used interchangeably with the term role assessment. The term assessment is used to conform with the frequently used term 'clinical assessment'.

THE DEVELOPMENT OF THE CHAPTER

In the next section of the chapter there is a discussion of the essential nature of a role. This is followed by an example of clinical work aimed at creating a clear impression of the application of role theory in one situation.

The more detailed discussion of roles and role assessment begins by focusing on the making of a role description. Various analyses of role relations and role clusters and discussion of the application of role theory take up the rest of the chapter.

THE ESSENTIAL NATURE OF A ROLE

We observe one person and we say: 'There's an adventurer'. Concerning another person we say: 'There's a creative town planner'. We are able to draw these conclusions through attending to the observable actions and emotions. These obvious expressions of a person are given a coherent form through their connection with a map of the universe that may be conscious or unconscious to the individual concerned. This map or picture of the way life works is the essence of any role or role cluster. An adventurer has one vision of how people relate to one another, a town planner another, a Michelangelo yet another. Some kind of vision of how life works is the controlling element in each role we fantasise or live out in the world. In the case of a person who experiences role conflicts, investigation brings to the light of day contradictory maps. A well-functioning person may become conscious of a multitude of pictures associated with each major role in their personality and of the fact that each picture complements the others and contributes to a larger vision. This larger vision is associated with a cluster of roles or with the totality of the roles in their personality.

In one piece of work a person created a dramatic portrayal of co-operative people building up one another in their work and personal interactions. This person had embedded in their consciousness a picture of creative beings interacting respectfully and this provided a motivating force for approaching challenging situations with relevant aims and well-planned objectives. A disciplined organisation and at the same time a light, free expression were characteristic of this person's functioning.

In another piece of work a resentful person operated in accordance with the laws of strict justice. In their view the universe worked best when individuals determinedly demanded justice and were hard and harsh in response to others. Those on the receiving end realised how unjust and wrong they had been. When this person participated in a dramatic enactment in which people were acting this way, there was an experience of absolute delight. 'Yes, that's the way things are', he said, 'and that's the way it should be.' There was an awakening of consciousness that this inter-active picture was the basis of their values. Subsequently there was a parti-cipation in interactive systems that portrayed quite different configurations, an experience of new responses – and the beginning of a development of other visions of life.

A person warms up to any role in response to the functioning of another person or persons in the here and now and the personal meaning of the role can be discovered by exploring the different dimensions of the situation. This may be accomplished by bringing about expression of what was not said and done outwardly. The hidden thoughts, feelings and aspirations which are above and beyond what is expressed in life itself are termed the level of surplus reality and it is through the exploration of this level of surplus reality that the various maps of the universe become apparent. There may also be value in enacting situations in which a particular role first came to birth, when a particular map of the universe was first formed, to become acquainted with the warm-up process of the individual as well as with the social and cultural matrix in which the events took place.

The outward manifestions of the map of the universe of an individual are a set of emotions and feelings and a set of actions. Role analysis takes into account these different elements of a role and determines whether they are congruent or incongruent with one another. Various techniques have been developed for the purpose of harmonising the different elements into a unified, working system. However, the most profound and lasting development of an individual normally involves an experience of living satisfactorily in accordance with a new map of the universe. Then the old map may be dropped and the old sets of emotions and actions become irrelevant and they, too, gradually disappear.

The centrality of a person's view of the universe has implications for where the focus of attention is placed. Some role descriptions emphasise the social dimension. Descriptions of the social roles of nurses, architects, lawyers, bank tellers, cooks, policemen or business managers highlight the development of these roles by a particular culture and when a person is addressed in terms of their social role, they experience themselves as part of a group. Other role descriptions portray more of the individuality of a person and touch their experiencing centre in such a way that their interest is greatly aroused. Role descriptions that accurately pinpoint the experience and aspirations of a person naturally enhance the conscious development of roles that are unique to them. Such roles may be termed psychodramatic. There are many examples of the use of psychodramatic role descriptions in everyday life. One person in a social situation was behaving in an adventurous way and his companion said to him: 'I like what you are doing. You're Marco Polo.' This person was slightly taken aback but continued acting in an adventurous manner with even greater enthusiasm and contributed even more to the occasion. Other roles are psychosomatic such as the roles of the eater or the sleeper.

EXAMPLE OF ROLE DEVELOPMENT IN CLINICAL WORK WITH A CONFLICTED PERSON

I wish to start by presenting a piece of work with an individual which took place recently. The purpose in doing this is so that you will be able to visualise the situation, comprehend the nature of the roles and the role relations, and the means by which a new resolution was found.

Scene one

These events took place in a group of ten people meeting together for the twenty-sixth time. The members of the group were well-motivated and had developed working relations with one another. Early in this session Barry was asked a question. He hesitated and sat thinking as though he were preparing what to reply. The group leader suggested that he was conflicted and Barry immediately said that this was the case. The group leader invited him to focus on this moment with a view to resolving the conflict and developing his ability to freely and immediately make his first response.

Barry indicated he would like to do this and the group leader assisted him to set out the situation as he experienced it.

The first scene he portrayed involved his father, mother, and two brothers. He selected four members of the group to be these people and enacted the roles of each person such that the group members were able to portray accurately what occurred. Barry stood at a distance from his father and brothers and his mother was further away behind his father. He became involved in the enactment expressing his emotions and his values very clearly. The theme of the interaction was one of severe criticism and withdrawal. The father acted as a cruel mafia boss in relation to his son Barry. Barry's two brothers sided with their father and acted as cruel rejectors. The mother was isolated. Barry himself was withdrawn and had concluded that there was nothing to be gained by communicating.

The group leader entered into a dialogue with Barry which began as follows:

> You have portrayed a situation that is associated with the cutting off of your immediate expression. But that cutting off is only one aspect of the picture. There is also the creative aspect that begins to express itself in its own unique way. When you were asked the question in the group just now we saw that you were interested to respond right away. So now portray another situation that is associated with the immediate free expression of yourself. Keep the scene that has just been enacted and choose another group member to be yourself in that scene. And create a new scene in a separate area.

Scene two

Barry, who was a part-time musician, quite quickly set out a new scene in which he was a member of an orchestra in a rehearsal that had taken place several years earlier. He created a strings section and a brass section and also chose someone to be the conductor and teacher. The other parts of the orchestra were not portrayed. In the enactment of the scene the timing of the brass and strings sections was not in harmony. Barry portrayed the conductor as humane, competent and able to bring the best out of the orchestra. The conductor made it very clear what was lacking and instructed the orchestra to repeat the section several times until he was satisfied with the timing. Barry enjoyed the practice very much. He liked the attitude of the conductor. He especially appreciated that he was not phased out by the mistakes of the orchestra but rather maintained an attitude of enjoyment while he trained them. The group leader characterised the conductor as a flexible and creative trainer and alternatively as an instructive artist. Barry was pleased by these descriptions and experienced greater love and gratitude toward the conductor.

Subsequent to the enactment of these two scenes, Barry asked someone else to play his role in the second scene and then stood in a position where he could see both of the scenes enacted at the same time. He was very satisfied to see himself acting in two quite different ways at the same time. He felt strengthened in his ability to express himself freely. He affirmed the value of his unique ideas and expression. He saw clearly that two quite different ways of functioning had been occurring one after the other and accepted this.

Visualising the situation

This description of these scenes and Figure 1 are aimed to enhance the visualisation of this brief piece of work and to enable any interested reader to begin to experience being there. Visualising any piece of work with people is of great importance and assists practitioners to maintain and deepen their contact with the original living situation, to keep seeing new facets, and to develop fresh perspectives. It is an advantage for a supervisor or interested colleagues also to be able to visualise a situation since this enhances their ability to be companions with the practitioner and co-operate in the creation of further effective work. Practitioners and supervisors have found that the utilisation of role theory both in verbal description and in diagrammatic presentation of work has also enabled them to picture and enter into situations easily and quickly. The practitioner who is well trained and versed in the use of the language of role theory can convey, through a very brief role description, a comprehensible idea of quite a large segment of the actions and emotions of a person and the view of the universe that is expressed by those actions and emotions. This economy of words has been a great boon in supervision sessions allowing more time to be spent on teaching and coaching.

The nature of the roles and role relations

An apt characterisation of the relationship between the protagonist Barry and members of his family is the term 'fragmenting role system'. Consistent with this is the fact that there is a mutual negative relation between Barry and his father and brothers which prevents intimacy.

The role system is disconnected from the fulfilment of Barry's life purpose and, according to him, fails to satisfy other family members. Barry's motivation is low, there is a sense of meaninglessness and his consciousness is not focused on the adequate aspects of his functioning. He indeed experiences fragmentation. One aspect of his personality is expressed and after that another and then another without much awareness of the relationship between the different roles. The term 'dysfunctional role system' also fits since the word dysfunctional highlights the contribution

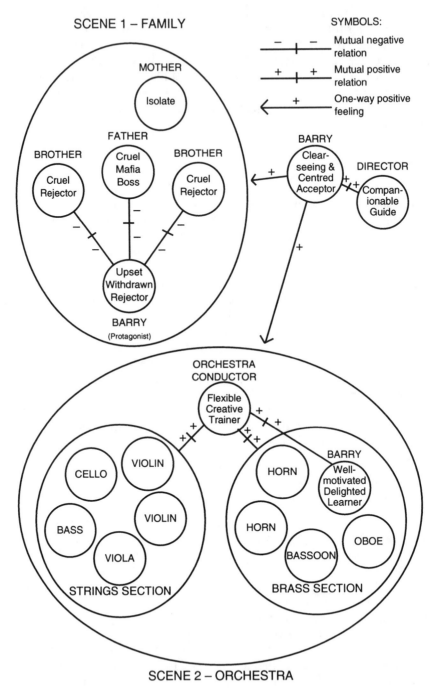

Figure 1 Barry observes family interaction and orchestra practice, simultaneously

that each person is making to the functioning and organisation of any family system. The term fragmenting, however, better portrays the inner experience of the people involved.

The roles and role relations enacted in the second scene reveal a positive two-way relation between Barry, the conductor and the members of the orchestra. The role system may be characterised as progressive since the fulfilment of Barry's purpose is being enacted. His functioning expresses his own unique individuality as well as social elements. This blending of the social and individual elements in his roles is one expression of his spontaneity and we may expect this to continue to develop through constant practice.

The means for developing a new resolution

At the beginning of this work there was a clear purpose, namely, to resolve Barry's conflict which emerged in the here-and-now group situation. The clear delineation of purpose was undoubtedly a major factor in the production of a new resolution. Human development involves raising into consciousness the purpose for which a person is involved in any situation. Purpose is an integrative factor in living and when a person is able to articulate their purpose the inner self awakens like a sleeping giant returning to consciousness. Sometimes the consciousness of purpose takes other forms such as an inner sense that life has a meaning or the form of an almost imperceptible feeling. In the work just described the consciousness of purpose increased as the protagonist valued his uniqueness while he continued to express himself.

A number of other factors contributed to Barry's development of a new role system. There was the bringing to consciousness, early in the work, the existence of progressive functioning. This increased his ability to resolve conflicts, to free himself from negative memories and to gain mastery over non-functional habitual patterns. Another factor was a willingness to enact his experiences. During the enactment there was an increase in spontaneous expression and a letting go of over-control by the mind. The structure of the session was also clear and this assisted him to feel safe enough, to enter a deeper level of feeling, and to let go of emotional reactiveness.

ROLE ASSESSMENT AND ITS APPLICATIONS

Assessment of roles and role relations has an important place in effective work. This may take the form of tentative role assessments made very quickly on the basis of intuitive observation or of well thought through role assessment based on lengthy and repeated observations of a person in different situations. A basic requirement for role assessment is the accurate identification and description of individual roles and this is focused on in the next example.

Example of role description increasing the involvement of group members

In many heterogeneous groups individuals have been invited to walk around the room several times. Other group members have been invited to observe them and to write down their immediate impression of the role of each person. In one group the following were some of the descriptions of one individual offered by the participants:

Harem girl
Indian dancer
Warrior
Priestess
Cavalier
Chinese lady with bound feet
Walking on the edge of a vast ocean
An animal – a spirited deer

Each of these descriptions was enlivening for the group member concerned and the others present. When they were stated out loud there was a greater level of enjoyment, discussion and exploration.

Those who presented each description focused their attention on the real essence of the person. The descriptions for the most part were not a product of the intellect. They represented an attempt to penetrate the surface level and to say something which made sense out of many different aspects of the person's functioning. Thus, we may conclude that each description was an integrative concept. When one group member said 'Harem girl' all the members of the group looked at the person from that point of view to see if all the movements, feelings, emotions and thoughts that have been expressed fit that description. The best descriptions are those which fit the present warm-up of the protagonist, their present life circumstances and the present challenges which life is throwing up at them. Projection is naturally a factor distorting perceptions but on the whole has not been very significant.

Examples of tentative assessment of roles and role relations during an interview

Example one: learning through viewing a person in relation to others

Like other professional people I regularly sit with a person in the first interview and listen to their story of what is motivating them to come and see me and what have been the particular circumstances of their life. I not only listen to the details of the story but also notice the person's way of telling the story and the effect this is having on my functioning.

During one interview George was very earnest as he tried to teach me something. I thought that maybe he fancied himself as a coach. I thought he probably coached various people with varying degrees of success from time to time. This musing and tentative assessment assisted in making sense of aspects of his functioning that might otherwise have been ignored.

Example two: developing a list of roles and identifying role clusters

In one case a person had finished telling their story and after a pause I suggested that we review all the different ways of functioning which I had noticed. I suggested that as I mentioned different kinds of functioning, they write them down on a piece of paper and that after I had mentioned five ways of functioning they would mention one and then we would take turns to identify roles until we had made a large list. In less than five minutes we developed the list of roles which follows:

Artist
Playful funlover
Coach
Companion
Adventurer
Manipulator
Teacher
Despairer
Self-doubter
Guard
Frightened, abandoned orphan
Anxious and suspicious fantasiser
Angry controller
Condemning critic
Friend
Father
Good listener
Lover
Perfectionist

We then engaged in the task of organising these roles into clusters and determining which role clusters are progressive and functional and which are fragmenting and dysfunctional and which are expressions of an effort to survive and thus are part of a coping system. This task was also completed in a short time. In the process this person became more organised, more thoughtful and began to make sense of a wider range of his behaviour.

Example three: listing progressive and functional roles

In a similar manner during my work with Louise in the first interview we made a long list of different roles. She was experiencing low self-esteem and in line with this was extremely self-critical. There was a low level of trust with me. I was the object of suspicious observation. When she had made a self-presentation including why she had come to see me I suggested that we make a picture of all their different attributes. I explained the concept of role and suggested that I would list a number of roles and also have her suggest some roles. In several minutes we had come up with the following list, each one being printed in capitals on a separate sheet of paper. The list is as follows:

Imaginative dreamer
Thoughtful planner/organiser
Warm self-appreciator
Sensitive caregiver
Playful enjoyer of life
Lover
Poet
Listener
Passionate dancer
Lowly and co-operative servant
Practical joker
Lone warrior
Ruminator (wishful thinker)
Mean street-fighter
Nature lover

Most of these roles are progressive and functional. I deliberately focused on all those aspects of her functioning which I personally enjoyed. As I concentrated only on these aspects and became increasingly successful at eliminating from my mind the dysfunctional elements, I found myself moving closer to her. Obviously I was finding points of connection. Subsequently I stated in a straightforward way the functional aspects which I observed and experienced and enjoyed and she began to argue, telling me that other people had not evaluated her in such a generous fashion and that she was not as worthwhile as I was indicating. I had already noticed an immediately positive response to my appraisal and so I said to her that she was clearly happy when I actively related to these particular aspects of her functioning which were real and that she was sufficiently in touch with herself to know that she had felt happy. She said yes, she did feel happy, but there were other aspects of her. I said that my first task was to build a good foundation and the best foundation was for us to give proper recognition to those abilities which she had built up over many years through much effort. She accepted what I said and her enjoyment increased. She stopped looking at me suspiciously. She simply enjoyed being with me just as I was enjoying being with her.

It appears that the simple and clear delineation of progressive and functional roles does, under appropriate circumstances, lead to the heightening of self-esteem. It also leads to the development of a positive two-way relationship or, using other words, a mutually positive tele relation, and to co-operative, purposeful work. Others may wish to see this in terms of the development of a positive transference.

Example four: example of maintaining emotional contact while making a lighthearted assessment

In another piece of work Luke was focused on his inability to refuse other people's demands. In the interview phase of the psychodrama he was distressed that he constantly gave in to the wishes of others. He was very sensitive to criticism. He focused on a situation with his wife where he felt constrained by her demands. He was unable to be centred within himself or to develop his own interests and activities while he was in his own home. In this situation the director and group members imagined him functioning in the submissive way that had been described and in this way became much more conscious of his situation. They also made a tentative assessment in a somewhat lighthearted vein even though the protagonist's plight was serious. The emotional contact with the protagonist was sustained at this time demonstrating that it is quite feasible to be lighthearted and to increase the level of emotional contact at the same time.

DEVELOPING AN ASSESSMENT PROCESS

Since the making of tentative assessments is so valuable for increasing the intelligent involvement of a director and group members, it is necessary to develop a workable process for carrying this out. The following is an outline of a possible process by which assessments may be made. The most simple and basic elements are considered at the start. First, there is the sociometric perspective and simple elements of sociometry:

- How many people are there in the person's social network?
- Are the feelings being projected towards the other people by this person positive, negative, or neutral and what is the nature of the feeling being projected towards them by the others?
- What is the strength of the feeling projected towards each of the others and the strength of the feeling from them to him?
- What is the nature of the person's feeling towards himself? Is it positive, negative or neutral? And what is the level of warm-up?

In the example just described Luke revealed that he is unable to refuse other people's demands. At this point it is possible to picture him in a situation with others, then picture him in another situation and then another. There are likely to be quite a few people in the man's social network. There are most likely to be negative feelings projected out from him towards these others as they make demands on him. The feelings are likely to be strong. He is likely to be negative towards himself for having these negative feelings towards others. Thus, he does not express his negative feeling overtly. He is conflicted. We may imagine that he looks at himself afterwards, sees himself caught up in conflict constantly and is angry with himself for being weak. This angry feeling will be strong.

After focusing on these simple basic elements it is necessary to concentrate on the sociometric perspective more fully and tentatively identify the roles and role relationships, the role clusters and the central role in each role cluster.

At the beginning of the interview Luke focused on his lack of ability and on the fact that he suffers because of this. Could we say that one of the well-developed roles in one of his dysfunctional role clusters is that of 'unhappy martyr'? Another role in this cluster will be 'incessant self-critic'. After this we may begin to see him as a person who has been seeking recognition in order to feel a greater sense of existence on the planet and also seeking approval and acceptance to build up his self-esteem. Could we therefore tentatively say that he has developed the role of 'distressed yearner'? Perhaps this is the central role in this role cluster. It would be in this role that he is so sensitive to criticism. And yet another role in this cluster would be 'helpful red cross nurse'. In this role he endeavours to relieve the pains and worries of others, including his children, his wife and his own mother. Through acting as a helpful red cross nurse he hopes to win the approval of others and gain the emotional closeness and affection which he lacks.

Other people in his life may have wittingly or unwittingly taken advantage of this dysfunctional role cluster. They may have avoided developing themselves in a well-rounded way. They may have asked him to do things for them which they would have been better off doing themselves. They may have assisted him in the creation of a strong system of dependency.

We might well speculate about what map of the universe Luke has created and which now sustains a social atom that produces such an inner sense of frustration and meaninglessness. The idea that he views the universe as a place where people are self-absorbed, needy suckers whose whims have to be indulged so that relationships can be maintained is consistent with the concern he has presented in the interview.

During this early stage of work in the initial interview there are several other areas on which the director may helpfully focus. A clear awareness that social-atom repair work needs to take place and identification of some of the functional roles in this man's personality will assist the director's warm-up. Being conscious of the existence of adequate roles at the interview stage is of great assistance during the setting and early development of the first scene in a dramatic enactment. This makes it much easier for the director to warm up a protagonist to roles that will be of assistance to him in bringing about a new resolution to any conflict. The director would also do well to keep in mind an additional factor, namely, that there is a central role in any progressive role system, a role that organises and harmonises a number of roles that would otherwise operate in isolation.

What is the central role in the progressive role system of Luke? Observation of other people who are functioning well provides a clue. This reveals that they have developed healthy, workable concepts about how any system including a family system works, are possessed of a good inner organisation, are able to formulate and execute plans and have an enjoyment of life. Observation of this particular protagonist reveals that he has at least begun to develop a concept of what will work in a family. He knows that it is necessary to be able to refuse another person's demands. He certainly has not developed this ability but at least he has an idea of it and is dreaming of taking a risk. Could we say he is beginning to develop as a daring planner? We also see him wishing to be able to organise creative activities of his own while at home. This ability is also very underdeveloped but again the motivation is there and therefore we may conclude that he is developing as a creative organiser.

Role analysis assists a person to develop a picture of their personality

A person recently came to me for a session and told me of the suffering they had experienced as a result of several tragedies and losses. This person was very upset indeed and spoke of needing to work on these things for a very long time. Already this person had done work with first one psychotherapist and then another every week for the past year and during this work had formed the notion that there was some very deep work that had to be done about early childhood experiences. I noticed that throughout the early part of my meeting with this person the roles being displayed in the here-and-now situation were becoming clear. I found that when I was aware of the different roles being enacted, my perception of what was being said developed. This person was telling me at one point of experiencing great fear and yet their actual functioning at that point was of a person who was quite angry about what had happened and who was determined to get on with life in a productive way. After a short time I said this:

> Let's just pause there and both get clear about the different things you have been saying and doing over the last few minutes. And, in

particular, let's set out the different roles you have been enacting so that you have a true picture of your present functioning and appreciate the abilities that you have developed.

So pretty soon we had set out in my office symbols of several roles. There were three roles that were taking her towards the fulfilment of her goals – one role was assisting her to survive, and the other roles were causing her to be stuck in a rut. She looked at the picture and soon was reflective and began to make a fresh analysis of herself. A while later she began to organise herself and plan some fresh steps so that her personality functioning was more attuned to her purposes.

Role analysis portrays the personality in different situations

A visual picture of the personality functioning of an individual in a specific life situation can be created through a role diagram. A series of role diagrams portraying a range of different life situations build a picture of the total personality functioning. A composite diagrammatic representation of all the roles and role relationships of an individual may be termed the cultural atom of an individual. In this particular section examples of role diagrams of the individual in particular situations are presented.

The person involved is a 35-year-old woman named Jean who participated in a number of psychotherapy sessions in a community clinic.

Figures 2 and 3 are of Jean's relationship with individuals in different situations. In the first situation Jean is at work. She has been presented with a new office machine and initially was overwhelmed with fear and did not use the machine. At the same time she knew that she had no option but to use it. She anxiously said to her boss 'I can't use it.' He firmly responded 'Do it!' She became acquainted with the machine's manual and slowly began to use the machine.

Figure 2 portrays the relationship between Jean and her boss. The roles of security seeker, panicky balker and withdrawing ostrich cause a sense of fragmentation within her own self and isolation from her boss and therefore are termed fragmenting dysfunctional roles. The functioning of the boss assists in the development of a fresh approach by Jean. Jean's new functioning as a problem solver, risk taker and pace setter is in the process of developing adequately and therefore these roles are termed a progressive role system.

Figure 3 portrays a second situation in which Jean is with her younger brother, Jack, who has moved into her flat after recently returning from overseas. He has little money, pays no rent, and is expected to do odd jobs around the flat in lieu of rent. He is a painter by trade. Jean asks Jack to paint a window frame for her and in response he looks helpless and says 'You know it's too stressful for me'. Jean gives up on Jack painting the window and walks off feeling helpless, inadequate and frustrated.

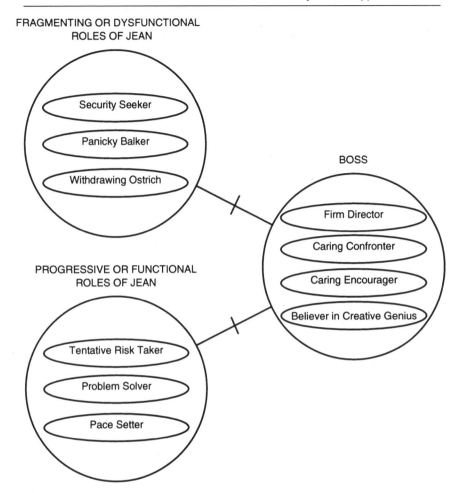

FRAGMENTING OR DYSFUNCTIONAL
ROLES OF JEAN

Security Seeker

Panicky Balker

Withdrawing Ostrich

BOSS

Firm Director

Caring Confronter

Caring Encourager

Believer in Creative Genius

PROGRESSIVE OR FUNCTIONAL
ROLES OF JEAN

Tentative Risk Taker

Problem Solver

Pace Setter

Figure 2 The relationship between Jean and her boss

Observation of the role system in Figure 3 reveals an absence in Jean's functioning of planning and organisation. Both of these are necessary for her further development and for a resolution of the conflict with Jack. It would be good for a director to be alert to the expression by Jean of any aspects of the roles of daring planner and creative organiser and to make appropriate interventions to develop these roles further.

Role analysis as a guide for further work

Many practitioners put together into a more complete diagram the roles that have been delineated in a number of sessions. The complete diagram charts the roles under three major headings, namely progressive, coping,

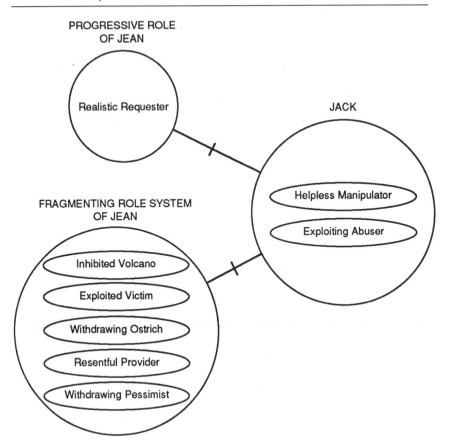

PROGRESSIVE ROLE
OF JEAN

Realistic Requester

JACK

FRAGMENTING ROLE SYSTEM
OF JEAN

Helpless Manipulator

Exploiting Abuser

Inhibited Volcano

Exploited Victim

Withdrawing Ostrich

Resentful Provider

Withdrawing Pessimist

Figure 3 The relationship between Jean and her brother, Jack

and fragmenting. In addition the diagram includes other subcategories which portray the dynamic movement of the person's development. Progressive roles are listed under the subcategories of well developed and developing and this assists a practitioner to develop a more fine-tuned analysis and to see at a glance where their interventions are best placed.

Figure 4 charts the roles of a person early in the work they planned to do and Figure 5 charts the roles after a good deal of work was completed.

An imaginative look at the roles listed in Figure 4 reveals a person who developed a number of progressive roles that provide a foundation for productive work and social living and, in fact, these roles show a person of quite considerable ability. This conclusion is confirmed by the fact that this person gave excellent guidance to school pupils with learning diffi-culties and was an effective consultant with teachers both individually and in groups. The two central roles are those of analyst and celebrator of life. The objectivity and precise computation which are aspects of the process

PROGRESSIVE FUNCTIONAL ROLE SYSTEM		COPING ROLE SYSTEM			FRAGMENTING DYSFUNCTIONAL ROLE SYSTEM	
Well Developed	Developing	Moving Towards	Moving Away	Moving Against	Diminishing	Unchanging
Science fiction buff	Observant astute analyst	Helpful fixer	Fearful defenceless wimp	Stubborn arguer		Ashamed self-doubting brooder
	Slightly wooden planner					Impotent rager
	Part-time organiser					Furious intolerant dominator
	Exuberant celebrator of life					Perfectionistic blamer
	Compassionate and encouraging friend					Anxious prophet of doom
	Flexible realistic teacher					
	Social pioneer					

Figure 4 Role analysis early in work.

PROGRESSIVE FUNCTIONAL ROLE SYSTEM		COPING ROLE SYSTEM			FRAGMENTING DYSFUNCTIONAL ROLE SYSTEM	
Well Developed	Developing	Moving Towards	Moving Away	Moving Against	Diminishing	Unchanging
Observant astute analyst	Imaginative writer	Helpful fixer	Fearful defenceless wimp	Stubborn arguer	Ashamed self-doubting brooder	
Imaginative planner	Expressive singer				Impotent rager	
Finely tuned organiser	Flexible realistic teacher				Furious intolerant dominator	
Exuberant celebrator of life	social pioneer				Perfectionistic blamer	
Compassionate and encouraging friend					Anxious prophet of doom	
Dramatic artist						
Science fiction buff						

Figure 5 Role analysis after completion of work

of analysis are balanced by a subjective involvement in the celebration of life. The other roles cluster around these two. The work of planning and organising are associated with the analytic ability. The expression of friendship is associated with celebration of life. The roles of teacher, pioneer and scientific fiction buff are associated with both analysis and celebration of life.

We also see a development of three roles for dealing with situations in which survival is threatened. These roles involve all of the means of coping and this is a distinct advantage. A person who relies on only one means of coping tends to develop a narrower range of personality functioning as compared to a person who is free to either move towards, or away or against. Someone who only copes by moving towards tends to overdevelop roles that include reactive elements such as submission. Likewise observation shows which roles a person tends to develop if they have learned to cope by only moving away or only moving against. The fact that this person has the ability to cope by acting as a helpful fixer or as a fearful and defenceless wimp or as a stubborn arguer brings about a warm-up to a much wider range of productive expression and therefore a more flexible personality.

The central role in the fragmenting role system is that of ashamed self-doubting brooder and the other roles cluster around this. The picture here is of an unstable emotionally determined person. Whilst brooding, much emotional pain is experienced and the other roles assist in the relief of this pain.

The role analysis provided a basis for planning further personal and professional development. The major focus of the plan was the much greater development of the roles of analyst and celebrator of life. It was predicted that when these two central roles in the progressive role system were well developed, all the other roles in the progressive role system would develop further, that new roles would develop, that the reliance on the coping role system would diminish, that much stronger working links would develop between the progressive and the fragmenting role systems and that as this occurred the fragmenting roles would move from the unchanging category to the diminishing category.

The work with this person was carried out in accordance with the plan and the predicted results were achieved. The chart in Figure 5 portrays the new role system.

The analytic functioning is now well developed. Organising no longer occurs on a part-time basis but is constant and finely tuned. Planning is imaginative and no longer wooden. The role of teacher is still in process of developing. New expression as a dramatic artist is already well developed and work as an imaginative writer, as an expressive singer and as a social pioneer has emerged and is integrated into professional functioning. Recent correspondence from this person included these words: 'I have a will, organization and energy which persist most of the time since February, in contrast to only occasionally before February.' This same letter also commented on the problematic aspects of personality which are all diminishing: 'Of course I still have trouble not going to pieces under stress.'

For both the practitioner and this client, role theory and the diagrams which were based on it were relevant to the ongoing work. Role theory assisted in the observation of this person in daily life, in the identification of what was adequate, overdeveloped, underdeveloped, conflicted and absent. It assisted in identification of the different elements of physical, mental and emotional functioning and in the assessment of how well these elements were harmonised. The diagrams assisted the process of discovering why their functioning affected other people in the way it did and what needed to be said and done in these situations. The diagrams made it easier to be aware of the complementary and symmetrical role systems that developed with other people and of the fact that there was an increase in complementary role relationships. As ability to analyse, plan and enjoy life came to the fore, so those roles pertaining to intimacy increased. There was a welcoming of closeness and an interest in complementing what others were doing. The aggressive approach to others diminished and along with this a lessening of symmetrical role relations and of the competitive dynamic that is associated with these. There was also a development of a real sense of being a role creator. Previously there had been much more of a sense of being a mundane person. A look at the diagrams also confirmed the ability to create forms of expression through which life purposes could be fulfilled. The experience of being a role creator was accompanied by an increase in motivation.

Application in role training

Role theory is relevant to every phase of a role-training session but is especially relevant during the assessment and planning stages of the session.

Role training aims to bring about the development of specific, limited aspects of human functioning so that a person's professional or personal goals are achieved more adequately and therefore it does not focus on a total personality reorganisation which is a major intent in a classical psychodrama session. A session normally begins with the delineation of specific aspects of functioning where development is desired and the dramatic enactment of a relevant situation. This enactment is followed by a role diagnosis and as has already been discussed this assists in the development of the organising ability of a person as well as appreciation of the self. The role diagnosis provides the basis for the detailed planning of the remainder of the session including the specific techniques to be used.

Role training is carried out in sessions specifically set up for this purpose or part of a session in which other modalities are used such as psycho-drama, transactional analysis, gestalt, or psychoanalytic methods. In the course of a series of psychodrama sessions with a protagonist, it may become clear that this person is very deficient in his or her organising ability. One or more role-training sessions could be conducted focusing on specific areas such as the development of a more effective warm-up to organising, development of greater awareness of specific deficits in the role of organiser, development of self-esteem while expressing this role or the generating of new forms of expression in this role.

A role trainer can make effective use of the total range of psychodramatic techniques and a session may involve the enactment of different scenes as in a classical psychodrama session. The factor differentiating role training from psychodrama or other methods involved in the reorganisation of personality is its sharp focus on building up a single role or one specific aspect of a role.

SUMMARY

Role theory may be understood and applied in the assessment of the functioning of individuals, groups and intergroup relations. A well-presented role analysis pinpoints where human functioning is fulfilling its purposes and where it has broken down. Role analysis also provides the necessary material for planning the means for increasing the effectiveness of human functioning and relationships. The examples given have aimed to assist in the integration of theory and practice and to confirm and stimulate the creative expression of professional workers.

With respect to the conduct of a psychodrama session, a working knowledge of role theory is of value in every phase of the session. During the beginning, or warm-up phase, of a group or individual session when interaction between people takes place or where group activities are organised, a range of individual roles and role relations emerge. These roles and role relations are an expression of different cultural systems and of the values of the individuals. An analysis of the role systems and of the level of warm-up of group members to each subgroup assists the process of identifying the best protagonist for the group. The director of a protagonist-centred psychodrama, who is clear about the roles and role relations expressed during the warm-up phase of the group session, is better able to generate ideas concerning the dramatic structure and which psychodramatic techniques may be appropriate during the action phase of the session. Thus, the director is more ready and able to work with the protagonist when he or she comes to enact similar role systems.

During the production phase of the session when the protagonist is enacting his or her situation, a role analysis makes clear which aspects of the protagonist's life are best attended to during the more detailed investigative phase. During the final therapeutic phase of the session, role analysis indicates whether or not the protagonist has arrived at a satisfactory resolution.

The psychodrama session concludes with the sharing or integrative phase and during this period role analysis is again of assistance. Observation of the roles of each group member and their relation with the director, the protagonist and with one another indicates what they have gained from the psychodrama and what areas are to be focused on in subsequent sessions.

REFERENCES

Batten, F. (1992) 'Magister Ludi, the master of play: a role profile of the playwright', Psychodrama thesis, Australian and New Zealand Psychodrama Association, Melbourne: ANZPA Press.

Biddle, B.J. and Thomas, E.J. (eds) (1966) *Role Theory: Concepts and research*, New York: John Wiley.

Clayton, G.M. (1973) 'Psychodrama with the hysteric', *Group Psychotherapy and Psychodrama* 30 (3–4): 31–46.

—— (1992) *Enhancing Life and Relationships: A role training manual*, Caulfield, Victoria: ICA Press.

Clayton, L. (1982) 'The use of the cultural atom to record personality change in individual psychotherapy', *Journal of Group Psychotherapy, Psychodrama and Sociometry*, 35 (3): 111–17.

Clayton, L. and Clayton G.M. (1980) 'Psychodrama', in D. Armstrong and P. Boas (eds) *Experiential Psychotherapies in Australia*, Bundoora, Victoria: PIT Press.

Crawford, R.J.M. (1984) 'The role structure of a patient', Paper for certification as Psychodramatist, Australian and New Zealand Psychodrama Association, Melbourne: ANZPA Press.

Di Lollo, L. (1987) 'The cultural atom as a dynamic concept', Psychodrama thesis, Australian and New Zealand Psychodrama Association, Melbourne: ANZPA Press.

Fowler, R. (1992) 'Using psychodrama in individual counselling and psychotherapy', Psychodrama thesis, Australian and New Zealand Psychodrama Association, Wellington: Fowler.

Hurst, S. (1992) 'The suicidally depressed person and psychodrama', Psychodrama thesis, Australian and New Zealand Psychodrama Association, Melbourne: ANZPA Press.

Mead, G.H. (1934) *Mind, Self and Society from the Standpoint of a Social Behaviourist*, Chicago: University of Chicago Press.

Moreno, J.L. (1939) 'Psychodramatic shock therapy', *Sociometry* 2, 1–3, reprinted in *Group Psychotherapy and Psychodrama*, 1974, 27, 2–29, and reprinted as monograph *Psychodramatic Shock Therapy*, New York: Beacon House.

—— (1940) 'Psychodramatic treatment of psychoses,' *Sociometry*, 3, 115–32, reprinted in J. Fox (ed.) (1987) *The Essential Moreno*, New York: Springer, pp. 68–80.

—— (1964) *Psychodrama*, vol. 1, New York: Beacon House.

—— (1978) *Who Shall Survive?*, New York: Beacon House.

Chapter 7

The measurement of human interactions

Commentary

There have been criticisms by some that Moreno's writing was not scientific enough, by others, that his writing was too technical. However, both these areas of concern continued to influence Moreno throughout his life. He himself saw the publication of *Das Stegreiftheater* in 1923 as marking the point at which he adopts a more scientific approach in his writing:

> *Das Stegreiftheater* marked in my work the beginning of a new period; the transition from religious to scientific writing. It initiated many characteristics found in my later work, such as the emphasis on measurement and charting of inter-personal communication, movement diagram, on operational procedure and situational analysis. As such it was a forerunner to the sociogram, the social atom diagram, the role diagram, the action sociogram etc.
>
> (J.L. Moreno 1947: 1)

Moreno argued for understanding preceding treatment, and with the tools of sociometry we have many useful diagnostic instruments. This chapter may remind us that the science of the measurement of the relationship was a creation of Moreno's, albeit one that he put down and let others adapt, whilst he devoted himself to developing the clinical method of psychodrama. The authors show just how useful a tool it can be to clinician and group-worker alike.

REFERENCE

Moreno, J.L. (1947) *The Theatre of Spontaneity*, New York: Beacon House.

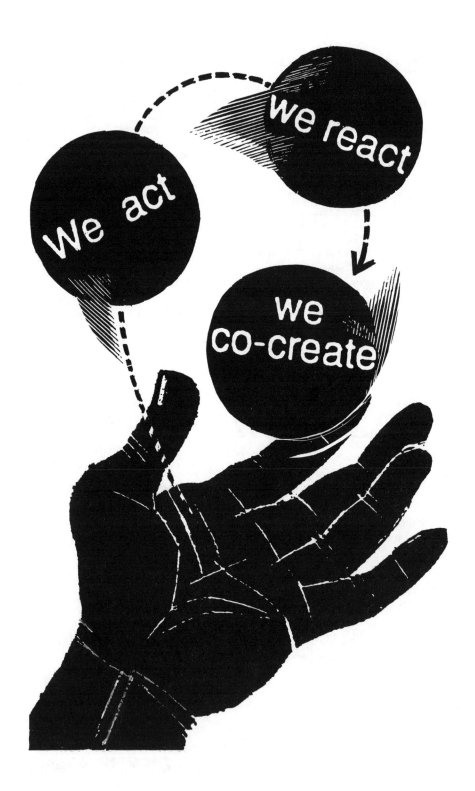

Sociometry and sociodynamics

Linnea Carlson-Sabelli, Hector Sabelli and Ann E. Hale

FOUNDATIONS

Goals: choosing partners, co-creating groups

Choosing a partner for marriage or work, gaining acceptance into a group, forming groups which can effectively accomplish their purpose, choosing a course of action, and electing political leaders, are some of the most important tasks we confront. Sociometry (Moreno 1978; Moreno 1942) and its offspring sociodynamics (Carlson-Sabelli *et al.* 1991; Carlson-Sabelli and Sabelli 1992b, c; Carlson-Sabelli *et al.* 1992a; Sabelli 1989) provide us with some useful tools to deal with such choices, and to understand the 'role we play' in our relations. They also illuminate and guide personal development, because our life is a co-creation with others. Who we become depends on the environment in which we live.

Sociometry studies interpersonal bonds by examining choices. Thus, Moreno generated a set of methods for empirical measurement of personal interactions in small groups, a series of principles relating to the development of the individual in groups, a number of experiments involving therapeutic regrouping of occupants of prisons, hospitals and schools into communities (Hare 1992), and a series of clinical methods that are, at the same time, assessments and therapies. The simplicity, versatility and richness of sociometric methods both as research tools and as practical techniques for understanding and organising groups, has found extensive application in business, education, community planning and health care systems.

Chance, cause, choice, co-creation

Sociometry is a therapeutic intervention (not only an objective measurement), to promote personal choice, and to foster insight into the physical, biological, social and psychological processes that predetermine them, and which may be largely outside the realm of free choice. Gaining insight into socioeconomic or psychological issues frequently reveals that what we believed to be a free choice was actually determined. The idea that illness can be a choice has been an ill-fated and cruel tenet of earlier psychoanalysis. Mental illness is the product of biological, social and psychological processes of causation, which includes chance, such as the genetic lottery. Manic-depressive illness, for example, is no more a matter of choice than diabetes. To seek treatment is a choice that all patients deserve. Since currently psychopharmacology offers fundamental, albeit not comprehensive, treatment for mental illness, it behoves every well-educated psychotherapist and educator to recognise when the protagonists, or their significant others, suffer from physical or mental illness that requires treatment. Chance events and causal processes pre-exist, coexist and outlast our personal choices. Choosing and creating may acquire supremacy only after recognising what physical, biological and economic causes have priority.

Stressing choice, sociometric tests neglect the biological, economic, social and psychological causes that determine and limit the range of (relatively free) choices. There is a priority/supremacy relationship in the process of choice, which, as in other cases, depends on the relations of power and of complexity: the more powerful processes (i.e. those with great energy) determine the universe of choice, whereas the most complex processes determine, within the range of the universe of choice, which choice is made. The formation of natural groups precedes choices, and their maintenance largely results from acceptance, which does not mean neutrality. In an enlightening pencil-and-paper exercise, persons draw their social atom, colouring each relation as being the result of choice (for example, one's spouse, business partner, teacher, doctor), of acceptance (brother-in-law, a student in my class), or of submission to necessity (a disliked co-worker). It is interesting to note where participants place their parents and children. Passive persons are often stimulated by this exercise to participate more actively in making choices.

It is important to study choice, because choice is a unique process of causation that distinguishes human behaviour from physical or socioeconomic determinations. Choice can be changed more readily, hence the importance of understanding the 'role we play' in our relations. However, choice is always embedded within other processes of physical and socioeconomic determinations, as well as in a web of reciprocities. Family ties and economic relations are not a matter of choice, but form the context within which personal choices are made. Biological (e.g. parent–child) and economic (e.g. employer–employee) bonds pre-exist, coexist and outlast personal choices, predetermining the range of choices and bias the outcome. The study of interpersonal bonds must then exceed and precede the analysis of choices.

The priority of biological and social roles, and the supremacy of personal choices

The interpersonal behaviour of individuals, and their collective behaviour in groups, is embodied in each individual first, as inborn patterns (such as infant care, harmonic and conflictual emotions, etc.) transmitted genetically, and second, as memories and rules introjected through experience. Moreno founded sociometry on role theory, postulating that social roles pre-exist the individual manner in which they are performed. Sociodynamics specifies that roles are created first by biological processes (e.g. woman and man, child and adult), and later created and conserved by social processes (nationality, class). Third, individuation differentiates a variety of styles within each of these roles, and may also create new roles which may be socially conserved. Before we develop as individual persons we are already assigned biological and social roles: a newborn baby already is a girl or a boy, and a member of a particular nation, class and religious faith. We exist as members of a population and of a family with which we share biological, economic, affective and ideological links. We play a role, the protagonist role, in our lives, but the 'role we play in' is in part determined by situations beyond choice, and by the choice of others. Social systems are not created by a mythological social contract between individuals, as individualistic economics and psychology pretend. Humans evolved from social animals, and only later became unique individuals. We begin life, and each interaction, as one of many members of a class of interchangeable *modules* (Carlson-Sabelli and Sabelli 1992a,c; Sabelli 1989) defined by age, sex, class, race and nationality. Our social self is attributed to us before we have the chance to develop our personal self. Before knowing each other as individuals, women and men, parent and child, teacher and student face one another as a function of their respective roles. In each *encounter*, you are the 'doctor' or the 'patient', the 'waiter' or the 'customer', the 'adult' or the 'child', the 'black man', the 'foreigner', the 'dumb blonde', before you have the chance to be known, and to know, the other. These social roles occur in pairs, in which the meaning of each member depends on its complementary opposite (an example of the *union of opposites*), and always imply a third role (child *vis-à-vis* mother and father; enabler *vis-à-vis* abused and abuser). Social roles serve as the ground for personal relations. The social role precedes the individual manner in which it is performed. There are many more individual personalities and life histories than the relatively small number of social roles. In this sense, we may say that the *social* has *priority* over the personal (individual and interpersonal psychological), and yet *personal* psychology and relations have *supremacy* over social but impersonal relations (Sabelli 1989, 1991a; Sabelli and Carlson-Sabelli 1989), for it is in the development of personal uniqueness that spontaneity and creativity come into being. Yet, the most fundamental encounter, usually our mother is, by its very nature, deeply personal, and in the normal course of development all relations become more personal: personalisation may be in fact the process through which large, impersonal groups move from exploitative to humane relations (Sabelli and Synnestvedt 1990). In the process theory view, interpersonal bonds predetermine the range of choices; bonds coexist and outlast personal choices, while personal choices have supremacy in that one may choose to create, modify or break bonds.

From sociometry to sociodynamics

Sociodynamics expands sociometry to consider both the priority of biological and social bonds, and the supremacy of personal choice. We define *sociodynamics* as *the comprehensive study of interpersonal relations as exchanges of energy* (physical and psychological). The analysis of energy flows connects sociodynamics to thermodynamics, economics and psychodynamics. Freud explained psychological processes as flows of psychological energy or 'libido'. Personal and interpersonal energy is also a central concept in Taoism.

Here we shall introduce sociodynamics through a series of new sociometric methods and practical exercises, which we developed clinically, and now also apply in education and organisational development. In earlier publications we have developed sociodynamics in the contexts of social psychology (Carlson-Sabelli and Sabelli 1984, 1992b,c) and of sociology (Sabelli 1991a; Sabelli and Javaid 1991), and presented its theoretical foundations in process theory (Sabelli 1989, 1991a,b,c; Sabelli and Carlson-Sabelli 1989, 1992) and in mathematical dynamics (Abraham *et al.* 1990; Thom 1975).

Moreno's sociometry owes its power to the combination of a clinical and therapeutic approach to social behaviour with simple mathematical techniques which can be readily applied by practitioners. Sociodynamics expands sociometry by using equally simple geometric methods recently developed to study processes which are too complex to be studied with metric methods, such as chaos (Baker and Gollub 1990) and catastrophes (Guastello 1988; Cobb and Zacks 1985). These methods expand sociometry by (i) investigating biological and social bonds, such as family ties and economic relations, which are not a matter of choice; (ii) studying conflictual motivations and emotions, and measuring the complex, contradictory nature of the dynamics underlying choice; and (iii) focusing on changes in individual pattern over time and in different groups, including natural open groups (this is in contrast to traditional methods that focus on snapshots of specific interactions in closed groups).

A simple example will illustrate the practical implications of the

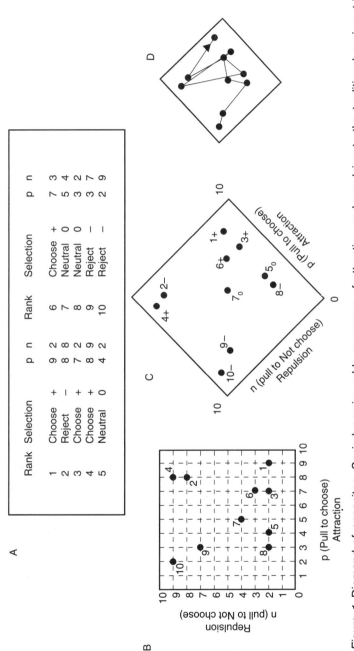

Figure 1 Diamond of opposites. Sociodynamics adds measures of attraction and repulsion to the traditional sociometric test. In addition to reporting categorical choices (+) and rejections (–), participants also report the rank order of their selections, and the degree to which they experience both a pull to choose (p) and a pull not to choose (n) each person (1A). It allows one to report the intensity of both opposites with a single point within a co-ordinate plane. (1B) The axes are a pair of orthogonal opposites. When this co-ordinate plot is rotated 90° counterclockwise (1C), the shared origin of the opposites is at the bottom, and the figure has a diamond shape, suggesting its name. This provides information about the range of intensity of contradictory feelings underlying interpersonal choice. The rank order, and actual choices (+) or rejections (–) or remaining neutral (0) made on the bases of the feelings of attraction and repulsion may be represented as a third dimension (1C). The trajectory (1D) indicates the sequence of rank.

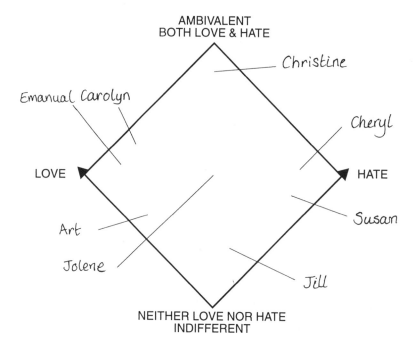

Figure 2 Name warm-up. In the example, Emanual and Carolyn both love their names, while Cheryl and Susan both hate theirs. Jill, Jolene and Christine all are alike in that they each like their name with the same intensity that they dislike it; however they differ from each other in the amount of intensity involved. Jill neither likes nor dislikes her name. She is indifferent. In contrast, Jolene is neither indifferent, nor highly ambivalent. She both likes and dislikes her name, to a moderate degree. Christine loves and hates her name with great intensity. Her name arouses conflictual responses inside her. Although she likes it a lot, Christine was a name given to her by her family when they emigrated, to replace her original name which was hard to pronounce. Finally, Art indicates that he likes his name very much, but he also dislikes some aspects of it. Following this example, each individual is asked to report his or her feelings regarding loving and hating their name, on a large diamond drawn on a chalk board. Those that think they understand the concept are asked to go first, providing further examples for those who don't quite grasp it yet. We have found that individuals, when taught, are equally able to report opposite feelings or motivations using either method.

sociodynamic perspective. Traditional sociometry conceives opposites as mutually exclusive categories (choice versus rejection), or as extreme poles of a continuum. This linear manner of thinking is embodied in the rank-order line from first choice to last rejection. Sociodynamics recognises that opposite feelings, for example, attraction and repulsion, harmony and conflict, almost invariably coexist, albeit in different degrees. Thus, it adds measures of attraction and repulsion to the traditional sociometric test. To report the intensity of opposites, participants in a sociodynamic exercise place themselves in a co-ordinate plane defined by such a pair of opposites (the *diamond of opposites* (Figure 1B)). The actual choice or rejections made on the bases of the feelings of attraction (p) and repulsion (n) represent a third dimension (Figure 1C and D, and there are other important dimensions to record and correlate with them, such as social status and age. This method requires participants to 'think in opposites', to consider the possibility that opposites may grow together. To facilitate this we have developed the 'name warm-up' (Figure 2).

Moreno identified spontaneity, role pairing and creativity as the three fundamental aspects of healthy functioning: We act we react, and we co-create each other's lives. Spontaneously, we act rather than remaining inactive; we are pulled by opposing motivations that lead us to alternative courses of action; we choose a behaviour that embodies our complex motivation, as well as our interaction with others. *Action, opposition and co-creation* are the three basic steps of the process of choosing. They correspond to the three fundamental patterns of all processes – the three laws of process theory.

ACTION, PSYCHOLOGICAL ENERGY AND SPONTANEITY

Action sociometry

A distinctive feature of sociometry, psychodrama, and related methods of evaluation, education and therapy, is that they occur in action, and in the present. Clinical experience indicates that action methods are often more powerful than paper-and-pencil tests to understand interpersonal choices and group dynamics. In our experience, action sociometry is more fun than paper-and-pencil counterparts, and also more revealing. Expressing choices in action offers a dynamic give and take, where the participants influence each other. However, public revelation also inhibits free expression. An inner choice and the choice expressed are not necessarily identical, as we have shown in a recent experiment (Carlson-Sabelli *et al.* 1992a; Carlson-Sabelli 1992). Our practice has led us to believe that interpersonal choices are revealed most fully in action when the process of choosing is incorporated as part of a larger activity, rather than the specified aim of the exercise. We have developed a series of fantasy play activities for children and adults to reveal connections and choices.

Co-created stories

We have learned from our experience with children that their fantasy play is always a story about how the players interact with each other, and, at the same time, reveals personal patterns of behaviour related to each child's unique life story. And the same principle is true for adults who engage in sociodramatic play (Blatner and Blatner 1988b). The metaphors, characters, interactions and story line, connect the life stories of each participant to the collective story generated in play. To facilitate the enactment of a story in which everyone contributes, we ask for a volunteer to become a character, set a scene and begin doing something. Through soliloquy and action a story line begins to develop. The other participants are told they may enter the action, one at a time, by taking any role they would like. Fantasy characters are not restricted to people, but can be inner thoughts – a fly on the wall, an antique mirror, anything that comes to mind. Persons are told not to enter just because they think they are supposed to, but to wait until they feel personally compelled to intervene. Anyone may exit the scene at any time, as long as they explain their leaving to the audience and other players in dialogue; for example, 'I am leaving to get pizza.' One can change to a new character in a new entrance, or remain the same. The fantasy might be allowed to take its own course, or be directed. The director uses all the techniques that might be used in a psychodrama, including role reversals among the fantasy characters. If the group has not done a story before, the members are warmed up to the co-created story by sitting in a circle and telling a story. One person starts, and brings into the story only one character. The story is narrated in the third person, and lasts until it has reached to its natural end. The group is then told to do the same thing in action, but to start with an entirely new story. A popular alternative is to start a verbal story, and move it into action when it comes back to the person who started it.

Revealing choices in action through fantasy play

'Howling wolves' is a story enacted in the children's theatre by four boys who had been hospitalised together on a child psychiatric unit. Previous sessions involved a central theme, with small variations, of wild animals, such as lions, tigers, wolves and cheetahs, helping each other survive the onslaught of hunters who wanted to sell their skins for fur coats, belts and shoes. The animals though wounded, always escaped. Dragged back to their cave, they were lovingly tended and healed. The four boys were the core of these sessions, which spanned several weeks and included numerous other children who came and went. It was the last theatre session for Mark, who was being discharged later in the week. He had been hospitalised the longest, and had initiated the 'jungle series' arising from his conviction that animals should not be killed for the profit of men. Once again, the jungle story unfolded. All four boys chose to be wolves, casting the staff as hunters. The wolf played by Mark ventured out too far, and was shot. Missing him, his wolf family began searching the jungle. He was eventually located by one of his 'brothers'. Soon all three wolves were

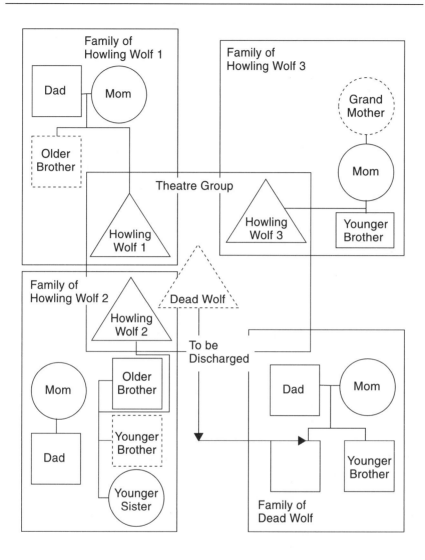

Figure 3 Sociogram illustrating the interconnections of a children's theatre therapy group and the family groups of each of its participants. Note that each howling wolf is mourning both the loss of his playmate (Dead Wolf) who is being discharged while also howling their pain at the death of a brother (Howling Wolves 1 and 2), and a grandmother (Howling Wolf 3) who was murdered. Broken line = dead; solid line = living; circle = female; square = male; triangle = hospitalised child.

hovering, nudging, and licking his wounds, but the injured wolf did not respond. 'I hope he's not dead', one wolf exclaimed. Activity increased to a frenzy, but nothing worked. Soon, a low-pitched noise, faint at first, but quickly rising in pitch and volume began to fill the room. The wolves were howling together, experiencing the agony of their loss. The boys were saying goodbye to a very special friend. The observer's eyes filled with tears, listening to their collective pain. During discussion following the play, we learned the full impact of its meaning. Extraordinary as it might be, the hospitalisation for each of the three 'howling wolves', had been related to the death of someone in their family. Mark's leaving aroused their personal pain and facilitated its uninhibited expression. The collective action is influenced and impacts the lives of the individual players in the group. The connections between the therapy group and the personal groups of each participant can be viewed in the mind's eye of the observer, as a sociogram, which can then be captured on paper, as illustrated in Figure 3.

Fairy tales, and other well-known stories provide structure to focus action. Permission to deviate from the story line facilitates the emergence of personal interpretations that have sociometric significance. Imagine a group of children playing a new ending to *Goldilocks and the Three Bears*. Unable to agree on who baby bear will be, we have twins. One of the twins invites Goldilocks, played by the newest child on the unit, to come and live with them forever, but the other loudly refuses. Occurring during therapeutic theatre on our child psychiatric unit, this scenario prompted a room change as the refusing bear was, at the time, Goldilocks's room mate.

'Connections': warming up energy through the exploration of the history of interpersonal bonds

Action requires a warming-up process. To highlight the subgroups formed by previous relationships and to illuminate the history of connections in long-standing groups for its newer members, we often begin by having each member of the group put a hand on the shoulder of the person in the room, they have known the longest. Starting from the oldest relationship, progressing to the newest, brief recollections from each participant about the time they first met, provide a history of a group in a very short time. Different directions follow, based on the configuration that emerges, the number of persons in the group and the purpose for doing the exercise. For instance, one might follow with the direction to touch the shoulder of the person they know the best, the least or with whom they would like to deepen the relationship. Using this technique with a group of trainees, for instance, highlighted a pair of men whose longest relationship was with each other. When asked to indicate the second longest relationship, one of the pair remained unattached to the group; his issue, isolation/inclusion was chosen for psychodramatic exploration. The exercise facilitated the most isolated person in the group to be chosen as protagonist, serving a therapeutic purpose for the group as a whole. Illuminating the bonds that already exist in a group, it provides every group member common knowledge about the existing structure of the group, before sociometric testing takes place.

In addition to exploring concrete bonds, rather than choices, this exercise also illustrates a process-orientated view which links events and choices in time, revealing the unity and continuity of spontaneous processes. In contrast, the structure illuminated by sociometric tests based on specific choices for selective, and often artificial criteria, is just a snapshot of the overall dynamics, a view of a very complex process, at one moment in time, which may or may not be representative of the rich complexity of the process as it develops in time. Having illustrated the concepts of process (in contrast to isolated events or permanent structures), of bonds (in contrast to choices) and of action through practical exercises, we shall now link them theoretically.

Action and libido

Action is not the result of a force or motivation; action and interaction, change and exchange, are spontaneous, while immobility and isolation are the result of inhibition. Although the term 'action' has an intuitive meaning in all realms of human discourse, it is worthwhile to define it as in physics, as the product of energy × time. The first law of process theory postulates the oneness of nature: everything is action. There is a unity to all processes that affect our existence. Both matter and ideas represent forms of action, i.e. of physical energy. Emotional, economic, cultural and other forms of motivation interact with each other as components of the same process, rather than remain separate in isolated realms of experience.

Freud described psychological processes as flows of psychological energy (libido), that includes affection, curiosity and anger as well as sexual energy, and is nothing more than a complex organisation of physical energy. His view has been validated by the fact that the density of energy flow in the human brain is 75,000 times greater than the flow of energy in the sun (Sabelli 1989: 87–9). We conceptualise interpersonal relations as exchanges of energy: *sociodynamics is the integrative study of interpersonal libido*. The circulation of psychological energy is both intrapersonal and interpersonal. Emotions are patterns of variation of energy, imprinted in physiological rhythms (heart rate, respiration, patterns of neurotransmitter release in brain) and expressed by interpersonal behaviours. In other publications we have discussed how intrapsychic and interpersonal patterns of energy flow are integrated in manic-depressive illness (Sabelli *et al.*

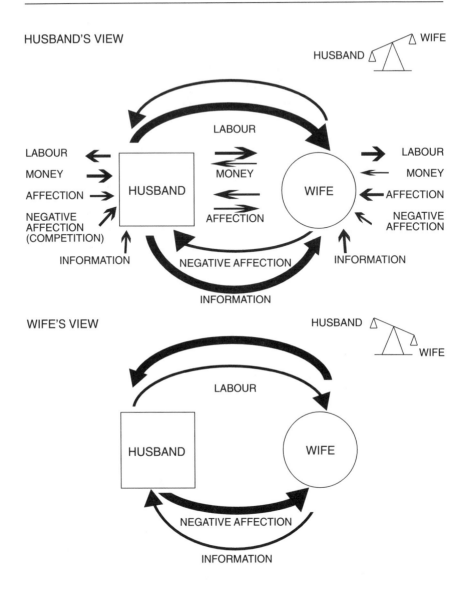

Figure 4 Action graphs. Exchange of energy (labour), matter (money) and information (affection and knowledge) for a married couple. After each participant draws her or his view of the exchanges, we ask each of them to draw how the 'scales of justice' are tilted for each of the relations depicted. Inequalities in the exchanges of labour, money and affection may produce conflict and separation. We use these diagrams to promote insight and congruence between the perceptions of each partner.

1990), unipolar depression (Sabelli and Carlson-Sabelli 1991), psychoses (Sabelli and Carlson-Sabelli 1989: 1548) and multiple personality disorder (Sabelli 1989; Raaz *et al.* 1992). These patterns may be revealed by mathematical analysis of longitudinal recordings of cardiac rhythms (Carlson-Sabelli *et al.* 1992b; Sabelli *et al.* in press) and of longitudinal monitoring of mood (Carlson-Sabelli and Sabelli 1990), and can also be studied sociometrically through the sociodynamic test (see p. 165) and action graphs.

Action graphs and personal justice

To examine interpersonal bonds in a comprehensive manner, we have developed the *action graph*, a paper-and-pencil diagram of interpersonal exchanges of energy (labour), information (about self and others, affection, entertainment, practical, social and intellectual skills) and matter (money and property). For instance, in a traditional family (Figure 4), the spouses exchange female labour (reproductive, raising the children and caring for the home) for male husbandry, energy for matter (money). In the majority of families today, both parents work within and outside the home, and so the exchanges are more variable and complex. Each person is connected to each other by a multiplicity of economic, affective and intellectual bonds. The thickness of the arrow serves to indicate the relative magnitude of intensity of flows each way. Bonds always go both ways, but the exchange is asymmetric. Diagramming these exchanges provides us with a dynamic 'action' model of personal systems and social nets. Affective bonds are thereby studied within the context of exchanges of energy, the intensity of the interactions in the relationship which carry material and information.

After the action graph of a family is completed, we ask the participants to examine it, and evaluate how justly they are being treated and how they treat others. We ask them to draw 'the scales of justice', tilted in one direction or another, regarding their relation with spouse, working partner, parents, society at large and 'life' (which many construe as God). In this manner we introduce a personal conception of justice, which often proves instrumental in modifying marital relations, as one learns to perceive how one contributes to our personal happiness and unhappiness, as well as one may learn to appreciate who treats us better than life in general.

OPPOSITION AND ROLE PAIRING

Choice and rejection, the sociometric test

To study interpersonal and social behaviour, Moreno examined two opposed actions – choice and rejection – between individual members of

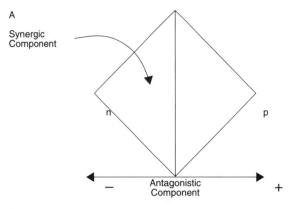

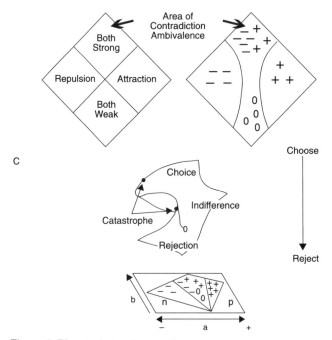

Figure 5 Phase plane of opposites.
A Opposite forces of attraction (p) and repulsion (n) are represented as mutually orthogonal vectors to illustrate they always coexist, and are in part synergic (vertical axis) and in part antagonistic (horizontal axis).
B Choice (+) is associated with higher attraction (right quadrant), rejection/ separation(−) with higher repulsion (left quadrant), neutrality (0) with weak attraction and repulsion (bottom quadrant); strong attraction and strong repulsion (±) (ambivalence, upper quadrant) creates unpredictable switches between choice and rejection.

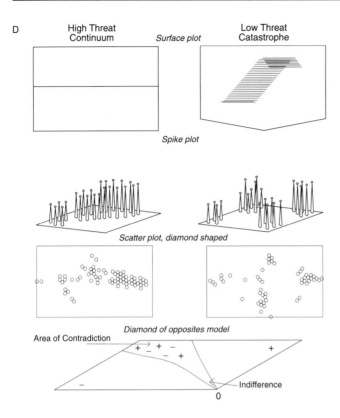

D

High Threat
Continuum

Surface plot

Low Threat
Catastrophe

Spike plot

Scatter plot, diamond shaped

Diamond of opposites model

Area of Contradiction

Indifference

0

C The distribution of outcomes (choice/union or separation/rejection) represents a third dimension (z) outside the plane of attraction (p) and repulsion (n). As ambivalence can lead to either choice or rejection, there is a fold in the outcome surface representing the distribution of outcomes. This is a catastrophe model, in which (b) the bifurcating control parameter is the energy provided by the union opposites ($b = f(p + n)$, where f = function, and the asymmetry (a) between outcomes is given by the difference between attraction and repulsion ($a = f(p - n)$).

D Catastrophe models comparing the distribution of sociometric outcome with attraction and repulsion, in conditions of high (left) and low (right) threat, illustrating the relationship of the distribution of the intensity of attraction (right vector) and repulsion (left vector) on the *diamond of opposites* (bottom plots) with the sociometric outcome expressed in spikes of different height (middle plots: tall = choice; medium = neutral; short = rejection), and corresponding three-dimensional surface (top). The high-threat criterion (left) yields a two-dimensional line (top left), indicating a polarisation of opposites along a continuum. Conversely, the low-threat criterion yields a surface with a fold (top right) associated with a catastrophe distribution. Note the coexistence of attraction and repulsion corresponding to neutrality at low intensities and with both choices and rejections at high intensity.

a group as partners for specific activities (sociometric criteria). The sociometric test (Hale 1981; Moreno 1978) is a self-report instrument where subjects delineate who, among the others present, they will choose to engage with in a specific activity. It involves real persons in actual interpersonal situations. Each group member is asked to assign other individuals in the group to one of three categories that they: (i) choose to participate with; (ii) choose not to participate with; or (iii) choose to remain neutral towards, and to rank their choices and rejections in order of preference.

In the sociometric test, the selection categories are assumed to correspond to the two underlying motivational forces, attraction and repulsion, or their presumed absence, neutrality. Moreno interviewed all of the subjects about their choices, adamant that a test should include the reasons for choosing. Such explanations uncover a multiplicity of reasons and feelings, which may be in part contradictory, creating various degrees of ambivalence. Yet, there has been no way to include this information in the traditional sociometric format, in which both the data-collection method and analysis are based on the either–or separation of opposites, choice and rejection and on linear numerical order such as rank ordering of choices. The sociometric methods that assume a linear continuum of attraction–neutrality–repulsion fail to disclose contradiction and ambivalence. This omission compromises their informational value (Hale 1989; Sabelli 1989: 405–6), a limitation that is not unique to sociometry. Empirical studies using regression analysis (Carlson-Sabelli 1992; Carlson-Sabelli *et al.* 1992a) indicated that attraction and repulsion are not inversely related. Hence, the linear continuum model of traditional sociometry distorts the data, and should not be used clinically.

The existence of ambivalence, contradiction and complexity in motivation and emotion is widely recognised, and the coexistence of opposites is taken as a basic feature of psychological processes at least since Freud, Adler and Jung. Likewise the principle of the union of opposites occupies a central place in process philosophies, and in quantum physics (Bohr's complementarity principle), but there has been no practical manner to apply it to empirical data.

The phase plane of opposites

Process theory approaches this problem by measuring opposites such as attraction and repulsion separately, using the phase plane of opposites (Figure 5A). The phase plane of opposites is a co-ordinate plane in which each axis represents the intensity of a pair of opposites. We originated the phase plane of opposites (which we call by the less technical name, the *diamond of opposites*) as a method to study the development of family relations of psychiatric patients (Sabelli 1989: 405), and later on as an action method with groups of patients and students (Carlson-Sabelli and Sabelli 1992b,c). Group members are asked to place themselves within a large diamond drawn in the centre of the room. The bottom vertex represents zero feelings (indifference or neutrality), and serves as the origin for the two axes along which the protagonists report their subjective estimate of the intensity of their opposing preferences, emotions, attitudes and feelings. Each group member is asked to stand within the diamond at the point determined by the intensity of both positive and negative feelings. The top vertex represents an area of contradiction, where opposing feelings are both intense and equal. Here there is a moving scenario, as those individuals with strongly contradictory feelings tend to pace near the top vertex, while the indifferent individuals stand quietly near the origin.

We use the diamond of opposites to measure separately the intensity of attraction and repulsion (the underlying opposing motivations involved in choice making). This is the first step in the *sociodynamic test*. By measuring attraction and repulsion in a bi-dimensional construct, the sociodynamic method provides an estimation of ambivalence behind each choice, making available for quantitative and dynamic analysis information found only in the reasons for choice on the sociometric test.

Introduced by the French mathematician Poincaré at the turn of the century, the phase plane has become a main tool of modern mathematical dynamics. The patterns of a complex process can be found by plotting its trajectory on a space defined by two (phase plane) or three (phase space) dimensions. The choice of the variables taken as co-ordinates is a difficult and critical step for which dynamics itself offers no suggestions. Process theory suggests that the most revealing plots will be obtained by choosing pairs or triads of complementary and opposite forces as the axes of the phase space. This is the phase plane of opposites, and it provides a practical method to study empirically, and numerically, contradictory processes. The phase plane of opposites is a generic method applicable not only in sociometry but also in psychological testing (Carlson-Sabelli *et al.* 1992a; Sabelli 1989) and in the natural sciences (Sabelli 1989, 1992). The diamond of opposites depends on the ability of individuals to report opposites, either by assigning a numerical number to the intensity of each opposite separately, or reporting each as a single point on a co-ordinate plane. We prefer to have individuals use the second method, to mark the place within the diamond intuitively, either in action (by standing in a particular spot), or in writing, without pre-assigning numbers. Why? It is the data plot, the configuration formed indicating the relationship of the opposites that we are interested in. The plot provides a way to envision the relationship of various combinations of opposites to outcomes. When opposites are plotted on a co-ordinate plane, the surface can be roughly divided into areas reflecting the mix of opposites. When the choice-making process is mapped, attraction and repulsion are the opposites, and socio-metric selection (choice rejection, neutrality) and rank order are the outcomes which can be plotted together on the surface as symbols (Figure 5B) or as a third dimension as spikes (Figure 5C).

It can immediately be read and interpreted, whereas numbers have to be plotted before they are useful. Indicating opposites on the phase plane simplifies the process and eliminates errors in scoring. If additional statistical analysis is to be done, the corresponding co-ordinates can easily be determined.

To create a phase plane of opposites: (i) decide which opposites are involved in the process; (ii) measure them separately (thereby allowing for an empirical evaluation as to whether they neutralise each other or grow together); (iii) graph them together as a point on the co-ordinate plane, noting the time; (iv) connect in order the points obtained at different times, drawing the trajectory of the process. Trajectories delineate patterns towards which processes converge when transient influences fade away (*attractors*), such as a consistent choice, *repellers* from which processes diverge (such as rejectees), as well as transitions from one attractor to another (*bifurcations*), such as switches from choice to rejection. Many complex processes converge to simple attractors, and can therefore be studied by examining plots in two or three dimensions (phase plane and phase space). Low energy is associated with decay towards equilibrium attractors (neutrality); moderately intense opposites produce bifurcations and cycles (periodic attractors) between them. High-energy opposites produce repeated bifurcations that lead to turbulence (chaotic attractors) and the emergence of novelty: creativity results from the union of high-energy opposites.

The union of opposites

Processes include both harmonious and antagonistic interactions between coexisting and similar opposites. Life itself is energised and procreated by the intercourse of opposite sexes; social processes are organised by the co-operative and conflictual interactions between administrators and workers; matter is constituted by positive protons and negative electrons. The union of opposites contrasts with the separation of opposites posited by logic (opposites as mutually exclusive categories, such as choice versus rejection), by linear thinking (opposites as polar extremes of a continuum, such as in the rank order of choices) and by dialectics (opposites as antagonists). The union of opposites has a number of important applications in sociometry.

First, roles are complementary. The ability to take on a desired role, depends on pairing with another person who plays the reciprocal role. One cannot mother without a child, teach without a student, or become a husband without a wife. When one is unable to play a role he or she desires to engage in, act hunger occurs. Second, opposites are more synergetic than antagonistic. For instance, it often appears that because resources are limited, one can gain only at the expense of the other; in fact, such economics do not apply to a marriage (where either both spouses gain or both lose) or to any other type of partnership, and, in last instance, we are partners of all those with whom we coexist. So, to benefit myself, I must benefit the other. Third, opposites are more similar than different. Hence, love to be loved, choose to be chosen, be tolerant to be tolerated, act non-violently to decrease violence. And yet, violence may also be increased by failure to defend oneself, tolerance may promote the development of intolerant groups and choosing may be one-sided. Harmony requires conflict, and conflict can create harmony. Fourth, opposites coexist: feelings of attraction and repulsion almost invariably underlie every important choice, and even opposite behaviours such as choice and rejection alternate and/or coexist in many interpersonal processes.

The principle of the 'union of opposites' has been known since antiquity; process theory adopts it as its second law, and operationalises it through the phase plane of opposites. The clinical usefulness of this method has been supported by experimental studies (Carlson-Sabelli *et al.* 1991; Carlson-Sabelli *et al.* 1992a; Carlson-Sabelli 1992) as well as by clinical experience. Opposites we often explore are inclusion and exclusion, feeling good and feeling bad, healthy and unhealthy, organised and creative, externally motivated and internally motivated, thinking and feeling, introverted and extroverted, feminine and masculine, grandiosity and low self-esteem (as characteristic of depression and of self-disorders) (Sabelli 1989).

The sociodynamic test

The sociodynamic test consists of the report of feelings of attraction and repulsion towards a given choice (person, activity, opinion), followed by the report of the categorical selection and the rank order of choices as customarily performed in sociometry. The sociodynamic test thus includes, and expands, the sociometric method, and can be performed in action as well as a pencil-and-paper exercise. Co-ordinates for attraction and repulsion are plotted as the opposites in the diamond (Figure 1B). As mentioned above, sociometric selection (choice rejection, neutrality) and rank order can be plotted as symbols (see Figures 1C and 5B) in the plane, or as a third dimension in space (see Figure 5C); when the test is performed in action, one may sit or stand to indicate choice or rejection. Choices are expected on the right quadrant where attraction is high and repulsion is low. Conversely, rejections are expected on the left, where repulsion is high, and attraction low. Along the vertical axis of the plane, attractive and repulsive forces are fairly equal; when neither opposite is dominant, but they are fairly symmetric in intensity, the person may express neutrality, but also may choose or reject, hence the selection is unpredictable. In such cases, the combined intensity of both opposites together is useful to understand the psychological process. The bottom low-intensity area, where there is very little attraction or repulsion, is associated with neutrality in sociometric selections. In contrast, when the pulls to choose and to reject the same person are both intense at a given moment, the protagonist may choose or reject, but does not remain neutral. Two different outcomes, sociometric choices and rejections, are associated with the same underlying condition, highly intense opposites, coexisting in ambivalence and contradiction. Because both opposites are strong, but neither dominates, a little nudge can cause a qualitative shift from a choice to a rejection, or vice versa. This is called a *catastrophe* (see p. 171), which is the simplest form of a bifurcation.

When motivations are highly contradictory, subjects often give a higher-rank order to rejections than to some choices (Carlson-Sabelli 1992). This discrepancy between choice and preference is particularly significant in view of similar phenomena in experimental animals: resection of the brain amygdala eliminates valuation regarding food consumption -- the animal eats not only food but also other kinds of objects, including harmful ones; however, the rat still eats everything in the same order of preference before the resection (Pribram 1990). This exemplifies that motivations, rank order and categorical values of choice are different measurements of the same phenomenon. Contradictory motivation dissociates preference from value in interpersonal choices. The discrepancy between sociometric choice and rank order of preferences exists only when underlying motivations are contradictory and indicates the value of measuring and mapping all three.

Clinically significant events occur in conditions of contradiction. Because of the instability, persons indicating activity in this area, are most susceptible to therapeutic action.

Using the diamond of opposites in psychodrama

We often use the diamond of opposites as a method to choose a protagonist for psychodrama, using the right axis to represent the intensity of positive feelings towards choosing oneself to be the protagonist, and the left axis to represent the intensity of feelings against becoming the protagonist. Those individuals with strongly contradictory feelings pacing near the top vertex are ready to change, and hence to become the protagonist, while the indifferent individuals standing quietly near the origin, are less motivated to change, and less ready to be the group's protagonist.

After reporting their underlying tugs towards and against being a protagonist the group can be polled concerning their pulls towards and tugs against each choice, once again, on the diamond. A chosen protagonist can poll potential directors concerning their desires for and against directing the drama. Once understood, the diamond of opposites can be used in any number of ways. For example, the exercise can also be used to ascertain those persons whose attention is not with the group. We do this by asking each participant to take an inward look and identify how much of their attention is focused in the present, and how much is focused in the past or future. Each person is asked to assign each of these opposites an intensity score from 1 to 10 and to report their scores by physically placing themselves on a co-ordinate plane drawn on the floor, stating the numbers assigned to each opposite and the reasons for their placement. The report identifies distracted individuals and allows group participants to articulate problems that are weighing on their mind. This exercise identifies persons who might need assistance, perhaps even a psychodrama, before being able to contribute to the work of the group. When selecting a protagonist based on this 'diamond of opposites check-in', we often ask the group to choose among the individuals in the 'focused elsewhere' (left quadrant) and high-intensity 'split focus' (upper quadrant) areas (see Figures 1C and 5B). The drama with a protagonist chosen in this manner addresses concerns that are blocking focus. The purpose is to facilitate inclusion, and contribute to the wellbeing of the group.

As other action methods, the diamond of opposites may be used as a warm-up to psychodrama. It provides a meaningful development of the central concern model (Buchanan 1980), widely used to discover and highlight issues of immediate concern in a particular group by polarising opposites from material expressed early in a session. In the central concern model, individuals representing the extremes of each opposite are placed at the ends of continuum. Other group members are asked to find their place in between, forming a spectrogram (Kole 1967: 53–61). Using the diamond of opposites serves to highlight the contradictions that are essential to the understanding of the process, and that are obscured by the linear continuum. Using the continuum to report emotions, attitudes or behaviours, forces participants, and the group leader, to think in black-and-white dichotomies. In contrast, the diamond of opposites gives insight into the coexistence of opposites. It provides a way for participants in the centre of the continuum to recognise that there may be differences among them, regarding the total intensity of the opposites. Some individuals place themselves in the centre of the continuum because they do not relate to either opposite very much. Others might be feeling a great deal of both. These situations are concealed by the continuum, and revealed with the diamond. Further, with the diamond, persons at either end, may be prompted to assess if they usually are in a polarised position with regard to the opposite being explored, or if they are also capable of modulating

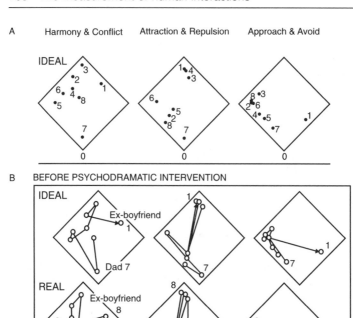

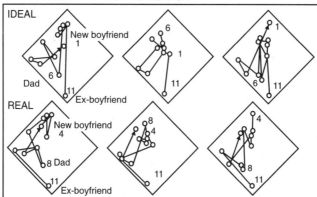

Figure 6 Interpersonal profile. A Diamonds of opposites depicting the intensity of harmony/conflict (left), attraction/repulsion (middle) and approach/avoid (right) in the interpersonal relations of one subject with the most important persons in her network numbered to indicate the order in which she would like to have contact (ideal rank order).

B Trajectory plots comparing the desired situation (top) with the real situation (bottom) concerning the amount of time one subject spends with significant others, before and after psychodramatic intervention.

their responses. Often they find that they belong in the contradictory quadrant, rather than in a polar extreme. The diamond includes the continuum, and provides a vehicle to acknowledge and report complex interactions of competing attitudes, thoughts and feelings underlying behaviour.

Interpersonal profiles

Attraction and repulsion is only one of the possible pairs of opposites relevant to sociometric choices; we also include harmony and conflict, and approach and avoidance, as opposite axes of the phase plane. We ask participants to generate a list of persons with whom they are emotionally connected, and to indicate (i) the order in which they would like to spend time with each person (ideal rank order); and (ii) the order in which they actually spend time (real rank order). Next, they are asked to indicate the intensity of their feelings regarding their interactions with each individual on their list by placing a point within each of three phase planes of opposites (harmony/conflict, attraction/repulsion and approach/avoid) (Figure 6A). Two sets of trajectory plots are made by connecting the dots according to ideal and real rank order from last to first; the arrow points to the person ranked first. In this way, the pattern indicating the real situation (Figure 6B), can be visually compared with the wished-for (ideal) situation (Figure 6B). We noticed in studies with twenty-two persons (Carlson-Sabelli and Sabelli 1992b) that the neutral quadrant was much more empty than the contradictory quadrant in all the plots in all subjects, indicating that coexisting opposites are more likely to create ambivalent bonds then neutrality. Thirty-six per cent reported at least three relationships in the contradictory corner of their plots denoting a process that is predictive of catastrophic switches between opposites, where one's choice might easily become a rejection, and vice versa. Finally, we were surprised when comparing information concerning real relationships with wished-for (ideal) relationships. We expected that the trajectories of ideal rank order would point to the extreme left vertex indicating a desire for pure harmony, attraction and approach, but such a pattern was observed only in 33 per cent of the subjects; apparently many people want some degree of conflict in their relations.

Because each reveals personally unique patterns, we use interpersonal profiles in our groups for targeting issues and measuring change in psychotherapy (Carlson-Sabelli and Sabelli 1992b, c). When used in conjunction with the social networks inventory (Treadwell et al. 1993), one can determine whether individuals dissatisfied with social distance in their important relationships wish to move towards or away from intimacy.

Identifying issues and evaluating the effectiveness of psychodrama with the interpersonal profile

Illustrated here are interpersonal trajectory plots before and after psycho-dramatic intervention for a young woman (Figure 6B). The 'before' plots (top) indicate a big discrepancy between this woman's wished-for (ideal) and real situation. Her first-ranked choice for contact (an ex-boyfriend), is the person with whom she reports having the least contact, suggesting potential unfinished business in this relationship. Further, she has more variance in the harmony/conflict and attraction/repulsion plots, than in the approach/avoid realm, suggesting a need to broaden her range of response.

After psychodramatic intervention, this subject's problematic relation-ship (ideal rank 1, real rank 8) shifted from the high-intensity contradictory area to the neutral corner and was replaced by a new one which is less conflictual (bottom), indicating that the unfinished business with her boyfriend had been completed. However there is still a lot of discrepancy in the ideal (1) and real (11) rank of the new boyfriend, indicating more work needs to be done to break the pattern regarding her relationships with significant others. This will likely involve psychodramatic work with early familial relationships from which this pattern emerged.

We are now in the process of creating an interactive computer program to provide immediate analysis and to track trajectories of change in every relationship reported on, over time, and to provide the capability to measure a variety of opposites.

Mutuality and accuracy of interpersonal perception

Interpersonal choices and bonds are two-way processes. Marriages, for instance, require a sustained mutual choice, and the ever growing creation of behaviours that accommodate both spouses. Mutual choices strengthen the bond between individuals and provide stability to groups; likewise rejections tend to become mutual. In the process of mutual interactions, how we feel for others becomes similar to how others feel about us, and vice versa. Attraction begets attraction, and repulsion begets repulsion (similarity of opposites). Attraction and repulsion involve a perception of how others feel towards us just as choice and rejection involve the antici-pation of how others would regard the decision. As social conflicts are introjected as fear and distrust for members of social groups different from ours (*para-consciousness*) (Sabelli 1989), we can create the conflicts we fear. Paranoids become isolated, while, in contrast, 'Pollyannas' become popular. Choices are also impacted by one's perception of the opinions of third parties. The Rockwell occupational approval grid (Rockwell 1987) has been developed as a tool to clarify this aspect for individuals considering various careers.

Fearing rejection, individuals may avoid choosing someone whom they regard highly, and so it is not unusual that a highly desirable partner be left without one. Choosing to go out with a girl my brother dislikes might be motivated by the response expected from him, or might take place in spite of his opinion. Attraction to one person may become rejection of another to whom we also feel attracted. These scenarios exemplify the complexities in the process of choice. Compounding it all is the fact that misperceptions can and do occur. Accuracy of interpersonal perception is important because choice is a two-way process, in which the choice of A by B favours the choice of B by A.

To measure the *accuracy of interpersonal perception*, subjects add to their reports of choices and intensity of opposing motivations, their guesses concerning the choices (Bonny 1943; Hale 1981; Moreno 1942) and motivations of the others for them (Carlson-Sabelli *et al.* 1991; Carlson-Sabelli *et al.* 1992a; Carlson-Sabelli 1992). In experimental studies, the ability of individuals to perceive correctly how much others are attracted to and repulsed by them (sociodynamic test) was greater than their ability to predict whether they were chosen or rejected (sociometric test), because choices and rejections are unpredictable when motivation is contradictory (Carlson-Sabelli 1992; Carlson-Sabelli *et al.* 1992). This suggests that intensity scores of attraction and repulsion should be used, instead of the actual decision, in computing and indices of accuracy (the degree to which one reads others accurately) and openness (the degree to which one is read accurately by others) regarding interpersonal perception. Perceptual sociometry can thus be developed as a measure of personal ability to understand and be understood by others, and may serve to evaluate the effectiveness of the role reversal technique used in psychodrama, and in family therapy, to improve empathy.

In attempting to understand two-way empathy, Moreno (1978) developed the sociometric test, and developed the concept of 'tele' as 'the reality-based feelings individuals have for one another in shared, here-and-now interactions related to roles and situations'. He thus contrasted 'tele' with psychoanalytic transference, which 'is not reality-based'. In our view, irrational transference feelings and objective economic bonds are as important as any form of empathy in the constitution of groups. We use interpersonal libido as a comprehensive construct that includes these various forms of bonding energy; action graphs are one method to study this process, while the measure of energy in the sociodynamic test (see below) is another.

CO-CREATION OF CHOICE

Catastrophes: how the interaction of opposites promotes creativity

Moreno's concept of co-creation is the core of the third law of process theory: Natural evolution and individual development result from the co-creation of opposites. The goal of sociometry (and of sociodynamics) is to measure and enhance our ability to choose, to create and to co-create harmoniously with others.

Metric models imply that selections are a linear outcome of attractions and repulsions; they are unable to deal with novelty and creativity, which are, by definition, non-linear. As discussed earlier, attraction and repulsion do not neutralise each other; their algebraic sum does not predict the sociometric outcome. On the contrary, the very nature of choice forces one motivation to overcome the other, and when both motivations are intense, selections are unstable, and likely to switch rapidly between choosing and rejecting, and thereby creating a more complex form of behaviour than either one or the other. Phase-space portraits allow us to analyse complex phenomena where gradually changing forces or motivations lead to abrupt changes in behaviour that do not fit unidimensional linear models. Discontinuous, sudden, qualitative shifts from one equilibrium state to another, such as from choice to rejection, or vice versa, are modelled in mathematics by a *catastrophe* (Thom 1975).

In experimental studies including thirteen different groups, we have observed a linear distribution of selections as a function of choices only in a few cases (Carlson-Sabelli *et al.* 1991; Carlson-Sabelli and Sabelli 1992b,c; Carlson-Sabelli *et al.* 1992a; Carlson-Sabelli 1992). In contrast, we have shown empirically that the distribution of interpersonal choices as a function of the underlying feelings of attraction and repulsion can be adequately modelled by a fold (see Figure 5C), one of the seven possible types of catastrophe (Thom 1975). Further studies may reveal that different criteria, different social circumstances, or different personalities generate other forms. Figure 5D illustrates the distribution of actual data obtained with criteria of differing threat: a linear distribution is the best fit when the sociometric criterion has a high-threat case, while in the low-threat case, data have a better fit with a catastrophe fold. Figure 5D indicates the expected correspondence of the co-ordinate plane of opposites with the catastrophe surface.

In mathematics, the term catastrophe does not have the connotation of a traumatic event: it describes a process where there is a potential for divergence because there are two competing point attractors. Consider, for instance, an animal confronting a threat. If frightened, the animal will retreat, whereas anger without fright predicts attack. When the animal feels the threat to be weak, and hence is neither frightened nor angered, the outcome is neutral, and the behaviour is more complex, either indifference or curiosity. When the animal is both intensely frightened and intensely angered, the outcome is even less predictable, and the animal may retreat or attack, or switch from one behaviour to the other. The direction of the switch is easily influenced by small external triggers. This switch between retreat or attack is an example of a catastrophe.

A catastrophe is the simplest form of non-linear change (bifurcation). When many bifurcations occur, there is chaos, which is not randomness but a turbulence that creates novelty and complexity. Chaos represents heightened spontaneity and creativity. As bifurcations serve as the basis for chaos, choices serve as the basis for creativity. Introducing catastrophe modelling into sociodynamics allows one to develop a strategy to promote creativity. The shape of a catastrophe is determined by two control variables: (i) a bifurcating function that at low values leads to a continuous outcome, while at high values the outcome is discontinuous; and (ii) an asymmetric variable that at mid-values is associated with large changes between the modes, while at extreme values is associated with small changes around the modes. We discovered that in our data the bifurcating function could be calculated as the sum of the underlying opposing forces of attraction and repulsion, while the asymmetric function was their difference. Intuitively, both opposing forces contribute energy (bifurcating factor) to the process: at low energy, there is neutrality, and at high energy, choice, rejection or ambivalence. The difference between opposite motivations provides information regarding the direction of the outcome (asymmetric control parameter). These results root sociometry in the powerful mathematics of catastrophe theory. They also suggest that catastrophes, the simplest form of non-linear, i.e. creative interaction, result from the union and difference of opposites (Sabelli 1989; Carlson-Sabelli and Sabelli 1992b; Seiden and Sabelli 1992).

We propose (Sabelli 1992; Seiden and Sabelli 1992) a *formula for creativity*: unite opposites (opposite opinions, perspectives, classes) such that both are of approximately similar and relatively high intensity. Testing the multiple motivations and conceptions that a person has at a given time, and as they evolve in time, in the phase plane of opposites, can reveal contradictions, and thereby promote creative solutions that include both opposites. In physical processes, novelty and complexity arise when a process is shaken by strong fluctuations leading to chaos, which in turn, create new and complex structures. Likewise, emotional contradiction does not arrest in balanced equilibrium or ambivalence, but the interaction of opposites co-creates novelty and complexity.

The co-organisation of groups

The complex process of organisation and reorganisation of real groups must be composed of a myriad of bonds and choices. Spontaneously formed groups may appear to exemplify 'self-organisation', but, in fact, groups are co-organised by the interaction of many, mutually contradictory, processes. As each person attracts and repels others in different respects and at different times, we may conceive of persons as being attractor–repellers in the interpersonal field. Each action and each choice represents the conjoint result of a multiplicity of personal and group processes. *Sociograms* are visual representations of the process of inter-personal choices among persons in a group (Moreno 1978; Hale 1981; Blatner and Blatner 1988a). Their value is limited because they are snapshots of a process, and only represent the conscious and public aspect of this process, and nevertheless are useful to the individual (who learns about her/his patterns of interaction, and gains access to roles and relationships) and to the creation and nurturing of groups. Sociograms can be expanded after the fashion of action graphs, to include not only choices but also other types of bonds between the individual members. In the standard sociogram, each person is connected to each other by a coded arrow denoting either choice or rejection, the thickness of which indicates its strength. The sociodynamic test allows one to draw in each case two arrows, attraction and repulsion, thereby revealing more cogently the dynamics of the group.

Data from the sociometric test provides information about the group including the existence of subgroups, and the identification of pivotal persons linking them with each other. The visual configurations of the bonds among group members reflect the way the group members organise themselves around a particular criterion in a straightforward manner, so persons unfamiliar with sociometric methods can understand a great deal about the group from it. With several tests, patterns of relating can be identified, and interventions to promote connectedness planned. The degree of connectedness with and isolation of an individual from other persons in a group conveys information about one's access to roles. Sociograms serve to identify stars (chosen by many), isolates (one who neither chooses, nor is chosen), rejectees, stars of incongruity (rejected by those he or she chooses or vice versa), and connectors. The study of sociograms sometimes reveals the existence of individuals who are both chosen and rejected more often than others. Plotting feelings of attraction and repulsion readily reveals in sociograms, or in the phase plane of opposites, the identification of four classes: indifferent isolates, attractive stars, repulsive rejectees and bifurcators. *Bifurcators* give and receive strong feelings of attraction and repulsion, and may be the target of many choices in some groups and of many rejections in others. They are, in general, high-energy persons, ranging from innovators and creators to bipolar personalities and manic-depressive patients, and other persons with strong personalities and/or strong convictions.

Sociometric asymmetry and social hierarchy

In all groups, interpersonal affection and choice is distributed unevenly. Some individuals are rich in choices, receiving far more love than they can reciprocate, while there is a number of unchosen, unwanted persons, who receive far less love needed for emotional growth and integration. Moreno discovered this asymmetry in the distribution of choices, and considered it the most basic sociodynamic law (Moreno 1978). Moreno's *sociodynamic asymmetry* is not a particular characteristic of processes of choice. The sociogram of an organisation does not make sense unless we distinguish levels of hierarchy, which are not determined by mutual choices, but by the choice of those in power. Likewise, social hierarchies are determined by reasons of birth and wealth, not by choice. Whereas greater equality is often desirable, one must also recognise that human asymmetries are just one particular case of Pasteur's *cosmic asymmetry*, that exists in every structure, and that is acknowledged as a fundamental feature of biological processes (Clynes 1969). According to process theory, asymmetry is the imprint that energy flow leaves on all structures, serving to store information (e.g. cultural conserves) and as a catalytic agent to direct change (Sabelli 1989; Sabelli and Carlson-Sabelli 1989). Just as in nature, high-energy systems tend to gain energy at the expense of lower-energy systems, so in society persons rich in energy, wealth or choice, draw from the weaker others. Here sociodynamic asymmetry reappears in its most fundamental form, as social hierarchy, economic inequalities, personal domination and, at times, oppression and abuse. Social status predetermines choices (priority). People who are rich or powerful are often chosen. This point is clinically important, as persons with low status often suffer a further decrease in their self-esteem because they receive few choices. Illuminating the biological and socioeconomic bases of sociometric asymmetries serves to heal many psychological and interpersonal wounds. On the other hand, people become rich and powerful because they are chosen by others (supremacy); it is thus of practical importance to learn strategies to improve our 'sociometric wealth', such as 'choose to be chosen'.

To explore these issues in action, group members may line up according to their perception of how often they are chosen, and interchanges between highly-chosen and seldom-chosen persons may elicit significant material. We add to this linear exercise a number of two-dimensional planes, including the frequency of being chosen and being rejected (revealing bifurcators), as well as (in groups of persons who know each other) subjective and collective estimates of these two parameters (widely differing for many types of personality). It is also therapeutic to understand that hierarchies are bi-directional. For instance, *male supremacy* is a reality, but so is *female priority* (Sabelli 1989; Sabelli and Carlson-Sabelli 1989; Sabelli and Synnestvedt 1990), as mothers are the first environment, the first love, the first authority and the first identification figure in the lives of most individuals. Moreover, women usually outlive men; hence older men have more choices than women (supremacy), but more women than men are alive to choose (priority). Recognising that women have power, sometimes even greater power than men in the family, does not deny the oppression of women in society at large, nor is intended as a compensation, but rather serves to recognise a reality, and to provide a basis for empowering the oppressed in each circumstance. To highlight the coexistence of opposing patterns of power in each relation, it is useful to request persons in a family or group to plot their intensity and extension in a plane of opposites. One may thus identify areas in which each spouse dominates the other, as well as areas in which there is equality or alternation of power. We discussed home economics in terms of interchanges of labour (energy) such as each person's contribution to home tasks, of information (practical, affective, intellectual) and money (matter) leading to relations of status. But labour and wealth not only have a use value; they also have a price or market value. It seems hard to look at the exchange value of people, but the reality is that groups are not closed, and that as many as 50 per cent of marriages end in divorce in the USA today.

Sociographs of family and group relations

Sociograms are also applied to study open natural groups, such as families and the 'social atom', the network of persons directly interacting with a given person. Social atoms are open systems, that extend indefinitely, without boundaries, but with decreasing exchange of energy and information at the periphery. The person is the one centre of a double cone that expands towards many in the past and towards many in the future. The advantages of the here and now indicate the usefulness of sociometric snapshots of groups under study, but when group members report about their outside relations such advantage is lost, while much can be gained by looking at relations historically. Sociographs plot the trajectory of the process of change in interpersonal bonds over time. These are constructed by plotting the intensity of opposites in a relationship, for example, attraction and repulsion, as a single point on a co-ordinate plane. Connecting the points from past to present, produces a trajectory depicting the pattern of the change for each relationship plotted. Figure 7 illustrates the evolution in time of the relation of a marital couple with the main significant other, over their life span. Sociographs can be obtained for natural groups such as families, or for the therapy or educational group in which the exercise is performed. We can thus compare the relationships of one person with others in different situations. Subjects are asked what they notice about similarities between the temporal patterns of their relations inside each of these groups (family, work, therapy group), as well as regarding the differences in pattern between their wished-for (ideal) and real situations. What can you do to move from the real towards the ideal? What are the barriers? What relationships need working on? What other issues does this exercise highlight for you? When we do this exercise in action, we ask the protagonist to reverse roles by standing in the site where she or he has

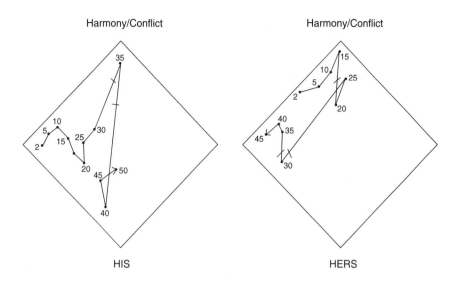

Figure 7 Sociographs. A sociograph is a trajectory constructed from connecting sequential measures (T$_1$, T$_2$, etc.) indicating a pattern over time. This trajectory indicates the amount of harmony and conflict reported by husband and wife regarding their most significant relationships over the course of their life.

placed mother, father, spouse, child, co-worker, at various points in time, and from that position spell out how they feel *vis-à-vis* the protagonist. This exercise illustrates sociodynamics as a sociometric method that focuses on long-term processes of interaction between coexisting contradictory feelings in the co-creation of situations and relations.

Colour sociograms

Seeking the *trifurcation* of opposites serves to understand patterns that are otherwise obscured by the tendency to think in pairs of opposites. The three primary colours serve as a model to understand the trifurcation of opposites. We use them therapeutically, to encourage people to go beyond the dichotomies of black and white thinking, shown by Adler (1954) and by Beck and co-workers (1979) to predispose to neurosis and to depression (Sabelli and Javaid 1991). We invite people to think of one possible pattern of behaviour that corresponds to each of the primary colours, and to their combinations.

In a typical group exercise, the participants are asked to assign a colour to (i) each other group member; and (ii) all persons in their family and social atom, by listing their names on labels of eight different colours (three primaries, three secondaries, black and white). We first examine

THE HOUSEHOLD METHOD

A

1964   1976   1985   1986

CHICAGO   EVANSTON

B

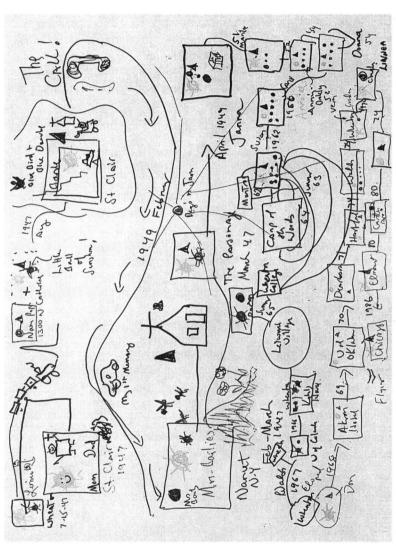

Figure 8 Households. Portrayed here (A) is the household of a 20-year-old woman (filled circle) still living with her parents. She was an only child, born when her parents had been married 12 years. At age 9, her half-sister, a daughter of her father from a previous marriage, joined the family and soon after, the family moved from the city to a suburb. A household changes whenever a person enters or leaves the household, or the person doing the exercise, moves, and can be embellished in a variety of ways (B).

the results in terms of correlations; for instance, many times participants unconsciously assign the same colour to the therapist and to one of their parents. Next we ask the participants to pair each colour with the names of coloured objects (fire, sun, water, earth, plant), emotions (anger, sexual arousal, tranquillity, etc.) and behaviours (aggression, escape, harmony, etc.). Then we ask the participants to interpret the colours chosen, under the assumption that colours do have some objective social meaning that have priority (as leading examples, we refer to red anger, depressive blues and cowardly yellow; to red left, royal and police blue, and the yellow of the Vatican theocracy) but individuals add personal meanings that have supremacy. Even at the social level, each colour has opposite meanings; for instance, passion is red, whether sexual or aggressive.

Colour sociograms serve to bridge the dynamics observed in the group with the dynamics of each person's social atom. This renders the study of relations within a therapy group more readily applicable to real life.

Household method

The household method (Figure 8) captures personal history as a series of sociograms which tap into a fundamental natural group. We ask participants to draw sequentially each household of which he was a member, starting with his parents' place before he was born, and defining a transition from one household to another by the entry or exit of one person, or changes in domicile (because these often imply a change in the circle of friends, school, work, as well as may reflect socioeconomic changes) (Figure 8A). Households most often are families, but in all cases represent economic units, and thus reveal significant sociodynamic factors. The history obtained using the household method is very rich. Individuals often embellish these with personalised illustrations (Figure 8B). It is a good exercise early in the life of a group to facilitate members to get to know each other quickly and highlight potential issues that are likely to emerge.

Co-creation games

We start co-creation games with an activity to increase energy and interaction. For example, we might play music and ask everyone to dance. When the music stops, the facilitator yells a number, and everyone has to form a group of that size. When the group is warmed up, we initiate an improvisation with 3 rules: (i) initiate, don't ask questions. Make statements and suggestions; (ii) say yes to whatever is offered, and introduce variations and embellishments; (iii) use partial contradiction; agree with what you can, and offer alternatives. In this improvisation, one person starts an activity in which he or she is doing something. It must be non-verbal. The group guesses what the person is doing. Once the activity is correctly guessed, another person in the group enters the scene, and it moves from non-verbal to verbal. The two players establish together, by their interaction their relationship to one another, and the reason they are together. For example, a person who starts a scene shovelling, might be joined by someone who says, 'I see you are digging a hole'. Person 1 might have had in mind that he was shovelling snow, but now shifts to accommodate the contribution of the other, through the conversation and action. Meanwhile the audience is responsible for stopping the players any time one of them breaks a rule, providing the opportunity for the rule breaker to try again. This activity goes on long enough for everyone to understand the rules. Next we break into groups of three, getting into groups by counting off by threes, so people are more likely to be with others they know less well than those they are sitting next to. The first person assigns a scene and a character for the other two. The two persons must start a dialogue that is within the scene. Again the rules must be kept, and person 1 is the judge. After 5 minutes, person 2 becomes the judge as persons 1 and 3 continue the dialogue, but with person 3 in the role he or she did not take in the previous dialogue. Finally the dialogue continues with persons 2 and 1, again, with a switch in character so that everyone plays each character and is the judge. A third activity can be added, which involves creating something together, a group co-creation. An activity that works well for large groups is to have a short guided fantasy in which each participant has a personal experience. The facilitator might ask people to relax, breath more slowly and imagine themselves walking in a serene place, a place where they might go when they needed renewal or were celebrating. As they are walking, their wise self comes and takes them by the hand. They come upon a huge cave that has a stone at its doorway. The stone rolls away, revealing a person or character, perhaps an archetypal character, whose presence has special personal meaning for the beholder at this particular time. The attention of the participants is brought back to the group, and each person is requested to draw a picture of the character that emerged doing something, to put a one-sentence title on the drawing, to tape it on the wall and to examine the drawings of others. Finally, each person is asked to draw their figure in someone else's picture, and add a sentence that says something about who it is and why the character has been added. There is no limit to how many characters can be in any picture. After this has been done, we find the pictures with the most characters in them, and have the persons regroup around these, breaking into one to five smaller groups, depending on the number of participants. These groups then are asked to create a metaphor or fluid sculpture depicting the picture they have joined. I have the person who initiated the picture be first in the enactment, and then come out and watch it from outside. The result is the immediate co-creation, a poetic dance with personal and collective meaning.

CONCLUDING REMARKS

Overcoming the individualistic focus of earlier psychotherapy, Moreno developed the *role-reversal technique* to provide insight into the other, and founded sociometry, psychodrama and family therapy on the unifying concept of the encounter. Sociometry and psychodrama are thus related as parallel developments within a *clinical philosophy* which regards *insight into the other* a necessary ingredient for interpersonal health. Understanding the 'role we play' in situations we dislike, we develop empathy for others.

Sociometry highlights the complementarity of roles. Psychodrama reveals them through the role reversal. Sociometry measures relations; psychodrama seeks to understand the causes and choices that lead to them, and provides skills to improve them. A psychodrama can be processed sociometrically, that is examine the reasons for role selections, and consider how one might increase access or gain role relief. Finally, sociometric portraits can be used to identify interpersonal issues, highlight a pattern within a psychodrama (Goldman *et al.* 1989) or evaluate psychodramatic work (Leutz 1992).

As the mathematical and clinical analysis of social behaviour, sociometry represents the product of a comprehensive, scientific and socially conscious clinical philosophy. Conceptualising social processes in terms of energy serves to unify sociometry with biology and economics (priority) as well as with psychodynamics (supremacy). Bridging mathematical dynamics with psychodynamics, sociodynamics embodies the process method of examining each problem from the complementary perspectives of the simpler, more fundamental levels of organisation, that have priority, and of the more complex levels, that have supremacy. The highest perspective is ethical, and hence we include in action graphs a consideration of 'the scales of justice'. Ethical concerns apply not only to individuals but also to society. In Moreno's vision (1978: 3), 'a truly therapeutic procedure cannot have less an objective than the whole of mankind'. In his quest 'to move within a rational therapeutic framework from small group psychotherapy to mass psychotherapy and mass Psychiatry', Moreno was interested in reaching the masses; in his spirit, we are developing sociodynamic exercises that challenge the participants to co-create a society at the service of persons rather than profit or power (Sabelli 1991b; Sabelli and Synnestvedt 1990). Moreno created sociometry as the ground basis for 'sociatry', the psychiatry of society. At this time when social visions are handicapped by a void of ideas, our generation must keep alive this historical mission. Mathematical method, clinical art, and social ethics, are three aspects of the Morenian tradition that should not be separated.

ACKNOWLEDGEMENTS

We thank Mrs Maria McCormick and other members of the Society for the Advancement of Clinical Philosophy, the students of the Rush Psychodrama Program, the members of the Sociometry Research Group, Renée Luecht, and Dr Minu Patel of the Bioscience Facility Resource Centre, University of Illinois at Chicago, for their generous support in this project.

REFERENCES

Abraham, F.D. (in collaboration with Abraham, R.H. and Shaw, C.D.) (1990) *A Visual Introduction to Dynamical Systems Theory for Psychology*, Santa Cruz: Aerial.

Adler, A. (1954) *Understanding Human Nature*, Greenwich, CT: Fawcett.

Baker, G.L. and Gollub, J.P. (1990). *Chaotic Dynamics*, Cambridge: Cambridge University Press.

Beck, A., Rush, A., Shaw, B. and Emery, G. (1979) *Cognitive Therapy of Depression*, New York: Wiley.

Blatner, A. and Blatner, A. (1988a) *Foundations of Psychodrama: History, theory and practice*, 3rd edn, New York: Springer.

Blatner A. and Blatner, A. (1988b) *The Art of Play*, New York: Human Sciences Press.

Bonny, M.M. (1943) 'The consistency of sociometric scores and their relationship to teacher judgements of social success and to personality self-ratings', *Sociometry* 6: 409–24.

Buchanan, D.R. (1980) 'The central concern model: a framework for structuring psychodramatic production', *Group Psychotherapy, Psychodrama and Sociometry* 33: 47–62.

Carlson-Sabelli, L. (1992) 'Measuring co-existing opposites: a methodological exploration', Doctoral dissertation, University of Illinois at Chicago, Order no. 9226372, UMI Dissertation Services, 1–800–521–0600.

Carlson-Sabelli, L. and Sabelli H.C. (1984) 'Reality perception and role reversal'. *Journal of Group Psychotherapy, Psychodrama and Sociometry* 36: 162–74.

Carlson-Sabelli, L. and Sabelli, H.C. (1990) *Psychogeometry*, Proceedings of the Thirty-Fourth International Society for the System Sciences, Pomona, CA, California State Polytechnic University, 769–75.

Carlson-Sabelli, L. and Sabelli, H.C. (1992a) *Modular Organisation of Human System: A process theory perspective*. Proceedings of the Thirty-Sixth International Society for Systems Sciences, Pocatello, Idaho State University, pp. 678–88.

Carlson-Sabelli, L. and Sabelli, H.C. (1992b) *Interpersonal Profiles: Analysis of interpersonal relations with the phase space of opposites*, Proceedings of the Thirty-Sixth International Society for Systems Sciences, Pocatello, Idaho State University, pp. 668–77.

Carlson-Sabelli, L. and Sabelli, H.C. (1992c) 'Phase plane of opposites: a method to study change in complex processes, and its application to sociodynamics and psychotherapy', *The Social Dynamicist* 3 (4): 1–6.

Carlson-Sabelli, L., Sabelli, H.C. and Patel, M. (1991) *Dynamics of Choosing in Small Group Systems*, Proceedings of the Thirty-Fifth International Society for Systems Sciences, Östersund University, pp. 7–11.

Carlson-Sabelli, L., Sabelli, H.C., Patel, M. and Holm, K. (1992a). 'The union of opposites in sociometry: an empirical application of process theory.' *Journal of Group Psychotherapy, Psychodrama and Sociometry* 44: 147–71.

Carlson-Sabelli, L., Sabelli, H., Zbilut, M., Patel, M., Messer, J.V., Walthall, K., Fink, P., Epstein, P. and Hein, N. (1992b) *Developing Electropsychocardiography as a Diagnostic Tool in Medicine and Psychiatry*, Chicago: Proceedings of Communication and Collaboration in Research, Rush University.

Clynes, M. (1969) 'Rein control, or unidirectional rate sensitivity, a fundamental dynamic and organising function in biology', *Annals of the New York Academy of Sciences* 156: 627–968.

Cobb, L. and Zacks, S. (1985) 'Applications of catastrophe theory for statistical modelling in the biosciences', *Journal of the American Statistical Association* 80: 793–802.

Goldman, E.E., Morrison, D.S. and Goldman, M.S. (1989) *Psychodrama: A training tape*, Phoenix, AZ: Eldmar Corporation.

Guastello, S. J. (1988) 'Catastrophe modelling of the accident process: organisational subunit size', *Psychological Bulletin* 103(2): 246–55.

Hale, A. E. (1981) *Conducting Clinical Sociometric Explorations*, Roanoke, VA: Royal Publishing Co.

—— (1989) 'New developments in sociometry', *Journal of Group Psychotherapy, Psychodrama and Sociometry*, 40: 119–23.

Hare, P. (1992) 'Moreno's sociometric study at the Hudson School for Girls', *Journal of Group Psychotherapy, Psychodrama and Sociometry* 45: 24–39.

Kole, D.M. (1967) 'The spectrogram in psychodrama', *Group Psychotherapy* 10 (1–2): 53–61.

Leutz, G. (1992) 'Sociometric–psychodramatic group psychotherapy in its methodic significance', *The International Forum of Group Psychotherapy*, 1 (5): 7–9.

Moreno, J.L. (1978) *Who Shall Survive?* 3rd edn, New York: Beacon House.

—— (1942) 'Sociometry in action', *Sociometry* 5: 298–315.

Pribram, K. (1990) *Brain and Perception: Holonomy and structure in figural processing*, Boston, MA: John M. MacEachran Lecture Series.

Raaz, N., Carlson-Sabelli, L. and Sabelli, H.C. (1992) 'Psychodrama in the treatment of Multiple Personality Disorder: a process-theory perspective', in E. Kluft (ed.) *Expressive and Functional Therapies in the Treatment of Multiple Personality Disorder*, Springfield, IL: Charles Thomas, pp. 169–88.

Rockwell, T. (1987) 'The social construction of careers: career development and career counselling viewed from a sociometric perspective', *Journal of Group Psychotherapy, Psychodrama and Sociometry* 40 (3): 93–107.

Sabelli, H.C. (1989) *Union of Opposites: A comprehensive theory of natural and human processes*, Lawrenceville: Brunswick.

—— (1991a) 'A synthetic approach to psychiatry's nature–nurture debate: a commentary', *Integrative Psychiatry* 7: 83–9.

—— (1991b) *Process Theory, a General Theory of Natural and Human Systems*, Proceedings of the Thirty-Fifth International Society for Systems Sciences, Östersund University, pp. 168–81.

—— (1991c) *Process Theory, a Biological Model of Open Systems*, Proceedings of the Thirty-Fifth International Society for Systems Sciences, Östersund University, pp. 219–25.

—— (1992) *God the Attractor: A scientific concept and a psychotherapeutic metaphor*, Proceedings of the Thirty-Sixth International Society for Systems Sciences, Pocatello, Idaho State University, pp. 1241–50.

Sabelli, H.C. and Carlson-Sabelli, L. (1989) 'Biological priority, psychological supremacy: a new integrative paradigm derived from process theory', *The American Journal of Psychiatry* 146: 1541–51.

Sabelli, H.C. and Carlson-Sabelli, L. (1991) *Process Theory as a Framework for Comprehensive Psychodynamic Formulations*, Genetic, Social and General Psychology Monographs 117 (1): 5–27.

Sabelli, H.C. and Carlson-Sabelli, L. (1992) *Process Theory: Energy, information and structure in the phase space of opposites*, Proceedings of the Thirty-Sixth International Society for Systems Sciences, Pocatello, Idaho State University, pp. 658–67.

Sabelli, H.C. and Javaid, J. (1991) *Depression and Conflict in Individuals in Social Systems*, Proceedings of the Thirty-Fifth International Society for Systems Sciences, Östersund University, pp. 175–81.

Sabelli, H.C. and Synnestvedt, J. (1990) *Personalisation. A new vision for the millennium*, Chicago: Society for the Advancement of Clinical Philosophy.

Sabelli, H.C., Carlson-Sabelli, L. and Javaid, J.I. (1990) 'The thermodynamics of bipolarity: a bifurcation model of bipolar illness and bipolar character and its psychotherapeutic applications', *Psychiatry: Interpersonal and biological processes* 53: 346–67.

Sabelli, H.C., Plaza, V., Vázquez, A., Abraira, C. and Martinez, I. (1991) *Caos Argentino: Diagnóstico y enfoque clínico*, Chicago, IL: Society for the Advancement of Clinical Philosophy.

Sabelli H., Carlson-Sabelli, L. and Patel, M. (In Press) 'Psychological portraits and psychocardiological patterns in phase space', in F. Abraham (ed.) *Chaos Theory in Psychology*.

Seiden, D. and Sabelli, H.C. (1992) *Co-creation: a process theory of form in art and life*, Proceedings of the Thirty-Sixth International Society for Systems Sciences, Pocatello, Idaho State University, pp. 720–9.

Thom, R. (1975) *Structural Stability and Morphogenesis*, Reading, MA: Benjamin/ Cummings.

Treadwell, T.W., Leach, E. and Stein, S. (1993) 'The social networks inventory: a diagnostic instrument measuring interpersonal relationships', *Small Group Research* 24: 155–78.

The transpersonal and psychospiritual dimension

Chapter 8

The cosmic circus

Commentary

The idea of the cosmos as being central to Man's existence, leads us into the first chapter of the next cluster of concepts. Martti Lindqvist explores Moreno's religious and philosophical background. He sees psychodrama as moving in two directions at the same time and argues for a reassessment of Morenian morality at a time of diminishing morality in the twentieth century.

Lindqvist and other authors suggest that Moreno's ideas on the nature of existence and the relationship between Man and God predate the work of the theologian Martin Buber and the later existentialists. There are many similarities between the philosophy of these two men and it is debatable which one influenced the other. It is now clearer that Moreno was one of the earliest of existential thinkers, even though Marineau sees contradictions in his advocating anonymity as well as fighting for recognition at the same time. The idea of a more direct experience of God in an I–Thou relationship, is perhaps more familiar to us now than when it was first expounded by Moreno.

Religion and the spirit

Martti Lindqvist

It is a sunny Sunday morning somewhere in the Finnish countryside. The group is sitting on mattresses in a big room which is full of light. The last day of the workshop has begun. As the group leader I gather some of the feelings and ideas from the participants. I say: 'You are in a circus. What do you see there? Look carefully what is of interest for you. When you have found something role-reverse with the thing you are looking at.'

The group creates several images from which I pick five for demonstration on the stage. In the centre of the stage lies a dying clown. He has decided to show his own death to the audience as his last performance. Further away there is a broken mirror on which an elephant has stepped. Very close to the clown is a beast, a very mysterious and frightening creature. And just on the edge of the stage lies a small child who has fallen from the merry-go-around. She feels very lonely and frightened.

The circus has no ordinary roof. The clear, blue sky covers the stage like a cosmic tent. The sky is eternal and unchangeable. It never lets you down.

The story starts to move when people, who are in the roles of the clown, the mirror, the beast, the child and the sky begin to interact spontaneously with each other. The story is very human and cosmic at the same time. It is greater than any explanation given to it. The mirror is the image of broken hopes and relationships. It symbolises the human soul that wants to be healed. Especially, it reflects the hurting feelings of the fallen and lonely child. The beast looks dangerous and starts to fight physically with the dying clown. When the struggle is over it shows that the beast and the clown are close friends, opposite sides of the same being. For the clown, the beast is his guide and companion when he approaches the unknown at the moment of his death.

What happens to the small child who embodies both the heart and the deepest purpose of the circus? The sky looks at her and gives her trust and comfort. The sky cannot move to the child but is able to create the contact between the child and an adult spectator in the group. The child finds the hope which she had lost and is given the courage to climb back onto the merry-go-around. What at first glance was just horror, loneliness, destruction and madness has gone through a metamorphosis and turned into joy, togetherness and beauty. It shows the magic of the drama and the magic of the life (Lindqvist 1992).

What has this unusual story of a circus to do with the great themes of religion, spirit and drama which gave J.L. Moreno his deepest inspiration in his thinking and when he created the theory and method of psychodrama? The circus itself is an archetypical image of life. There are all the different feelings which a human being can experience. There is much sharing, excitement and magic present. People and other creatures on the stage have different roles which they develop to the full. The stage itself is a place with a touch of special magic. Everything is possible. The borderline between reality and surplus reality disappears.

The symbols are important. The name 'circus' refers to the circle-shaped stage ('arena') which is the focus of all that there is and happens in the circus. Therefore, it was not an accident that Moreno himself created a circular stage for psychodrama. The circle is the symbol of eternity, wholeness and life which returns to its origin. The same symbolism can be seen, for example, in the use of the wedding ring or funeral wreath. In the beginning the stage is empty but at the same time the atmosphere around it is in a state of pregnancy. It is as it was in the very beginning of the universe: 'The earth was without form and void, and darkness was upon the face of the deep and the Spirit of God was moving over the face of the waters' (Genesis 1: 2). In the circus, the first creative action takes place when the public form an emotional contact with the empty stage. Expectations rise in the warm-up process.

Life itself can be described as a cosmic stage. At birth we enter the stage and in the moment of death we leave it. Life means that we have the possibility to play our own stories on the stage of life and that our stories are seen, shared and received by others. Life is rich if the roles are manyfold and fully played. There are times when cathartic action takes place giving the opportunity for metamorphosis, a qualitative change in one's own core.

From the very beginning of human culture, drama has served as an important means of human encounter with 'the greater life'. Drama has united people, healed them and given them the possibility to participate in the common myths of human history. As a matter of fact most rituals, religious and secular, are means of describing, mastering and changing life in dramatic form. There is a wide variation of different forms of drama, but what unites most of them is the emphasis on the spirit, experience, interaction, spontaneity and creativity.

MORENO'S RELIGIOUS ROOTS

It has been asked, whether Moreno's religious and metaphysical ideas are a necessary part of the theory and practice of psychodrama. Could one work with psychodrama successfully without taking notice of its religious roots? Different people have different answers. What remains clear is that we could not think of Moreno himself without his own history and his personal way of thinking which has profound religious overtones. Historically, religion gave Moreno in many ways his basic inspiration, the motivation for his practical work and the basic metaphors and concepts to describe the human drama in the universe.

In my opinion, it is possible to understand the relevance of religion to psychodrama at three different levels: (i) the metaphysical foundation of spontaneity/creativity theory; (ii) the moral commitment to work for people; and (iii) drama as a means to deal with religious/metaphysical issues. In what follows, all three aspects are briefly discussed.

It is widely known that Moreno had profound ideas about religion, God, spirit and cosmic processes. This is understandable partly because of his historical and religious background: his origin was Jewish. One of the famous stories from his childhood tells how when he was playing God with other children he tried to fly but in the attempt fell down and broke his right arm. Surely, there is some symbolism in this story given his cosmic ideas and his later self-interpretation as a man who was going to make a profound revolution in psychology and to transform the social institutions of human kind everywhere.

In his early adolescence Moreno also had deeply religious experiences. He tells about his vision when he was in his fourteenth year living in Chemnitz. He calls it 'his epiphany'.

> I found myself in a little park standing in front of a statue of Jesus Christ illumined by the moon's faint light. It drew my gaze and I stood transfixed. In the intensity of this strange moment I tried with all my will to have that statue come alive, to speak to me. . . . Standing there in front of the statue, I knew that I had to make a decision, one which would determine the future course of my life. I believe that all men have to make such a decision in their youth. This was the moment of my decision. . . . I decided for the universe, not because my family was inferior to any other family, but because I wanted to live on behalf of the larger setting to which every member of my family belonged and to which I wanted them to return. . . . The small statue before me symbolized that Jesus had gone the way of the universe and had taken all the consequences which were involved.
>
> (Marineau 1989: 23)

Moreno, at least later, understood that this was the beginning of his calling for a special task in the world.

> Standing before Christ in Chemnitz, I began to believe that I was an
> extraordinary person, that I was here on the planet to fulfil an extra-
> ordinary mission. This state of mind is usually called megalomania. That
> is a nasty name. It's really name calling.
>
> (Marineau 1989: 24)

The next step in his religious development took place in the early years of
his time in Vienna when he established with friends 'The House of
Encounter'. Some authors call that period of time Moreno's hassidic
period (Fox 1987: xv; Williams 1989: 10–11). Moreno wanted to establish
'a religion of encounter' based on love, voluntary giving and anonymity.
The emphasis was on the community work with the simple and needy
people who were displaced and without help. Moreno says:

> My new religion was a religion of being, of self-perfection. It was a
> religion of helping and healing, for helping was more important than
> talking. It was a religion of silence. It was a religion of doing a thing
> for its own sake, unrewarded, unrecognized. It was a religion of
> anonymity.
>
> (Fox 1987: 205)

At that time Moreno also had religious debates with his friends. Marineau
describes in his biography of Moreno how members often met to talk about
subjects such as the return of Jesus Christ and everyone had his hypothesis.
Moreno claimed that Jesus would come back nude, or jump from a tree,
and tried out these hypotheses himself. It is even possible that he might
have thought of himself as Jesus at one period (Marineau 1989: 27–8).

Although Moreno had a Sephardic Jewish background he read widely
different religious authors and often identified with them strongly. Among
the names to which he refers frequently are Jesus, St Paul, Socrates,
Mohammed, Buddha, St Francis, Pascal, Kierkegaard, Swedenborg,
Tolstoy, Dostoyevski and Schweitzer – all of them great prophets or
religious teachers who put more emphasis on life than on intellectual/
theological expertise.

From the year 1910 onwards Moreno formulated his idea of God who
is not only a distant creator but an active force in the universe, who is
manifested everywhere where spontaneity and creativity are at work.
Blatner's evaluation is that a review of the complete philosophical writing
Moreno produced during these years shows that he deserves to be included
among the early existentialists (Blatner 1988: 18).

Moreno's religious concerns gained more philosophical overtones when
he, together with other intellectuals established and published the famous
periodical *Daimon* (later *Der Neue Daimon*) in Vienna during the years
1918–20. It was a journal mostly for existential literature and expression-
istic arts. Its name was allegoric: the Greek word *daimon* meaning the

ambiguous spirit which is creator, adviser and the source of inspiration. At that time Moreno also had contact with the famous philosopher and theologian Martin Buber (1878–1965) who had also a strong Jewish background. Buber's famous 'I–Thou' philosophy of encounter is in many ways very close to the ideas which Moreno had in his mind. According to Buber's view, God, the great Thou, enables human I–Thou relations between man and other beings. A true relationship with God, as experienced from the human side, must be an I–Thou relationship, in which God is truly met and addressed, not merely thought of and expressed. The opposite of an I–Thou relationship is the I–it relationship where other beings are reduced to mere objects of thought and action. It is typical of Moreno's life history that there was controversy between him and Buber, because Moreno thought (obviously without convincing evidence) that he had expressed the idea of the I–Thou relationship before Buber did (Marineau 1989: 48–9).

The high point of Moreno's religious thinking was certainly the publication of *The Words of the Father* in 1920. It is a fascinating, subjective and very poetic book which is easily misunderstood. As Marineau says 'it was the logical conclusion of Moreno's childhood and adolescence, a long search for life's meaning and a truthful representation of the universe' (Marineau 1989: 65). In a way, the book is Moreno's 'Song of the Songs' partly written in the poetic form. In the book he argues for a cosmic view where man takes responsibility of his own life and becomes the 'I–God'. Moreno says later:

At a moment of greatest human misery when the past seemed to be a delusion, the future a misfortune and the present a fugitive pastime I formulated in the 'Testament des Vaters' the most radical antithesis of our time by making my 'I', the 'I' and 'self' of the weak human bastard the same and identical with the I and self of God, the Creator of the World. There was no need for proof that God exists and had created the world if the same I's whom he had created had taken part in the creation of themselves and in the creation of each other. If then God was weak and humble, unfree and doomed to die, he was triumphant just the same. As the I–Self–God it was he who had made himself unfree, in order to make a universe of billions of equally unfree beings possible outside of himself, but depending upon them. The idea of God became a revolutionary category, removed from the beginning of time into the present, into the self, into every I. It is the 'Thou'–God of the Christian Gospel who may need the proof of meeting but the 'I'–God of the Self was self evident. The new 'I' could not imagine being born without being his own creator. He could not imagine anyone being born without being their creator. Too, he could not imagine any future of the world ever to have emerged without having been its creator. He could not imagine any future of the world to emerge without being personally responsible for its production.

(Moreno 1983: 12)

The book *The Words of the Father* is the most controversial in Moreno's production. Some people consider it to be Moreno's main work, while others take it as a sign of his insanity and megalomania. Nobody can forget the impressive opening words of the poem: '*I am God, the Father. The Creator of the Universe. These are My words, the words of the Father.*' Marineau says: 'Following Swedenborg's example, Moreno, the doctor of medicine, was allowing his inner "voices" to speak, in an attempt to unite religion and science' (Marineau 1989: 67).

Although Moreno referred often to the concept of God, he dissociated himself from traditional theological ideas. He wanted to find a new understanding of God as an active and all-covering creative principle in the universe.

> When God created the world in six days he had stopped a day too early, He had given man a place to live but in order to make it safe for him he also chained him to that place. On the seventh day he should have created for man a second world, another one, free of the first world and in which he could purge himself from it, but a world which would not chain anyone because it was not real. It is here that the theatre of spontaneity continues God's creation of the world by opening for Man a new dimension of existence.
>
> (Moreno 1983: 7)

Moreno distinguishes between the 'God of the first status' and the 'God of the second status':

> All the affirmations and denials of God, all His images, have revolved around this, the God of the second status, the God who had reached recognition in the affairs of the universe, so to speak. But there is another status of God, which even as a symbol has been neglected, that is the status of God before the Sabbath, from the moment of conception, during the process of creating and evolving the world and Himself.
>
> (Moreno 1985: 32)

It is typical of Moreno's thought that even here he wants to go back to 'the first universe', to the 'status nascendi' where everything is possible and where everything is in process – even God.

In his later years Moreno was not writing so much about his religious ideas. He did not want to be a theologian or the founder of a new sect. But he incorporated a religious, transcendent dimension into all of his ideas and thoughts. He also had the opinion that secularisation and materialism were great dangers for humankind. Moreno says:

One of the greatest dilemmas of man in our time is that he has lost faith in a supreme being, and often in any superior value system as a guide for conduct. Is the universe ruled by change and spontaneity only? The psychodramatic answer to the claim that God is dead is that he can easily be restored to life.

Following the example of Christ we have given him and can give him a new life, but not in the form which our ancestors cherished. We have replaced the dead God by millions of people who can embody God in their own person. This may need further explanation. The outstanding event in modern religion was the replacement, if not the abandonment, of the cosmic, elusive, Super-God by a simple man who called himself the Son of God – Jesus Christ. The outstanding thing about him was not scholarship or intellectual wizardry, but the fact of embodiment. There lived in his time many men intellectually superior to Christ, but they were flabby intellectuals, instead of making an effort to embody the truth as they felt it, they talked about it. In the psychodramatic world the fact of embodiment is central, axiomatic, and universal. Everyone can portray his version of God through his own actions and so communicate his own version to others. . . . It is no longer the master, the great priest, or the therapist who embodies God. The image of God can take form and embodiment through every man – the epileptic, the schizophrenic, the prostitute, the poor and rejected. They all can at any time step upon the stage, when the moment of inspiration comes, and give their version of the meaning which the universe has for them. God is always within and among us, as he is for children. Instead of coming down from the skies, he comes in by way of the stage door.

(Moreno 1975b: 21–2)

In this famous statement Moreno is already making a direct application of his concept of God into very practical psychodramatic work. God is not abstract and absent. He is on the stage in the role of everyman.

METAPHYSICAL FOUNDATION OF THE SPONTANEITY/ CREATIVITY THEORY

Moreno's spontaneity theory is closely connected with his idea of the 'first universe' whereby he means the matrix of 'all-identity' as the framework in which a small child experiences his existence. In the first universe a child sees everything as part of himself. At a psychological level, of course, the relationship between the child and the mother is decisive. For a child, there is no difference between him or her and his or her mother. In a similar way humankind has originally understood itself as an integral part of the cosmic process. This experience is mostly felt at the level of the collective unconscious without intellectual reflection or fixed roles (Leutz 1986: 40–2,

71–4). For Moreno the first universe is a magic realm and man has the opportunity to keep contact with it through his whole life:

> Why I chose the course of the theatre instead of founding a religious sect, joining a monastery or developing a system of theology (although they do not exclude each other), can be understood by taking a view of the setting from which my ideas sprang. I suffered from an idée fixe, from what might have been called then an affectation, but of which might be said today, as the harvest is coming in, that it was by 'the grace of God'. The idée fixe became my constant source of productivity; it proclaimed that there is a sort of primordial nature which is immortal and returns afresh with every generation, a first universe which contains all beings and in which all events are sacred. I liked that enchanting realm and did not plan to leave it, ever.
>
> (Moreno 1983: 3)

The warm-up process is in the last instance a manifestation of the 'cosmic hunger' to maintain an identity with the entire universe. Through that process we become reconnected with the creative sources of life and its unlimited opportunities. It is not only a hunger for self-realisation of an individual man. It aims at 'world realisation' (Moreno 1975a: 154).

This means that the distinction between 'reality' and 'illusion' becomes problematic. Everything is possible and nothing is pre-determined: 'millions of imagined worlds are equally possible and real, of equal value to the world in which we live and for which metaphysics is constructed' (Moreno 1983: 35). There are illusions of a real world which are of equal importance as 'the reality of an illusionary world'.

The roots of Morenian drama are deeply philosophical – even theological. The basis of Moreno's cosmology is the concept of a continuous cosmic drama, which God himself both directs and acts. This is the very beginning of all creativity and spontaneity which exists in the universe (Moreno 1953: xvi–xvii). The idea of creation is 'status nascendi' which is inherent in chaos.

> The creative definition of 'Godplaying' is the maximum of involvement, the putting of everything unborn from the chaos into the first moment of being. This preoccupation with the status and locus nascendi of things became the guide of all my future work.
>
> (Moreno 1953: xvii)

It is a state where no 'cultural conserves' (fixed products, structures, roles, definitions and theories) still exist. God creates, making opposite roles to himself. Thus, totally new things appear. God interacts with his own nature.

Moreno goes so far that he even speaks of a divine theatre and gives his imagination the permission to visualise God as an actor.

Can God be an actor? How should the stage be constructed upon which God, the perfect being, acts? He who loves himself loves illusion still more. He who loves reality loves play still more, that is why children love playing. He who has created the world after himself, could it not be essential to his greatness that he loves to repeat creation like a playwright on a cosmic scale, not only to his own enjoyment which hardly requires any confirmation, but to the enjoyment of his creatures?

The repertory of the heavenly stage consists of the eternal repetition of one play, the creation of the universe. Numberless stages are necessary in order that this drama may be enacted. It is a stage with many levels, one higher than the other and one leading up to the other. On every level is a theatre and on the highest level there is the stage of the creator.

(Moreno 1983: 95)

Moreno emphasises that the theatre of the creator does not produce any reduction of suffering: 'In reality, life and death, love and misery are underscored, multiplied in proportion and enormously increased. The repeatability of creation makes being immortal nonsensical' (Moreno 1983: 96). What is special in God's theatre is that in God all the spontaneity turns into creativity. All that he says turns immediately into actual reality.

At this point we meet the key concept which is perhaps the most misunderstood idea in Moreno's thinking. This is the concept of 'I–God' which he introduced in *The Words of the Father* in 1920. What is not usually seen, is the close interrelation between the concept of Man and the concept of God in Moreno's theory. As a matter of fact, dealing with the 'I–God' Moreno is speaking of Man's self-interpretation:

The modern apostles of Godlessness, when they cut off the strings which tied man to a divine system, a supramundane God, they cut in their enthusiastic haste a little too much, they also cut off Man's very self. By the same act by which they emancipated Man from God they also emancipated Man from himself. They said God is dead, but it was Man who has died. My thesis is therefore, that the center of the problem is neither God nor the denial of his existence, but the origin, reality and expansion of the self. By self I mean anything which is left of you and me after the most radical reduction of 'us' is made by past and future retroductionists.

(Moreno 1983: 8)

That means that the I–Self–God process has no relation to the idea of the Man–God and similar anthropomorphic concepts. The issue is not the godlikeness of a single individual, but the godlikeness of the total universe, its self-integration (Moreno 1983: 11).

Williams sees correctly that for Moreno psychodrama is the practical means to make people 'I–Gods', 'part of the supreme power ruling the world by spontaneity and creativity' (Williams 1989: 222). In this way transcendent becomes immanent – or, using a Christian metaphor, the divine incarnates into human existence. Moreno is not understood if one does not see that he was very serious in his belief that psychodrama provides a concrete tool to enter into the divine cosmic drama.

What has been said means that the core of Moreno's metaphysics is the intimate relationship between God and the spontaneity/creativity process. On the psychological level we can speak about human emotions, energies, imagery, vitality and freedom. However, for Moreno this is not only a psychic process but a real manifestation of the cosmic drama where human beings fully participate (Blatner 1988: 14–15).

Moreno explains his new insight in this way:

> When I found the proud house of man, on which he had worked for nearly ten thousand years, to give to it the solidity and splendour of western civilization burnt to ashes, the only residuum which I detected in the ashes portent with promise was the 'spontaneous–creative'. I saw its fire burning at the bottom of every dimension of nature, the cosmic, the spiritual, the cultural, the social, the psychological, the biological, and the sexual, forming in each sphere a nucleus from which a new urge of inspiration could arise. But instead of falling into an orgy of admiration before the new discovery, as thousands of other similarly affected men have in the past, considering the spontaneous–creative as an irrational gift of nature, as something mystic which some people have and others do not, around which a cult could be built, I was inclined to treat the matter with the same detachment as the scientist examines a new element. . . . I thought of the prophets and saints of the past who appeared as the most shining examples of spontaneous creativity, and said to myself 'This is what you have to produce first and you yourself have to give flesh to it'. Thus it began to 'warm-up' to prophetic moods and heroic feelings, putting them into my thoughts, my emotions, gestures and actions, it was a sort of spontaneity research on the reality level.
>
> (Moreno 1983: 5)

In his theory of man as 'I–God' and spontaneity/creativity Moreno openly gives the therapeutic process a cosmological task.

> A therapeutic method which does not concern itself with these enormous cosmic implications with man's very destiny, is incomplete and inadequate. Just as our forefathers encountered these changes by means of fables and myths, we have tried to encounter them in our time with new devices.
>
> (Moreno 1975b: 20)

This also means that even strict psychodramatic concepts and methods have cosmic implications. For instance, the warm-up phase of psycho-dramatic production is not a technical 'foreplay' of the dramatic act but a process where the group is reconnected to the 'first universe' and to the cosmic process of becoming 'I–Gods'.

RELIGION AS MOTIVATION FOR THERAPEUTIC AND SOCIAL WORK

From Moreno's life history it has become clear that he had a firm belief in his special calling. For him, the whole purpose of psychodramatic work was human liberation, democratic society, world peace and cosmic trans-figuration. He found this vision during a long process where he identified himself with great prophets and religious leaders. He has been blamed and stigmatised for that, but on the other hand it was also the most powerful sign of his moral greatness. Therefore, it was not an accident that he gave so much of his time for work with outcasts, refugees, prisoners, prostitutes, young children and delinquent adolescents. He had a moral vision and he had a concrete mission.

Moreno could not understand why he was accused of being egocentric and megalomaniac. He wrote referring to the criticism concerning his book *The Words of the Father*:

> It is amusing to think retroactively that my proclamation of the I was considered as the most outstanding manifestation of megalomania from my side. Actually, when the I–God is universalized, as it is in my book, the whole God concept becomes one of humbleness, weakness, and inferiority, a micromania rather than a megalomania. God has never been so lowly described and so universal in his dependence as he is in my book. It was a significant transformation from the cosmic God of the Hebrews, the He–God, to the living God of Christ, the Thou–God. But it was an even more challenging transformation from the Thou–God to the I–God, which puts all responsibility upon me and us, the I and the group. Another aspect of the micromania of the book is its anonymity, which blatantly proclaimed that it is not the I of a lonely, singular person, but the I of everyone. The embodiment of the I was practised by me in life itself, long before it took psychodramatic form.
>
> (Moreno 1975b: 21–2)

The natural consequence of this was that Moreno did not respect an intellectual enterprise for its own sake. His interest in knowledge was emancipatory. Until his death Moreno expressed his admiration for great persons in history who committed themselves totally to the human predicament. He wanted to become one among them.

Men like Josiah, Jesus, Mohammed and Francis of Assisi had a sense of the drama and knew a form of mental catharsis incomparably deeper than that of the Greeks, one which comes from the realization of great roles through their own flesh and blood, singly and in groups, from the daily meeting of bold emergencies. Their stage was the community proper, every situation which they entered challenged their therapeutic genius. They knew of spontaneity, immediate solution, of the warming up process and of acting in roles, first hand and not from books. Jesus, like a chief therapeutic actor, had his auxiliary egos in his apostles and his psychodramatic director in God himself who prompted him what to do.

(Moreno 1985: 8)

No wonder that Moreno admired the Swedish mystic Swedenborg, who had an excellent scientific background but saw his proper calling in making the mysteries of God known to people.

Moreno seems also to have been aware of the pathological side of this kind of self-understanding but he did not make any excuses for that: 'I was an experimenter and experimenters like Jesus, Buddha, St. Francis often look inadequate even pathological, but they are trying to live a life of truth and prefer an imperfect existence to a perfect theory' (Marineau 1989: 120).

Even much later, when Moreno was already in the United States and had accomplished his major life work, he referred to religious figures as examples to follow. In the mid-1950s Moreno wrote on Kierkegaard:

For Kierkegaard existential involvement of the subjective actor was axiomatic; it validated itself – it did not require further proof. Underlying his credo was the problem of validation. Religious behaviour in order to be valid and meaningful has to involve the entire subjectivity of the religious actor. It has to fill and vitalize the religious ritual with it. This is a special case of spontaneity familiar to psychodramatists; a new response to an old situation, the requirement to re-experience a repeated situation with the same intensity as if it had happened for the first time, the revitalizing of religious conserves as a ritual or a prayer.

(Moreno 1975a: 209)

What is special in Moreno's moral insight is that he also wanted to incorporate his basic moral ideas to the scientific concepts and practical methods of his psychodramatic theory. For him, sociometric movement was a source of democracy and social justice. According to him sociometry is a process of the people, by the people, and for the people. Also the introduction of the method of role reversal was a major revolution in a moral sense. Through role reversal Moreno concretised the famous golden rule principle according to which one has to put oneself into the position of others in order to understand what are their rights and their view of life.

Moreno gives also three basic ethical rules for sociodramatic and psychodramatic work: (i) Give truth and receive truth. (ii) Give love to the group and it will return love to you. (iii) Give spontaneity and spontaneity will return (Moreno 1953: 114).

DRAMA AS A MEANS TO DEAL WITH RELIGIOUS/ METAPHYSICAL ISSUES

Using drama in dealing with 'spiritual' issues was by no means a secondary concern for Moreno. Actually, he started his dramatic work with 'axiodrama' from which he later developed psychodrama and sociodrama. For instance, his three major works from the years 1918–19 were papers written in axiodramatic form: 'The godhead as author', 'The godhead as orator or preacher' and 'The godhead as comedian or actor', which were published in *Daimon* and *Der Neue Daimon*. Axiodrama is a dramatic exercise where issues of ethics, cosmic relationships or values are dealt with using action methods. In Moreno's words it 'deals with the activation of religious, ethical and cultural values in spontaneous–dramatic form' (Moreno 1953: xxvi).

In axiodramatic work Moreno also had great role models. For instance, Socrates himself was, in Moreno's opinion, a good axiodramatist using the famous 'maieutics' method, including role reversal when speaking with people in the agora of Athens. 'I was interested in the ethical more than in the intellectual Socrates, in the "changer" more than in the thinker' (Moreno 1953: xxii–xxiii).

Psychodrama and sociodrama give the opportunity to visualise and concretise all possible metaphors, images, symbols and creatures on the stage and promote interaction between them. The roles taken can be, for example, religious, philosophical, mythical or aesthetic. The purpose of the work can be the clarification of the concepts, to try to understand the different levels of their meanings or to promote cathartic processes in the realm of religion and world view.

PRACTICAL EXAMPLE OF RELIGIOUS SOCIODRAMA

For six years I have run an ongoing group for theological students dealing with moral and religious issues using sociodrama/axiodrama. In this context I give just one example of our work.

The last sunday of the Church year is approaching. Its religious theme is 'The Last Judgement'. The sociodrama group has gathered for a three-hour session. The general theme of the winter term in the group has been the problem of evil. As a warm-up the director tells the group the story of a preacher who based his sermon on the topic of the last judgement. The preacher said that the Church had lost its credibility and failed in its mission-ary task because the priests no longer spoke about hell. The preacher told the congregation that each person who has not personally repented and converted in the proper Christian way will go to hell after his or her death.

The participants are asked to imagine that they have just been listening to that sermon. They are divided into two groups to discuss their feelings and thoughts concerning the sermon. Most of the students are very critical about the sermon. They say that the preacher put himself above the congregation. In their opinion, it represented an old-fashioned way of interpreting Christian teachings which leads to the situation where more and more people withdraw from the church. They say that the Christian faith is not something that is based on people's own choices and decisions.

One student takes an opposite view (partly in order to provoke heated discussion). He says that it is good when somebody still has the courage to preach in pure form what is said clearly in the Bible. The Bible says that after death there are just two choices – either heaven or hell. One participant insists that belief in hell is a sign of bad exegetical knowledge.

After the warm-up the group makes a sociodramatic study on different concepts of God, heaven and hell. The ideas are taken from the viewpoints presented in the discussion during the warm-up. A sociometric triangle is made in the room the corners of which show the three main attitudes among the students towards the issue concerning hell. The first corner symbolises the idea that hell means an eternal separation from God. The second corner represents the opinion that hell means eternal damnation by God. The third corner shows the place where the issue of the hell has no relevance in life and faith. Of the nine students three take places very close to the first corner. For them, hell means separation from God. Two students show through the choice of their places that the whole issue is almost irrelevant to them. Three students stay in the middle of the triangle. One student (the one who had defended the preacher during the warm-up) steps outside the triangle. He says that his concept of the world as a creative and frightening chaos cannot be demonstrated by a point within the triangle. Nobody takes the stand that hell means eternal damnation.

The students describe one by one what their positions mean to them. 'Hell means for me a life without Christ.' 'There is eternal separation and suffering without hope.' 'I cannot decide. Earlier I thought that hell means separation but now this issue is irrelevant for me.'

Maarit says: 'I stay in the middle because in my thinking I find the issue irrelevant but my fear moves me towards eternal damnation.'

The director decides that the group should move to work on Maarit's response because it reflects a high ambiguity between thoughts and feelings which might be true also for other members of the group. Maarit reverses roles with her fear and goes to the place of eternal damnation. Maarit says:

'The atmosphere here is depressing and condemning. When I was there I would not guess what this would be like . . .'

The director asks Maarit to build hell. She takes three students to be the fire in hell and three others to laugh at her suffering. Maarit says: 'I miss my feelings. I just have the idea that I have done something wrong.' The director asks Maarit to concentrate and find out what is going on inside her. Maarit (making a spontaneous role reversal) goes suddenly away from hell and says: 'I have done something to cause me (Maarit) to be in hell.' In role reversal Eero takes Maarit's place in hell and Maarit becomes the person who is responsible for Maarit's being in hell.

MAARIT: (in role reversal) There is not such a thing as evil or hell. Don't be afraid. We have a loving God.
DIRECTOR: You have preached the loving God and Maarit has believed in what you said. Now she is in hell. What do you think about it?
MAARIT: (still in role reversal) I don't believe it. It is not possible.
EERO: (in Maarit's role in hell) I trusted you. You said that there is no hell. I cannot get rid of this.
MAARIT: (in role reversal) I have nothing to say. I am guilty. I have let her down.

The Director asks Maarit to build heaven. Maarit makes a circle using five students to demonstrate it. They show togetherness and warmth. She goes to the circle but says that she is still aware of the reality of hell.

Maarit goes back to hell. The director asks whether she knows about heaven while being in hell.

MAARIT: Yes, I am aware of it like the rich man in the Bible saw Lazarus in heaven. I would have liked to go to heaven if it would have been possible.
DIRECTOR: Why was it not possible?
MAARIT: I could not do anything. It's God's business.

Jussi is taken into the role of God.

MAARIT: (addressing God from hell) I want to know whether You are a marionette or not.
MAARIT: (in God's role) I am not a puppet. I am the ruler of the universe, I represent justice but unfortunately everything went wrong.
DIRECTOR: How did it happen?
MAARIT: (as God) This was not my purpose. I did not want to have this kind of segregation.
DIRECTOR: What do you mean?
MAARIT: (as God) It has happened in people's heads.

The director asks Maarit to build the human head according to her own understanding of it. She makes the head in the form of a circle and puts six students there representing (i) fear and aggression; (ii) other feelings; (iii) humour; (iv) intellect; (v) empathy; and (vi) human weakness. The director asks Maarit what issues the head is thinking at this moment. Maarit says: 'It wonders whether a man has the right to condemn another man.'

The director asks different parts of the head to have a dialogue with one another.

FEAR/AGGRESSION:	There is no need to condemn others. In that way yourself will not be condemned.
HUMOUR:	All are condemning each other.
HUMAN WEAKNESS:	We all are limited beings.
OTHER FEELINGS:	How on earth could one condemn others?
INTELLECT:	It is like a car theft. It is natural that criminals are condemned.
OTHER FEELINGS:	But hell is quite a different thing!
FEAR/AGGRESSION:	It is just natural that one protects oneself.

Maarit follows the discussion in God's role and says that it is quite understandable.

The director asks God to say something to the human head.

GOD:	It is interesting to watch the head which I myself have created. It is a small but also a very confused thing.
DIRECTOR:	But you have made it.
GOD:	Yes, but strange things are happening there. It would, of course, be easier if it was not so confused.

Different parts of the head start asking God questions.

FEAR/AGGRESSION:	Have you created me, too?
GOD:	Yes.
FEAR/AGGRESSION:	Where has Sin come from?
GOD:	It's a good question.
HUMOUR:	Oh, God . . .!

The director asks students to find where Sin is. Tiina role-reverses with Sin. Tiina takes a place opposite to God.

SIN   If God would not be there, I would not be here. (to God) I think that I have been born from something which belongs to you.

The director role-reverses Sin with God.

GOD: (played by Tiina who speaks to Sin) I have not created you. You have been born inside the human mind.

Tiina is reversed back to Sin. She says that her duty is to create chaos, to turn everything which is good into bad. The director asks Tiina, as Sin, to bring about chaos.

SIN: The evil is in me, not elsewhere. I am deceiving all the time. I pretend to be good. I can wear the mask of empathy. I can understand people's lives so well that they do not need to bear their responsibility. I am mothering them. I take the mask of different feelings. They do not see me.

The parts of the head are taken away from their roles. A new triangle is formed consisting of God, Sin, and Evil.

GOD: I am freedom.
SIN: I have fun.
EVIL: (to God) You created everything, but it all ends with me.
GOD: I make everything new. Evil has its limits. I see Christ.
EVIL: Nations go down, all is under my power, everything ends in death.
GOD: Death is part of life.
EVIL: Man wants me.
SIN: Life would be boring without me.
EVIL: This is a joke.

In the process of the sociodrama three students have role-reversed with God. They are asked to give names to the side of God they have played.

GOD 1:   Goodness.
GOD 2:   Blind forgiver, Christ.
GOD 3:   Humanity, Yin and Yang.

Evil identifies himself as 'Hopelessness and Despair'.

After deroling, the students discuss their experiences and thoughts. Some comments they made were:
'Sociodrama opened my eyes to see things in different light. Our thoughts about God are usually too clean and sterile, too distinct from the real world.'
'The issue of choice is a burning theme for me.'
'Sin has to do with God, in a way it is in God.'
'Death is not necessarily bad.'
'God is helpless and theology is boring.'
'Only poems can express religious truths.'

When the group met for the next session, the contents of the drama were discussed. The students said how illuminating it was to see the discrepancy between their theoretical/theological ideas and their inner feelings. Most of them said how they had changed in their religious opinions from the time when they had their first strong religious experiences and internalised basic religious symbols like heaven, hell and sin.

A long discussion ensued about the relationship between God and evil on the one hand and God and sin on the other hand. Many participants agreed that God cannot be totally separated from evil otherwise reality would be divided into two separate parts. Controversy is inherent both in the image of God and in man's self-image.

This drama shows how, in a sociodramatic process, rigid dogmatic concepts of God can be turned into dynamic interplay between various creative aspects of universe and history. In a real Morenian sense, in the sociodrama, there was a touch of mystery connected to the eternal struggle between good and evil in the whole of creation.

CONCLUSION

We have seen that Moreno's fundamental idea of the spontaneous–creative process in the form of drama has a much wider background and scope than just the clinical setting of therapeutic psychodrama. Moreno's vision was essentially a theological one. This also shows how Moreno's approach differed from that of Freud.

> Freud has failed in two respects, first by the rejection of religion. This cost him the opportunity to learn in an existential way of the contribution which saints and prophets (who are not identical with theological theorists – one can be a saint without any or a minimum rationale) have made towards psychotherapy. Some of the most ingenious agents of psychotherapy before the advent of natural science, were saints or prophets. Second, by his indifference towards social movements such as socialism and communism. His ignorance cost him another opportunity – to study group structure. It remained for psychodrama to take the God-act seriously and to translate it into valid therapeutic terms, and for sociometry to take the group seriously – as a process sui generis – and so to broaden and deepen the scope of analysis beyond any visions Freud ever had on the subject.
>
> (Moreno 1985: 8)

In his famous anecdote Moreno reveals what he said to Freud: 'You analyzed their dreams, I try to give them courage to dream again. I teach people how to play God' (Marineau 1989: 30–1).

Williams emphasises, rightly, that the metaphysical side and the therapeutic side of psychodrama need not compete with each other. There is a difference between psychodrama as therapy and psychodrama as revelation.

> In psychodrama as revelation, the 'full subjective onesideness' of the protagonist is totally supported and explored. The drama is a personal epiphany, a revelation of personal history and potential, an education

and support for the passion to know the meaning of one's experience, and the drive to find, show forth, and enhance the inner spirit. These are all excellent pursuits. Psychodrama as therapy is neither 'higher' nor 'lower' than psychodrama as revelation: it merely has a different purpose – the solving of problems. The difficulty emerges if the two are confused, and revelation, or therapy for that matter, becomes part of the client's problem-causing system.

(Williams 1989: 225)

In the last instance Moreno sees Man's alternatives as either becoming a robot or restoring his original spontaneity.

Why should man want robots? It is perhaps the same reason, in reverse, as the one which at an earlier period made us want a God to whom we were robots. Therefore, if we could understand what we mean to God, we could understand what robots mean to us.

(Moreno 1975b: 263)

According to Moreno the fate of man threatens to become that of 'the dinosaur in reverse'. The dinosaur perished because he extended the power of his organism in excess of its usefulness (Moreno 1975b: 266). We extend technological control of the world into an extreme without seeing how the living creative process inside us is diminishing. This is not a concern for therapists only. The survival of humanity is at stake.

REFERENCES

Blatner, A. (1988) *Foundations of Psychodrama: History, theory, and practice*, 3rd edn, New York: Springer.

Fox, J. (ed.) (1987) *The Essential Moreno: Writings on psychodrama, group method, and spontaneity by J.L. Moreno, M.D.*, New York: Springer.

Leutz, G. (1986) *Psychodrama. Theorie und Praxis. Das klassische Psychodrama nach J.L. Moreno* (First revised reprint), London, Paris and Tokyo: Springer-Verlag.

Lindqvist, M. (1992) *Unelma rohkeasta elämästä. Ryhmämatkoja luovuuteen*, Helsinki: Otava.

Marineau, R.F. (1989) *Jacob Levy Moreno 1889–1974: Father of psychodrama, sociometry, and group psychotherapy*, London and New York: Tavistock/Routledge.

Moreno, J.L. (1953) *Who Shall Survive? Foundations of sociometry, group psychotherapy and sociodrama*, New York: Beacon House.

—— (1975a) *Psychodrama*, vol. 2, New York: Beacon House.

—— (1975b) *Psychodrama*, vol. 3, New York: Beacon House.

—— (1983) *The Theatre of Spontaneity*, Ambler, PA: Beacon House.

—— (1985) *Psychodrama*, vol. 1, New York: Beacon House.

Williams, A. (1989) *The Passionate Technique: Strategic psychodrama with individuals, families, and groups*, London and New York: Tavistock/Routledge.

Chapter 9

The global task
Sharing time and space

Commentary

Mónica Zuretti also sees a way forward out of the materialistic, atheistic society at the end of the millennium. She emphasises the cosmic in a way that highlights just how much it lies beneath all of Moreno's work and brings it closer to the surface in a way that makes it clearer. There is scope to argue that the Morenian concept of the co-unconscious has connections with Wilfred Bion's ideas of the unconscious processes of a basic assumption group (Bion 1961). Like Bion, Zuretti's work is rooted in clinical practice, and her chapter reflects her psychoanalytic background, as well as that of a psychodramatist who studied with Moreno. However, Zuretti's chapter also stresses, in a way similar to the systems theories of family therapists, how all of us network in the past, present and future.

REFERENCE

Bion, W.R. (1961) *Experiences in Groups*, London: Tavistock.

The co-unconscious

Mónica Zuretti

J.L. Moreno defines the co-unconscious as the unconscious link between people who share their life processes, as, for example, couples, groups, families, friends, co-workers, or psychotherapist and patient.

> We must look for a concept which is so constructed that the objective indication for the existence of this two-way process does not come from a single psyche but a still deeper reality in which the unconscious states of two or several individuals are interlocked with a system of co-unconscious states. . . . Co-conscious and co-unconscious states are by definition, such states which partners have experienced and produced jointly. . . . A co-conscious or co-unconscious state can not be the property of one individual only.
>
> (Moreno 1977: vii)

The co-unconscious is developed during a shared time and space which belongs to a particular relationship. It includes, as well as the creation of that special relationship with all its vicissitudes, the history of the individuals involved in it. Our ancestors are gone but humankind as a whole will only be recognised when awareness of these individuals has reached the point where planetary consciousness is achieved.

Man develops his life in successive matrices – genetic, maternal, identity, family, social and cosmic – a continuous body of relationships which allow the drama, the action of life, to evolve. From those matrices will emerge the roles which will be the builders of a differentiated ego capable of forming part of the chain of relationships which allow continuity of humankind.

Each one of these matrices is a network, an intricate knot of links formed by a protagonist and his auxiliary egos. Depending on the perspective from which these roles are considered their position may change and the individual who was a protagonist from one perspective may well become an auxiliary ego in another. This knot of relationships will have in action a co-conscious process which will be engraved at different levels of consciousness in the individuals who form these matrixes.

All these relationships are based on tele, a two-way process which is enacted and at the same time registered.

The treasure of the co-unconscious is formed by the part of the relationship not acted (or acted but not named with words), not expressed, not known because it belongs to the secret realm of the genetic or cosmic knowledge, but nevertheless present in the net formed by the sum of the different matrices.

Personal discovery is the way into maturity, is a continual unveiling of the mystery hidden in the realms of the co-unconscious and will follow the path marked by the creative acts of each person's life that, like small pebbles of brilliant light, show the way from matrix to matrix.

BIRTH, A CREATIVE ACT

Birth, considered as a creative act, takes place at a knot formed from the different relationships which belong to diverse matrices. The spirals in which these different matrices develop cross each other at different space times. At the moment a creative act is taking place all matrices coincide at one point and a change is achieved which affects the whole structure.

This change may occur in the direction of expansion, evolution and creation or follow the need for contraction of the gravitational energy. A creative act will always be a decision to choose between two possibilities: life or death.

At the instant of conception, there is a disjunction between the unlimited experience of the universe and the limited, progressive potential of the genetic code. At the moment of birth there is a crossroads, if one considers the infant to be the protagonist. There exist opposites formed by the encompassing experience of the cosmic matrix and the restraining matrix of the maternal uterus. There must be a decision to act and risk the adventure of the unknown.

It will be the genetic co-unconscious knowledge hidden in the baby's cells, joined to the co-unconscious knowledge shared with the mother during the pregnancy, which will resolve the outcome of the birth.

If both coincide, action emerges and the complementary movements which belong to the profound knowledge of the body will allow the magic of creation. The baby, gaining access to the many co-unconscious experiences lying in the deep reserve of his or her relationships, will place him or herself in the position required for his or her change of matrix and his or her subsequent entrance into the new dimension of an independent biological being in search of learning in a new life.

This position will have to respond and be responded to, by the mother, who will have to resort to her own resources of genetic and cosmic knowledge and her unique learned experience of family and social life. These resources come from her conscious learning of the roles in her many relationships and the co-unconscious knowledge which will enable her to develop, without words, the link with the baby, a link that will lead her to understand easily, in a correct tele relationship, the needs of that particular baby looking for an answer to its needs.

This life experience, this creative act, will be the beginning of the co-unconscious active process because it will be the first action performed by two individuals deeply linked in the same space and time on which both lives depend. The creative act will include the long warming-up of the pregnancy as well as a prospective project. From then on every action will include the presence of the other. Human life exists only in a matrix of relationships that hold and contain it.

The family matrix is expressed by the father's role. His presence will facilitate the development of the act of birth and constitute a protective presence in the co-conscious understanding of the process, based on his own co-unconscious experience reactivated in the present situation.

The social matrix will give this particular act, taking place in its milieu, all the technological possibilities and care which are its patrimony regardless of the form through which they are implemented. In every culture the acts of birth and death are the most important ones, even if recognised and expressed in different ways. Part of this explicit expression and recognition belongs to the conscious realm, but its great secret is hidden in the shared co-unconscious which is carried from generation to generation.

Every single creative act, like the act of birth, takes place in a knot of relationships and will evolve by feeding from and creating a co-unconscious process.

Psychodrama, as the method based on the concept that every person is his or her own creator, will constantly work with and within the co-unconscious knowledge present in the structure of the social atoms that form the different matrices in which an individual's life unfolds.

Sociometry, the science of human relationships, will always take into account the way in which the different matrices participate, as well as the ways in which their complementary existence relates to each other. This will allow individuals to fulfil their spontaneity and creativity growth processes and become active members in each one of these matrices. Successive matrices will create and be created in a double co-conscious and co-unconscious process which will harbour the development of each particular individual. The circle of constant feedback between individual and matrix or individual and group will become a growth spiral.

DEVELOPMENT OF THE CO-UNCONSCIOUS

The cosmic matrix is the reservoir of those experiences which belong to the planetary existence of the human race. From this matrix every human being brings the knowledge, engraved in his or her particular genetic code, of the actual life experience of his or her ancestors, especially that of his or her parents, including their nutritional habits and the added data furnished by the environment in which they are living – the earth.

After the instant of conception the growth and search developed through out his or her life will enable him or her, following the creative act of his death, to re-enter at a different level the spiral of the cosmic matrix. The circular movement of life will be transformed into a pyramid of transmutation transferred to infinite relationships by the co-unconscious.

Acceptance of the above concept depends on the cultural recognition of this knowledge which is present in Celtic, Inca, Egyptian and oriental societies but which is, however, very limited in western cultures. This reservoir will nevertheless be reached implicitly or explicitly through co-unconscious experiences.

In the genetic matrix a very subtle process of acceptance between the spermatozoon and the ovum expresses the existence of a tele relationship prior to the existence of a human being. For the first psychosomatic role, preceding even that of the breather, is the contacting role which appears at conception: 'The appearance or not of a zygote will be determined by the acceptance or rejection between cells when they contact each other. Tele in action at the microscopic dimension' (Giorgiuti 1988).

If acceptance is achieved, the genetic matrix will acquire concrete existence and an embryo will be formed. Its future development depends on the acceptance of all the matrices involved. This tele process will be the seed of the development of the co-unconscious.

The conjunction of a need for materialisation of the energy present in the cosmic matrix (which might be called spirit in some cultures) and the possibility of two cells coming together in the planetary realm, will create the genetic matrix producing an egg in search of a home. The maternal matrix will provide the egg with the holding and protection of the contacting role for the time necessary before self-sufficiency is reached.

Before birth, the deep connection between mother and child will take place between two bodies walking the path of differentiation towards the creation of the co-unconscious which will be created at the moment of birth.

FIVE PHASES OF EVOLUTION

The identity matrix, formed by the relationship between mother and child, evolves from undifferentiation towards differentiation through five phases of evolution.

The first stage is complete spontaneous all-identity.
The second stage is that of the infant centering attention upon the other stranger part of him.

The third stage is that of the infant lifting the other part from the continuity of the experience.

The fourth stage is that of the infant placing himself actively in the other part.

The fifth stage is the infant acting in the role of the other towards someone else.

(Moreno 1977: 61–2)

Moreno's description of the identity matrix shows it proceeding from an all inclusive co-unconscious relationship, from the baby's perspective, to a two-way relationship with others.

The mother will acquire a differentiated status from the baby when in the co-unconscious there appears the co-conscious link that will maintain a secret co-unconscious shared knowledge between them. The mother will be the pole of the dyad capable of differentiation and, helped by the father's constant inclusion, will provide for the psychic health of the baby. The aim of a human being is to bring the secret unrecorded part to light with his or her own acting in life and the establishment of correct tele relationships in the subsequent matrices. The task of humankind is to understand the laws which rule the planet and their relationship with the cosmos.

The father will bring into the identity matrix the constant presence of the family matrix. During the undifferentiated stage of the identity matrix the father's role will give the mother–child dyad the necessary support for its evolution which will be of the utmost importance in the differentiation.

From the third phase on, the father's role will help in the process of differentiation to be established between fantasy and reality which will separate the co-unconscious from the co-conscious: 'The transition from the first to the second universe (that period when he becomes aware of reality and fantasy) brings about a total change of sociodynamics in the universe of the infant' (Moreno 1977: 73). The co-unconscious, until that moment built within one relationship in all its dimensions, will now become part of a complex knot of relationships to be understood and developed. From now on the co- unconscious will be like the submerged part of the iceberg, allowing for the movements and actions of the ego in relationship with others in a group.

The family matrix as the social placenta will provide the child with the training ground for his or her social roles. Formed from the conjunction of other family matrices it will be the relative space time in which its members will form and create the roles through which they will be included in the social matrix.

The social matrix will give the family matrix the cultural patterns on which it will be based. Within this social matrix the cosmic and genetic matrices will express themselves and the family matrix will find a contained space for its development. In the social matrix, a network of relationships which is in constant evolution, will be created, according to the needs of the particular time, the social organisations (political, religious, scientific, etc.) which form the human social framework.

It is possible to consider therapeutic groups as part of this organisational matrix. The organisational structure will have deep roots in the co-unconscious network, and will not always be recognised and admitted by the rational part of our understanding of institutional development.

The co-unconscious is a process which will be active and in continuous change during individual and group life.

UNIT OF EVOLUTION

The individual social atoms, intricately related to each other throughout the matrices, create a network of social matrices connected to each other by human relationships, a sociometric network which goes beyond the formal structure. This sociometric network can be considered as a jungle of several species which grow into a magnificent group of trees. Under the ground the roots dig deeply into the earth and stretch out over long distances. The sociometric co-unconscious network is the hidden energy that like the jungle with its roots, allows evolution in the planetary matrix to continue.

THE CO-UNCONSCIOUS PROCESS IN GROUPS

Within a group the co-unconscious of the sociometric network in the here and now is the energy which sustains the group process. This process of continuous discovery, unveiling, creation and recreation, like the knitting and unravelling of Penelope's mantle, selects the positive and creative aspects from the destructive ones and allows the development of the group.

The continuous action of recreating the fabric of the group permits the different patterns that each individual draws to be part of the whole, while the total picture awaits the personal voyages of discovery of its members to reach the fruition in self-discovery and reunion.

When a group is created, there is already a tele structure existing before the group comes together that includes the personal history of all the members. This forms the basis of the particular tele structure that will later be developed.

The term 'group' was originally used in Italy to describe a number of sculptures, each one of them with a particular form depicting a theme created from different perspectives, but all together conveying a unique message. Each part of those sculptures has its own history, its own way of becoming an expression of life through the creativity of the viewer. The message, as a door onto new possibilities, will depend upon the way in which the sculptures are placed and the relationship between them. If they are separated the whole gestalt of that system will stay lost.

The here and now of a particular sculpture group expresses a moment, the mood of the person that looks at it, the history of humankind as seen by the viewer in relationship with who is looking at it. But at the same time each one of the pieces displayed will transmit the moment of its creation, the story of the material on which it was created, the evolution of the earth in the particular place from where it came. All these relationships will build, between them, a network in constant change.

Every time we work with human beings their many relationships are present, as when we look at a single piece of a sculpture group the whole complex appears. When the different parts are placed together, they will create a network of relationships, a tele structure of the moment, just as the sculptures in the Bigeland Park in Oslo do for the viewer walking around them on any afternoon. But this tele structure will have an obscured aspect, the co-unconscious tele structure that will be hidden within, just as the image of the park on the night of a full moon will contain the dark side of the moon.

This structure in a group will be the actual link between the members who will connect themselves through attractions, rejections or indifference, and all the in-between possibilities, which will be the product of the here and now as much as the result of previous experiences.

This structure will have a parallel co-unconscious one based on the same forms of relationships. It will become apparent in psychodramatic work, when constantly creating and recreating the network of the group, whether it be a psychotherapy group, a family, a couple, a team or the internal group of relationships which form the perceptual social atom of each individual.

The energy that binds this structure together was well known to the Incas when they built a stone wall: to make a wall that will be strong and secure it is necessary to study the nature of the stones and to know their sex and the knowledge they have accumulated during centuries to be able to understand the possibilities of their staying together or breaking apart. This knowledge is considered even more important than their form or actual material. In this way walls have survived centuries without any addition to the energy between the pieces.

The energy that holds human beings together was described by Moreno in his 'Introduction' to the third edition of *Psychodrama*, vol. 1:

Tele (from the Greek: far, influence into distance) is feeling of individuals into one another, the cement which holds groups together. It is *Zweifühlung*, in contrast to *Einfühlung*. Like a telephone, it has two ends and facilitates two way communication. Tele is primary, transference a secondary structure. After transference vanishes, certain tele conditions continue to operate. Tele stimulates stable partnerships and permanent relations.

(Moreno 1977: xi)

These relationships include a co-conscious as well as a co-unconscious recognition of the link, this aspect being much more extended than the conscious one. It includes the unrecognised body reactions, unknown social experiences, the religious and ideological activities and the long history of our ancestors, elements that link human beings through common experiences, many of them unconscious even to the individual but still forming part of the hidden co-unconscious of the relationships established as part of the life of one individual, one family, one race, one planetary inhabitant: 'Individuals who are intimately acquainted reverse roles more easily than individuals who are separated by a wide psychological or ethnic distance. The cause of this variation is the development of co-conscious and unconscious states' (Moreno 1977: vi). These two parallel phenomena are constantly present in any relationship. As in the act of birth two processes will be present in any action. Life will continue when these two processes relate to each other in a harmonious way, allowing the tele relationships to evolve, the creation to emerge and the constant exchange between the individual and his or her matrices to occur.

Psychotherapy intervenes at the moment at which this process meets with a resistance in any member, or the group, which can be expressed by painful suffering, absence of reaction or some other manifestation. It will supplement what the real relationships have not until that moment been able to provide or to resolve.

The understanding of these concepts makes it clear that it is necessary to include the development of the co-unconscious in any therapeutic intervention.

CLINICAL EXAMPLES

Cosmic matrix

The cosmic matrix appears in memories of events prior to the moment of birth or even to conception.

During a meeting the mother of a young over-developed 12-year-old girl says: 'When she was 4 years old she told me: "I chose you from the sky when I saw you with the children. I knew I was going to need love because of my differences, it is not easy to be accepted when you are different."' The mother is a teacher of handicapped children.

In another dramatisation the protagonist was recreating a scene in which she was holding her dog in her arms while her partner, from whom she wanted to separate but could not, was telling her: 'You are destructive, you are the one who is ruining my life.' The director asks her to think about another scene in which something similar may have happened. Her answer is: 'I can't remember, it never happened before, not with my parents', suddenly she starts to cry. 'I see my mother with a baby in her arms.' Sobbing copiously she says 'The baby who died before I was born.' She then takes the role of the mother and adds: 'It was not my fault, I just fell from the bus when I was pregnant and he got hurt.' Taking the father's role and still crying she says: 'It was terrible but it had to happen.' The director asks if the father is angry and the protagonist from that role answers that he is not the angry one but the baby is.

DIRECTOR: How do you know?
PROTAGONIST: I saw him.
DIRECTOR: Where?
PROTAGONIST: In the sky, there are only lights white lights and he looked at me very angrily and said . . .
DIRECTOR: Reverse roles.
PROTAGONIST: (in the role of the brother) I did not want to go.
PROTAGONIST: But it is not my fault. I saw him then, before I arrived. That is why I have been so afraid of babies and could not have one.'

This meeting of brother and sister created on the stage gives the protagonist an answer to many questions about her life.

During the sharing the group exchanges similar experiences and remembers especially the first scene played by the group, six months before. In it, after the dramatisation of the death of a family – father, mother and baby – known to some of the participants, the protagonist from the role of the baby had said: 'Do not cry any more, I am happy, we went away all together.'

This memory changes the group's perspective about life and death and brings forward the difficult situation of another baby about to be born without a family, who expresses his fear of coming into the world.

The protagonist of the previous psychodrama, teacher of the mother of this baby, sensing the continuity of life, realises then the possibility of becoming a protective figure to mother and child, without the fear of becoming too involved. After continuing the work for some months the baby was born without any problems. Once the psychodrama was finished it was felt that the subject we had been dealing with, since the beginning, related to all the members in one way or another.

It is possible to consider in these examples the presence of a process which starts its development prior to the moment of birth, a knowledge shared by the future human being and the significant others which is co-unconsciously transmitted. What is important from the point of view of the group is that this deep knowledge will appear at the moment the group's development allows the expression of these fantasies or realities.

UNKNOWN KNOWLEDGE ABOUT BIRTH

The moment of birth, previously described as a creative act in which a knot of relationships come together, is frequently present in therapeutic work. It expresses the co-unconscious manifestations from different matrixes.

Example

Warm-up

In a group that has been working for nine months, one member is selected to work on her feelings of uncertainty that cannot be placed in any actual life situation. It is a group of psychodrama directors in training. After being selected, the protagonist chooses the director who happens to be the oldest member of the group and who will direct for the first time.

Dramatisation

Scene one

The protagonist describes her difficulty in seeing the scenery because everything is white-coloured and cold as marble. She is asked to reverse roles with that marble. She says:

PROTAGONIST: I am cold and white, I am a table in a surgical theatre.
DIRECTOR: Do you have a message?
PROTAGONIST: It is cold and needs care and love. (out of the role) It is so strange it seems to occupy the whole space, I feel very small.
DIRECTOR: Where are you?
PROTAGONIST: (lying on top of the marble) This is very big . . . it seems so, so big . . . no, I am very small. I am so cold. I have just been born. (she starts crying)
DIRECTOR: Are you alone?
PROTAGONIST: Yes. (the crying continues) My head seems to be open, I feel something that comes from that side. (she signals to her right talking in a very low voice)
DIRECTOR: Reverse roles and become that which you are feeling.
PROTAGONIST: I am standing beside the table, I am silent, I do not need words to talk to her, I know her deeply, deeply inside of

	me. (she turns round to the nurse) Please bring something to cover her, she is very cold after the bath.
DIRECTOR:	Reverse roles.
PROTAGONIST:	It is warmer. I hear a voice inside my head that says: I know her, she belongs to the Healers' Fraternity, she has always been with us. Poor baby, why did you take this difficult path? I know about it, we are all one. The secrets I am teaching you, passing over to you at this moment, will become yours later, much later. You will learn through the common way and you will discover later this secret knowledge of union, connected to other realms of healing powers, later, but now I say to you: welcome to the Healers' Fraternity as my ancestors welcomed me before. (she has talked in a clear voice, the sobbing has stopped completely and now without moving transmits this message in a different voice) I hear many other things but I cannot tell them, they seem to enter my body through my head and expand, then keep silent for a moment.
DIRECTOR:	Reverse roles.
PROTAGONIST:	I am the grandfather.

She holds the baby tenderly, covering it with care, hands it over to the nurse and without saying a word walks away. She goes out of the room, sits down and covers her forehead with her hand.

DIRECTOR:	Grandfather, are you worried?
PROTAGONIST:	Yes, I know what a difficult path this one will have to tread, but it will be as it has to be, it is also beautiful.
DIRECTOR:	Is there someone else here?
PROTAGONIST:	Yes, the aunt but she will never understand.
DIRECTOR:	Can we bring her in?
PROTAGONIST:	Yes.
DIRECTOR:	Reverse roles.
PROTAGONIST:	(as the aunt) Are you happy Doctor, you seem preoccupied?
DIRECTOR:	Role reversal.
PROTAGONIST:	(as the grandfather) It is such a responsibility.
DIRECTOR:	Do you want to hear the dialogue from the baby's role or from outside?
PROTAGONIST:	From outside, in a mirroring position. Now I understand the message. It is a shared responsibility and a shared knowledge. Grandfather, thank you.

Very slowly she walks to the auxiliary ego in the Grandfather's role and embraces him.

Sharing

The protagonist says: 'I am not cold any more and I am calm. I always knew about the scene between my aunt and my grandfather and felt very rejected, now as I understand it and also understand the deep connection with him, my search as a healer makes sense.'

The other members of the group talk about their own births and share from the deep knowledge of being a healer. The director talks about her wish to become a grandmother and the responsibility of directing for the first time.

This responsibility or this worry was shared by the whole group. One week later the protagonist comes to the group with the news that she will be a grandmother.

Processing

In the processing in the next session, the group's relationship to the roles of the psychotherapist and healer were considered, the consequence of the co-unconscious warming up to the choosing of the protagonist.

The individual matrices show in this dramatisation the existence of a very deep co-unconscious relationship between grandfather and child, kept secret in the body language up to the moment in which the conjunction of the group matrix in need of a scene to express its anxiety, warms up the hidden memory and brings it into action.

At the same time, the strong co-unconscious link in the protagonist's actual family appears when she is able to relate the psychodrama, with the news given to her after it, about her daughter-in-law's pregnancy.

At the time of this psychodrama session the social matrix in Argentina was facing a dangerous situation: the country was suffering hyperinflation and it seemed only very radical action or magic could correct this. A possible way out appeared to require a different understanding of old messages. Money was not security any more. Society needed another system of values to be reborn in order to find the lost links between its roots and new projects.

When this psychodrama was considered, with regard to this particular social situation, there was a message to follow intimate inner knowledge and not the badly misunderstood programmes of reform.

The strong co-unconscious link in the group showed that the social co-conscious was in need of space–time relationships which could express the group's deep worry and bring to the surface the hidden resources kept in its co-unconscious.

In conclusion, it is possible to consider that the theme which emerges from a group will be played by a protagonist at the moment in which the group's co-unconscious warm-up coincides with an individual's, and that this in turn will always be interlocked with his or her family's matrix.

The group as a network is a real social atom deeply connected to the social matrix. It will have a co-unconscious network formed by the actual relationships within it plus the social atoms of its members rooted in the social matrix.

The subject dramatised by a protagonist, as in this example, will bring forward the group's theme and will always express the group's social concerns and their possible resolution.

PLANETARY INCLUSION

The description of the co-unconscious includes the need of a shared space and time to create it. The changes in planetary communications have been expanding their boundaries more and more.

It will be possible to amplify the lens of the co-unconscious much more with the evolution of humankind, as what used to belong to an imaginary realm clearly appears more and more as a shared experience of groups of people at a particular time or space, re-enacted or transmitted through generations.

The American continent has the privilege of being the first crucible where this unveiling of real knowledge of the common experience of humankind takes place.

The next example will describe the conjunction between the individual, group, social and planetary co-unconscious.

The space: an International Conference; the time: the year of the commemoration of the discovery of America, and the five hundredth anniversary of the admission by the scientific and political powers of that time of the existence of a 'New World', knowledge already present in legends, sagas, and myths since very old times.

First theme

People arrived from all over the world. After the introductions, the enactment of a world map was used as warm-up. The image of this world was different according to each one's perspective. It was seen differently by people living in China, Vietnam, Australia, Europe, North or South America.

It was important to understand that there was a difference in the way people from different continents placed themselves in relation to others. A crucial moment arose when someone coming from Asia placed himself at the far end of the room and located the American continent in the middle. The image accepted by the Americans was not felt to be correct by the Europeans who considered the centre the right position for their own continent.

After some discussion the map was finished by taking into account the reality of being at the moment in the Northern part of the American continent, a situation that allowed for a compromise.

A conversation started about the work to be done: a sociopsychodrama. The contract between the group members and the leader was clarified and the sociodramatic and psychodramatic approaches accepted. The socio-dramatic work would relate to the group's concern including the social reality of the here and now and the psychodramatic work would enact personal protagonist work related to the theme.

The reality of the world at the moment was discussed, the tearing down of the Berlin wall and the encounter of the east and the west were both considered an advancement that stretched around the world. This brought forward the economic differences, the misuse of power and the appearance of racial, ethnic, ideological and religious violence.

Wars were still being fought in several parts of the world and were considered evil, but there was a feeling that the rich countries regarded them as a necessity which maintained the status quo, even if these same countries happened to help in the development of the poorer countries.

This statement was very badly received by members of the western community, who felt it unjust and undeserved. All these subjects became very important in the group's dynamics and were brought to action.

The scene was set by a Slovenian. He created a scene where a group of Moslems and Christians were seen. The Moslems were being thrown out of their homes. They did not belong, even if they had lived in the same place for many generations.

It was very important to notice that although the majority of the group's members did not know one another or one another's history, the auxiliary egos chosen for the different roles were closely related to the theme being enacted. This showed the presence of a clear co-unconscious link underlying the scene.

Two members enacting the role of soldiers were asked by the director what in their personal experience had prevented them from acting such a role in real life. What began as a sociodramatic scene changed into a personal one, involving feelings and relationships, which although present in social events, are commonly regarded as outside individual awareness.

Both soldiers commented on personal situations which had stopped each of them from going to war. One, a member who came from Israel, mentioned a teacher. The other, the protagonist, said that his own son had been the reason. This boy had taken the rifle from his father's hand and declared that peace had to be kept above anything else, even if it meant losing one's own life.

The whole group regarded this statement as not only very profound because of its content, but also because of the emotions involved in the meeting of father and son. The strong reactions of both, which spoke of their mutual love, of the need for the father to meet his son with a different set of values and of the hope of the advent of a future world bore the imprint of an important change in the co-unconscious value system.

Part of the group was ready to conclude that peace must be maintained regardless what risks it may include. Others took a stand over the need to defend oneself in case of attack and the last group oriented itself towards confrontation.

The first group was the bigger one and sociodramatically the group was taking a position of commitment towards peace. The negative position of those against them, especially a small group of women, saved the wish for peace from being an illusion.

Second theme

The second theme was economic power and dependence between poor and rich countries.

It was brought forward in a dramatisation in which the great demand surging from the Third World was changed into a sudden discovery of its own plentiful resources, which made it unnecessary to seek help from the first world and thus removed the reason for resentment.

This group found its own identity in individual and family relationships. Support was given by the care and love present in their small tribe.

An interesting phenomenon was observed when the other group, which represented the developed world and which was looking at the others, felt itself unnecessary. The group members turned within themselves to discover that their own security also depended on their close relationships. A great relief was experienced by the western community, especially by the European members, who said they were rather tired of being responsible for the development of society.

After this dramatisation the two groups were ready to recognise each other as human beings with the same needs and possibilities and realised that their supposed differences were limited to ideological, religious, or political positions.

Fundamentally, they concluded that if one group was capable of hearing or understanding the other, there was less room for manipulation and misuse of power.

Third theme

The need to understand existing secret societies, such as the Mafia, was considered by the group to be an important issue. The question was presented by a psychologist who worked in Sicily and was interested in analysing the phenomenon.

As a warm-up to the process the world map was again brought into the room. Sicily was placed in the centre. Very soon it became apparent that this central position connected the island with the four directions of the compass, especially with North America.

The scene enacted was the funeral of a judge, very much involved in the subject, who had been murdered some months before. The real funeral had been a private ceremony attended, out of fear, by few people. The public ceremony was reserved for the burial of the policemen and the woman who had been killed during the attack on the judge. It was felt that the large public participation in this ceremony was due to the injustice of their deaths.

This funeral was enacted in the session and the protagonist reversed roles with one of the dead policemen. From this role he talked in a very calm voice. He described himself as a seed: 'I am a seed getting deeply into the soil. I reach the centre of the earth. It is very hot. I am expanding, I am the continuity of life. Each one has to describe his own circle: dying and being reborn.'

The group surrounding him fell into a total silence in profound quietness and peace. The message was felt to be a sacred one.

The protagonist was then asked to reverse roles with the earth. The role of a containing mother was immediately taken and with an act of birth the scene was transformed into a new dimension of awareness that touched the whole group.

It is important to point out that the woman chosen to be the mother belonged to the group that had been more upset about the commitment to peace made before. She was a few months pregnant and the scene enhanced her tender and loving attitude.

The whole group formed a circle. They were facing the mystery of life and its continuous flow. In their deep planetary co-unconscious level they were connected to the mysterious rites of the matriarchal Mother Earth, worshipped by agricultural, primitive cultures.

A very important contribution towards the understanding of the co-unconscious process, was the protagonist's discovery, the next day, that his best friend had drowned in the Mediterranean. In a very strong co-unconscious connection, he received a last message from his dead beloved friend, whilst enacting the psychodrama.

It is possible to look at the Mafia process as the last manifestation of a very old culture which worshipped, especially, the maternal and feminine power – the Earth. This continuing worship is not expressed through open war, but by the deep unacknowledged struggle between brothers for a place within this Mother Earth, transforming that seed of love into hate.

The next scene enacted was the meeting, as brothers, of a Hungarian and a gypsy whom the first considered to be his friend. Their meeting occurred after a long walk that had begun in India for the gypsy and in the north of Europe for the Hungarian and taken them five hundred years. This period symbolised the long way that mankind has walked to enable people of different races and cultures to meet as equals through the breaking of internal and external walls.

Fourth theme

Finally, the group had to deal with the inclusion of new members who had arrived during the two days of the pre-congress. The group in which they joined, overcoming differences, provided a basis at the congress for the recreation, in the reality of the here and now, for permanent inclusion of everyone into humankind. This will only take place peacefully with acknowledgement of the common memory of our origins kept in the planetary co-unconscious.

The importance of this dramatisation lies in realising that what is looked upon as the worry of one particular individual, in fact includes the problems of many. This group's work made clear that the wish for peace and encounter throbbing in everyone can be fulfilled only if the basic needs of connection, love and understanding are met, balancing the need to express the aggression that the development of life generates. Hate and love must be transformed into the seeds of life and birth of a new planetary structure. This structure will allow the inclusion of those who have been separated by ideological, political or religious reasons. It will reveal that the misuse of power constantly creates the myth of brothers in permanent war with each other, which separates individuals from the deep connection with the co-unconscious shared links and forgets the reality of love.

This chapter purposefully ends without the processing of the technical aspects of these sociodramas. This is in order to allow the reader to link in with the co-unconscious process that maintains the continuity of life and opens new ways of relating to the realities of the world.

REFERENCES

Giorgiuti, E. (1988) Genetica y Psicodrama, lecture given at the Centro de Psicodrama y Sociodrama, Buenos Aires (unpublished).
Moreno, J.L. (1977) *Psychodrama*, vol. 1, 5th edn, New York: Beacon House.

The personal and unconscious dimension

Chapter 10

Disintegration
Its role in personality integration

Commentary

Dag Blomqvist and Thomas Rützel challenge the usual emphasis on order, sanity and rationality, arguing that disintegration is both therapeutically and philosophically important. Their chapter reveals a developmental line which is important in Morenian psychology, in which disorder and psychosis are valued rather than diagnosed. Taking the conventional notions about what was already an unconventional concept, and developing their themes of surrealism and alienation, they show just how powerful and exciting such ideas can be. Their chapter questions perceived cultural and psychotherapeutic norms in a similar way to that which characterised Moreno's earlier creative period in Vienna.

Surplus reality and beyond

Leif Dag Blomkvist and Thomas Rützel

AN EXTENDED CONCEPT OF SURPLUS REALITY

The psychodrama stage is often described as an instrument having three time dimensions: past, present, and future, and also as an instrument that does not differentiate between fantasy and reality. These descriptions make it difficult to understand fully the concept and the content of surplus reality; what it is, as well as what it is not.

It would be more appropriate to say that on the psychodrama stage there is no differentiation of time at all. There is also no differentiation of different kinds of realities with one regarded as more real, valid or true than another. Surplus reality can be defined as an intersection between different realities, known and unknown, where the ego's ability to control and distinguish ceases. This state determines ecstasy[1] which we understand from its etymological root as *leaving the limits of one's individuality*.[2] This is a state in which one does not experience things as one used to do, but looks upon them from another unfamiliar perspective. This perspective can either belong to an unknown part of the self, to another person, known or unknown, or to an impersonal force.

Psychodramatists nowadays often work with surplus reality without taking into account its philosophical perspective. The psychodrama usually starts with the protagonist's problem and during the session the drama goes back to early childhood experiences to heal the wounds. Surplus reality is in this case often used as a technique to complete and heal something, to have an integrative effect upon the ego so that the protagonist feels better and can get on with his or her life. To bring on stage a dialogue between the protagonist and someone dead or giving him a new father or mother are only two examples of this way of using surplus reality.

However, we feel this orthodox concept and application of surplus reality as a technique to act out fantasies and wishes and, therefore, the ego's needs is very restricted and has little to do with the full potential of surplus reality. Surplus reality is more an instrument of disintegration and should be regarded as a theatrical instrument for the director to create discomfort, uneasiness and tensions on stage. The dramaturgist Dyfverman states that the key to drama is uneasiness and not the idyll.

A concept of reality that consists only of conventional dialogues and where there is just politeness and lack of confrontation leads to a drama that does not bring life onto the stage. Therefore, we have to look upon surplus reality as an *extension* of reality in the original sense of the word: the aspect of a widening of reality. The word wide is derived from the Indo-Germanic word *ui-itos*, meaning in German, *auseinandergegangen*. The literal translation into English would be: one did go from another, or more simply: to fall to pieces. Here, we see the perspective of surplus reality as a form of disintegration or falling to pieces.

Unfortunately, we look upon our failures in life or our insecurities as something to be got rid of in order to return to our 'normal' selves. That many people come to psychotherapy and psychodrama because of their failures only enhances the demand on psychotherapy to make them return to normal: their normal life, their normal state of mind and their normal success. People are usually trying to find a reason why something or other happened and what can be done about it. Very rarely do we consider failure itself as being meaningful. We thus explore our failures to a very small extent and consider falling to pieces as being negative. It is the opposite of being strong and of knowing what one wants to do. When we start to fall to pieces and enter surplus reality, nothing makes sense any longer.

As therapists we often ask ourselves in a rational way such questions as: How can this brave woman stay with this man who drinks, beats her up and abuses her? Why did she or he commit suicide so unexpectedly? In surplus reality, however, we move from a rational point of view into the dimension of no sense and of no predictable meaning.

We experience a sense of falling to pieces or disintegration when something unexpected happens to us which throws our life out of its regularity. Such incidents could be, for example, separation, losing a partner through death or losing one's job. After such an incident we fall to pieces into many different figures, for example, the one with murderous impulses or the one who wants to heal, and these figures do not seem to co-operate. In German people say: *'Ich fühle mich hin- und hergerissen'*, which means: 'I feel pulled into different directions'. Speaking with a forked tongue is another aspect of this. One says one thing and means something else. In the world of surplus reality things do not fit together.

However, it is very important not to confuse the world of surplus reality and the unknown with the world of the unconscious. The principle of opposites influences the world of the unconscious whereas surplus reality or the surreal world is truly Dionysian. That means it is the world of chaos and not the world of opposites. In Jungian psychology the principle of adversity is a central concept whereas in the surreal world of the unknown, the right or wrong of this principle is an open question. In this Dionysian world the opposite to male is not necessarily female, the opposite to death is not necessarily life, the opposite to consciousness is not necessarily unconsciousness.

Most of us suffer from an incurable mania to return the unknown to the known, of bringing back things into the 'light' so that they can be classified and so our brains can then go to sleep.

In the world of surplus reality a protagonist *has* to think, *has* to work, and *cannot* go to sleep. Just as a dream can never be dreamed twice, the protagonist cannot bring back his or her experiences in surplus reality into everyday reality although they will have an effect upon his or her life.

ENTERING THE WORLD OF SURPLUS REALITY

People often have inner dialogues. Usually these occur in situations when the body is occupied with some kind of activity, like walking home from the bus stop or knitting, and when the mind is running idle. Mary Watkins writes:

> I shall place before you the view that imaginal dialogues do not merely reflect or distort reality, but *create* reality; that the real is not necessarily antithetical to the imaginal, but can be conceived of more broadly to include the imaginal; and that personifying is not an activity symptomatic of the primitivity of mind, but is expressive of its dramatic and poetic nature.
>
> (Watkins 1990: 58)

When such dialogues are projected onto the psychodrama stage and when the substantial figures behind such dialogues and their interactions take place, we can say that these dialogues *create* the person or the substantial protagonist.

The most important thing in psychodrama is not to look upon the world from the protagonist's point of view, but to create an opportunity and a platform for the protagonist to encounter his or her antagonists and look at himself or herself with the eyes of the antagonist, from the antagonist's perspective. This refers to the basic psychodramatic technique of role reversal. These dialogues and different perspectives, through role reversal, will challenge the protagonist. When working with schizophrenics or with people who hallucinate and one wants to know more about the figure behind a certain voice the schizophrenic person can rarely give you information about it. Neither can he or she antagonise the voice that attacks him. A psychodrama director working with surplus reality will therefore substantiate the figure behind the voice, whatever it may be, and encourage a dialogue in which the figures are reflecting one another. Some of these figures might represent different known or unknown parts of the protagonist. However, as mentioned before, other parts could belong to other people, known or unknown, or even to an impersonal force. These dialogues can *only* appear when the phenomenon of disintegration has taken place.

Another important aspect that we have to add to the concept of surplus reality is the dissolution of inside and outside. We cannot say that the inner world is a reflection of the outer world or vice versa. We rather must ascribe the phenomena of figures and voices, mentioned before, to creatures or beings with their own consciousness and unconsciousness, be they personal or non-personal. Surplus reality can only be experienced through surplus reality.

Our idea of surplus reality is related to the philosophy of the Surrealists who were always in search of the unknown and were not, as many people now believe, a movement of expression or expressive arts. To relate to these unknown worlds was more important to them.

> The expressive function is, however, mentioned in positive contexts as well. That which is expressed is in such cases not conceived of as preexistent ideas or subjective emotions but as something unknown and difficult to grasp. According to one line of thought, it exists only through its expression and is entirely distinguished from the person expressing himself, in contrast to emotional symptoms, for example. Expression in this positive sense (according to Surrealism) is informed by absence of expression in the usual sense of the word. This aspect of Surrealist theory has almost escaped notice, still less been accepted by contemporaneous critics in whose conception of art the idea of expression appears to play a fundamental role.
>
> (Sjölin 1981: 410)

Entering the world of surplus reality means the psychodramatist must leave the world of the law of cause and effect behind. He or she also must give up the idea of a certain structure of a psychodrama session such as those described by the psychodramatic spiral by Elaine Goldman or the Hollander curve. The psychodramatist even has to leave behind the traditional aspect of a drama with a beginning or an end.

The dramatic tension of surplus reality exists because the protagonist moves on unfamiliar territory in his or her psychodrama. This is very important because it describes his or her feeling of the surreal experience: He or she is waiting for something. It is a search where even the purpose of the search is unclear. When the drama enters the stage the protagonist and the director are in the hands of the drama and *not* vice versa.

SURREALISM AND THE WORLD OF DREAMS IN PSYCHODRAMA

The psychodrama stage and the unconscious have similar structures or characteristics as both are beyond time. On the psychodrama stage the past is not in opposition to the future, but rather past and future meet one another and unite. Fantasy and reality are also not one another's opposites, but unite in Moreno's concept of surplus reality. The concept of surplus reality is one of the strongest psychotherapeutic dimensions of psychodrama. Surplus reality also contains the key for working with dreams from a psychodramatic point of view. By challenging the ego's usual tendency to differentiate things and put them opposite to one another, the protagonist and the group are introduced to a mystical world filled with another knowledge, infinite wisdom, beauty, risks and danger.

This world, where opposites do not exist, is, for instance, represented in the art of René Magritte. In our lives we will occasionally return to this surrealist world which is beyond rational understanding and reach. In it we mix people and places that we usually keep separate; we will find ourselves in situations and carry out actions that our usual ego would never dream of doing. Strangely enough it is the energy arising from this dream world which is vital for us to be able to cope and deal with our life. In other words, in this timeless world, in this kingdom of darkness, man is connected to the so-called world-soul.

It was a general belief for the alchemists that the soul was partly personal and partly divine, and thus immortal. In this way the personal soul was linked to the world-soul. For the soul, death is as insignificant as it is for the unconscious. For the ego, however, death is a vital threat. It is the soul that adds meaning to life and provides us with the *élan vital*. Not to be connected to the soul leads to a lack of substance and energy for life.

There is also an old belief that time and the world-soul are connected or even, in a way, one and the same. In ancient Greece Aion was the god of time. Originally Aion denoted the vital fluid in living beings, their life span and allotted fate. This was a generative substance like all waters on earth. One can say that Aion was the basic substance of life. M.-L. von Franz writes about Aion: 'Aion, the god of time, is here clearly an image of the dynamic aspect of existence, or what we might call today a principle of psycho-physical energy' (von Franz 1978: 6). Time, from this perspective as a creative source of substance, has great importance on the psychodrama stage. It is related to Moreno's principle of the moment, or his concept of here and now. In this sense Moreno's principle of spontaneity and creativity is also such a life-giving substance. By freeing man from the borders between reality and fantasy, as well as time, Moreno believed that the person could become a creator.

Death is a serious matter for human beings and everything living on earth, and, therefore, one of the basic concerns for the ego. However, relating to Aion, death is a part of a greater principle.

The task on the psychodrama stage is to free this energy and unite man with the cosmos. Moreno wrote in *Invitation to an Encounter*: 'In the unconscious state where the dreams are created also a regenerator of energy must be included. In the sleeping dreamstate we regenerate' (J.L. Moreno 1914). When a dream picks its material it absolutely ignores the logic of our daily ego and its divisions and controls. A dream can pick up places and people that we usually keep separate in time and space. A dream also puts us in the most shameful situations and conflicts.

Since the unconscious was never an important issue for Moreno, he certainly did not consider dreams as being a *via regia* to our unconscious, or that dreams were something that must be decoded from their manifest dream context to understand the latent dream thought. Moreno regarded this as wrong, or as a resistance towards the here and now.

Moreno considered dreams as something man and his ego had to relate to from the dream's point of view. Since the creator of the dream is the *unknown*, something out of the ego's control according to Moreno, we should experience the unknown rather than try to force it under the control of the ego. This unknown is related to the deepest root of nature and existence of man and, consequently, the ego is ruled more by it than admitted. To become acquainted with this world is to become close to the unknown or the surreal.

Dreams connect man to Aion and create a field of force between what the ego has experienced and what is never seen. René Magritte believed that what was never seen or experienced becomes present through its absence. In this way a dream is a reality for the surrealists. *What the ego would never dream of doing has already been done.* To see dreams in this way is contrary to the modern analytic tradition, but not to the psychodramatic. The analytic tradition sees dreams and symbols with a somewhat latent content that, through certain analogies, will become better understandable. That is to say that dreams would represent something else other than what is manifest. Even many psychodrama directors continually relapse into psychological interpretations and into finding analogies. If they intend to work with dreams from the perspective pointed out in this article, they must be aware of this attitude.

However, one branch of the Surrealist movement, represented by René Magritte, was also sceptical about the analytical interpretation of symbols mentioned above, since it watered down the symbol. A symbol contains a certain energy that will always be unknown to man. However, this energy can be experienced, but will not be explained by any logical thinking and rationalisation.

We experience this in Magritte's painting, in which the object is always taken out of its normal context. Magritte called this technique of disturbing the senses the 'art of the non-related object'. That is, to put things together which we usually see separated or in other contexts. From this point of view, since we are forced to look upon the object itself, everything can be regarded as a potential symbol. Symbols only represent themselves. According to Sjölin (1981) the surrealists express themselves in the following way: a long-standing belief exists saying that nothing exists without cause; on the contrary, every being and every phenomenon of nature contains an enciphered message that gives life to every cosmogony.

Relating to the object as such rather then trying to make it understandable for the ego is an exercise and experience for the mind that Magritte provokes. By using familiar interpretation systems one tries to make the latent dream content understandable to the ego. Magritte's critique to such a procedure was that the wisdom of the dream would get lost in the ego's rational logic. In that sense the surrealist experience, as well as the relationship to the unknown, would get lost. An enigma does not hide anything because it already contains all the necessary information. It is only a matter of finding a new way to relate to the objects that one can get the image; all the material is accessible.

Regarding the concealed meaning of, for instance, a dream, the question whether the meaning is latent or not is not of interest, as from the surrealists' point of view the meaning is there in its manifest form, accessible for everybody to participate in. The surrealists were more focused on the experience of the dream and the participation in the irrational. Surrealism meant to participate in disharmony and disintegration. Dream psychodrama encourages this experience of the enigma through dialogue and action in the different aspects of the dream. Since Moreno wanted to teach the protagonist to be a better dreamer, this form of dream psychodrama is not restricted to acting out the dream as the ego remembers it. Several scenes of such a dream psychodrama, acted out in the here and now, were often not present during the night but are created impromptu and in relation to the protagonist's presentation of his or her dream. This process is called dream evolution where the spontaneous play directs the development of the dream psychodrama. The dream presented on the stage will be a new production and can go many steps away from the original dream. Production in the here and now is a piece of art in itself and the person is a creator of art within the moment. Sometimes this will lead to relief, sometimes to further confusion and sometimes, nowhere at all. (An example of such a dream psychodrama can be found in the last section of this chapter.)

This kind of dream psychodrama is a way to encourage and train the ego to relate to the absurd rather than to find a latent meaning. This will encourage the feeling of estrangement and prepare us for the so-called surrealist experience. This experience is described as a field of force full of suspense, as *rites de passage* from one condition to another, whatever it will be. They are the *rites de passage* into the unknown. By following the dream and the unreasonable wisdom we hope to make the ego more flexible, tolerant and spontaneous. The meaning will reveal itself through the Dionysian experience of the irrational. Following the wisdom of the unreasonable is to work with an extended perspective of Moreno's surplus reality.

To get in touch with these unknown worlds, surrealists use a technique that they call automatism, which is described as follows:

> The experience of estrangement has been described by the Surrealists chiefly in connection with automatic writing. It appears that the person writing feels estranged from, in particular, the meaning of the words he has heard inside himself or which flow from his pen. The experience of estrangement can also be caused by the intonation of the interior voice or by feelings and moods connected with the words written. Sometimes the feeling of estrangement is aggravated by the fact that the words strike the person who has written them as the expression of another personality or even of an impersonal force.
>
> (Sjölin 1981: 407)

Another important aspect of the surrealist experience is the one that things, like words in automatic writing, are robbed of their conventional qualities and put into a new estranged context. This also means that not only the object is robbed of its conventional qualities, but also the relation in which it is put is totally changed.

An object only represents itself and does not stand for any hidden thing. What is more important than explaining and interpreting is that one becomes involved in these new unfamiliar experiences and bears the tension. The ego tries to be logical and explain tensions. Surrealism teaches us to bear them. This condition of tension is the surrealist experience. Freud's dream analysis offers explanations that satisfy the ego. However, the surrealist experience is incompatible with an ego-centred psychology. In both surrealism and surplus reality the phenomenon of disintegration is more important than the integration process. Therefore, surplus reality will remain a mystery and a source of creativity.

MADAME BLANCHE AND HER MIRROR – A DREAM PSYCHODRAMA

The following dream 'Madame Blanche and Her Mirror' is an example of how surplus reality can be used in dream work. The method used in this dream psychodrama was created by a group called the Liechtenstein group. The Liechtenstein project started in 1985 in Vaduz (Principality of Liechtenstein) and consists of professional psychodrama directors from different countries. Its goal has been to develop knowledge and skills regarding the directing of dream psychodramas. In the research and development of Moreno's concept of surplus reality the group has studied ancient Greek theatre and tragedy in relation to the cult of Dionysus and psychodrama.

For a deeper understanding of surplus reality the group has also made a great effort to understand the mystical world of the surrealists. The attention has, therefore, been focused on the manifest dream as surrealistic painting or experience and the group members believe that symbols only represent themselves, whatever they may be.

The dream is not reproduced on the stage as the dreamer remembers it. It is rather a locus nascendi for a new surplus reality experience on the psychodrama stage. Many scenes that are dramatically produced did not exist in the dream as the protagonist remembers it. This form of dream work has been inspired by the surrealist painter René Magritte. The surrealistic and the Greek theatrical art have very distinct techniques to prepare for the Dionysian journey to these hidden dimensions of the mind and the word protagonist can be understood as the 'initiated to the divine madness' (*theia mania*). These techniques were converted into psycho-dramatic techniques and cannot be seen as isolated techniques as they cover the whole philosophy of surplus reality.

To maintain the spirit of the psychodrama we did not correct the English of the protagonist or the auxiliary egos very much.

At the beginning of each day group members who dreamed the night before share, if they so wish, their dreams with the rest of the group and without further comments by the group.

After the dream sharing, Roland is selected as protagonist. He is a tall blond man of 30 from Germany; he is a rather quiet person. He has been in the Liechtenstein project from the beginning. At the time he attended this year's seminar he felt down and was looking for new opportunities in his life. He is a psychologist and psychodramatist; he is employed and also works in a private practice. He is married and has one child.

The director of this session is the leader of the project, Leif Dag Blomkvist, and he asks Roland to come up on the stage and sit on a chair next to him. Everybody closes their eyes, and Roland tells of his dreams. He presents them in *tempus praesens* and is instructed not to try to remember things that don't come to his mind spontaneously. He relates his first dream as follows:

> Some people are on the run like in a movie. There is a camping lodge like those in the Yugoslavian mountains. There is a man and a woman and Napoleon and I. Napoleon and the woman fall down into a valley. But I feel this is not so dangerous.

Two nights later the following dream emerges:

I enter a villa or mansion and shall repair or paint something there. A sophisticated lady lives in this place. The frame of a mirror has to be painted in white. I paint the frame but on some parts the wood doesn't accept the paint. I try to put several layers of colour on these parts, but, however, the frame rejects the colour and I am dissatisfied. The sophisticated lady, as well as others, is dissatisfied. They say Günter should do it.

The dreamer is associating these dreams together, referring to his inability to do jobs correctly or knowing what he should do. In his first dream he had to take a group of people through the mountains and did not do his task properly: people fell off the mountains. In the second dream, he failed to paint the frame of the mirror.

The protagonist starts immediately by setting the most important scene of the second dream on stage. Contradictory to the orthodox Morenean dream work, the Liechtenstein school doesn't warm up the protagonist to the role of the dreamer by working on residues of the day previous to the dream. It starts immediately in the dream and, thus, in surplus reality.

Letting the protagonist tell the dream once before the action takes place gives the director a clue of where to enter into or how to warm up for the session. The director, as well as the protagonist, can, in case the dream is very long and has many scenes, select the scene that seems most appropriate to start with.

Roland chooses to start with the second dream. The director asks him to set up the scene in the mansion and Roland moves different chairs and changes the coloured lights to create the right atmosphere of a sophisticated bourgeois mansion in France. The sophisticated lady stands by the entrance door of the room with the mirror's damaged frame. The protagonist calls this woman Madame Blanche. The protagonist reverses roles with Madame Blanche.

MME BLANCHE:	I am all alone in this building here in France and it has 15 rooms. A large staff is working for me and I like them, so I pay them well. I am a very nice lady.
DIRECTOR:	What is special about the mirror?
MME BLANCHE:	It is beautiful. The frame is beautiful. It is baroque. It is hanging in the entrance hall beside the staircase to the gallery. Unfortunately, it has got old and dirty. It is more than 200 years old.
DIRECTOR:	Is it from the time of the French revolution or Napoleon?
MME BLANCHE:	Yes, something like that. I found it in the cellar.

The protagonist now goes from the role of Madame Blanche into the role of the mirror.

MIRROR: I was made before the French revolution. I was built for use. Everything was breaking down during this time. I was in danger and I am lucky that I did not get smashed. (Mirror turns its head to Mme Blanche)

MIRROR: (to Mme Blanche) I hang here on the wall so you can have a final look before you go out. My glass is very nice but I would like to look better. How wonderful it was in the old times. We had a lot of parties and gatherings here, only the high society, baronets, dukes, etc.

Dream evolution is the expansion of a certain symbol or an aspect of the dream. In this case a scene at a party in the good bygone times is selected. However, this scene never existed in the original dream. The group members prepare themselves for the respective roles. The king and the queen are there, some intellectuals and many more. The protagonist chose the role of a Marquis de Longgelan with his wife. The protagonist also wanted the ordinary hungry people of that time on stage.

MARQUIS: It seems that many people are travelling abroad these times. Especially those who have to pay taxes.

MME DU PONT: Disgusting how the lumpenproletariat is shouting and why are they all so hot for money. They don't know what to do with money anyway.

PROLETARIANS: You are not earning your own money.

KING: Neither do you have anything in your head. You don't know what it means to live because you eat shit the whole time.

PROLETARIANS: We are going to get you.

The scene ends with the storming of the Bastille. The psychodrama theatre looks like a battle ground and the whole group participate in the spontaneous play. It is a principle that catharsis is reached through participating in the action on stage. This playful aspect of the spontaneous drama is often forgotten. The scene returns to Madame Blanche's villa. Madame Blanche sits alone in her room, thinking about life.

MME BLANCHE: I am sitting here alone. Once I had a husband, but he went a long time ago. The friends that I have I don't regard as adequate for me. I feel life has lost its substance.

DIRECTOR: Well, your craftsman is here, Roland Berger (the protagonist) to fix your mirror. How do you feel about him?

MME BLANCHE: He is good and he is very careful. I got his name from an aunt and she said that he works well.

ROLAND: I feel good coming to you because this is a beautiful house and I will fix your frame.

Monologue technique in psychodrama means that the protagonist expresses different thoughts or feelings that are hidden and not shown in his action on stage. This technique is excellent for expressing the dream ego's action.

ROLAND: (monologue) I am a little bit insecure because I am not a professional. However, I might be able to do it. If I have a little luck it will work out. I have not spoken about the price with Madame Blanche and maybe she can't pay what it costs. This repair is going to take much time, and I don't know what to charge. I feel uncomfortable.

DIRECTOR: Do you like this job?

ROLAND: Yes, I like doing things like this for myself.

DIRECTOR: You did not set a price!

ROLAND: I can't because I am not a professional. A professional person would have done it in his own *Werkstatt* (workshop).

These remarks give the clue to introduce a figure that was not present in the dream, but will enter the psychodramatic dream production in the here and now. That will be the figure or archetype of the 'professional', whom the protagonist calls Mr Schneider. The purpose of such a dialogue is to bring the shadow out in to the open and make visible the shadow figures' projections on to Roland. Mr Schneider, as a shadow figure, projects incompetence on to Roland which is, to a certain extent, true. However, the dream ego does identify itself as competent.

The subjective content projected into the object is not what the object identifies itself with or defines itself as. Rarely, if ever, is anything of what is projected present in the object (von Franz 1980).

Roland takes the role of Mr Schneider, the professional. Mr Schneider has a diploma and much experience in his field. He can prove what and who he his. Roland's role is played by an auxiliary ego.

SCHNEIDER: You idiot, get away from that mirror. You are destroying it. That is what you get when you hire these moonlighters. They do not only steal work, they also do a bad job. Madame Blanche, I don't think you will be satisfied by the work of such a little shit as Mr Berger. I had to learn for 10 years and I am older than him. I will charge you 1500 DM. You might get it cheaper by Mr Berger, but he will ruin your mirror.

ROLAND: I have have often done this. *I know how to do it!*

SCHNEIDER: Ignorance, ignorance. You can't even take half the price!

Roland tries to work while Mr Schneider is looking at him with a big smile and Madame Blanche is also watching him. The work starts to go badly, and the mirror is not turning out very well.

Roland is now in the role of himself and Mr Schneider is played by another group member.

MME BLANCHE: This doesn't look very good. The closer I get to the mirror the more dissatisfied I become. This man doesn't do a good job!

ROLAND: I see that the work is not that good. The criticism is correct. The mirror and the frame don't look good. I have over-estimated myself. I have tried, but I can't do it better. I am humiliated. I feel ashamed. But this is not my regular job. I wanted to do a favour.

Shame and humiliation are the feelings experienced when people start to integrate their shadow. The ego that has been too blown up and, therefore, has left the ground is coming back to earth. Lyn Cowan writes:

> The word 'humiliation' comes from the Latin word *humus* which means 'earth' or 'ground'. Humus is the dark organic material in soils, produced by the decomposition of vegetable and animal matter. It is essential to earth's fertility. Humiliation, then is a process of decay and decomposition, of matter's feeling rotten. That which is dark and soiled in us, which decomposes and causes us to lose our composure, becomes fertilizing material, life giving, vital.
>
> (Cowan 1982: 36)

Symbolically one can say a mirror never lies. The shadow reflects itself upon the ego and that creates the feelings of shame and uneasiness. The work on the frame is not very good. Up to this point the protagonist has been concerned with the frame of the mirror belonging to Madame Blanche.

He has not looked into the mirror itself. Madame Blanche represents a female aspect reflected upon Roland. The frame, in its female aspect, is also a symbol of the self.

Roland plays the role of the mirror and cries out:

MIRROR: Once I was so beautiful. Everybody was impressed by my beauty and I hung in a very important place in the house. But times have changed. Nowadays I can only live in dreams.

DIRECTOR: How do you feel about Roland now, with the work he did on you?

MIRROR: (to Roland) You need more experience. You look tired and pale. You must achieve a better condition. Are you sick? I think it is your damned job in the school. All you do in the morning is read the newspaper, that is what is important for you. You don't have any interest in the classes. All you do is kill time. When you work as a psychologist in your practice all you do is think: When is the time of the consultation up so you can go home and eat.

The mirror is warning Roland about the danger of his psyche's female aspect. If the female aspect, the so-called anima, takes over it can make men sentimental, make them live on dreams, think about how it could be, make them lazy and lacking initiative. Anima can be a *femme fatale*, poisoning the male ego.

ROLAND: All right, but I don't do that all the time. I am not always bored. But the mirror is right: When I feel weak I polish my mask and feel weak.

In the psychodrama of dreams the director has to be aware of the fact that on one level the dream only symbolises itself. It is like a theatre of life and existence. The old Greek dramas were nothing else than reflections of man's relationship with one another and the gods in daily life. In experiencing the dream psychodramatically daily life often attends the spontaneous production, being mixed with the dream and, therefore, a new dream production is performed on stage in the here and now. It would be wrong to keep daily life out of a dream production in a dogmatic manner. Dreams can help us to understand daily life, just as daily life can help us to understand our dreams if we are willing to look a bit closer to our irrational components of daily existence.

Roland tells the director that he feels this way about his work as a teacher and a psychologist in a school for unemployed people. He has the impression that everybody there is lacking in any interest. He also experiences a lack of initiative.

Roland sets up his room at work. It is 8.45 in the morning. He puts the newspaper on his desk, has his basket with food beside him and sits in front of an enormous flipchart. The flipchart takes up the whole room. Roland reverses roles with the flipchart.

FLIPCHART: I am wonderful, I have all these grids and timetables, all these different colours for different activities. When one looks at me one may think the whole place is full of activities. Roland loves to close his door and put plans on me. It is wonderful. I am impressive but who in hell is knocking on the door. Right now when Roland and I are having such a good time?

As Roland has locked the door from the inside he has to unlock it to let his colleague Peter in.

PETER: (outside the room) I would like to talk to you about the situation in the school and in the classes.

ROLAND: (monologue) What a bore and so tastelessly dressed in a red jumper. This idiot is always toadying. It doesn't help the situation that he is from Hunsrück (rural countryside in Germany). And above all, this idiot is only a social pedagogue. With what rubbish am I surrounded? The staff is not much better than the clients.

ROLAND: Come in!

PETER: The flipchart is looking better and better. But it doesn't really reflect reality. Only a few things are taking place. It is an over-exaggeration. Probably I don't understand it. It is so complicated.

ROLAND: My flipchart is not complicated. It is a plan, it is a *frame of our work that we have to work on*. It is a suggestion for our future and how we should work. You are boring and dry. You drain me.

The next move in the psychodrama has to refer to the frame. The frame already appeared in the dream as Madame Blanche's mirror that Roland had to work on even though he was no professional. The frame now appears as his *frame of work*, as the flipchart.

Madame Blanche's mirror was approximately 200 years old dating from the time of Napoleon. Also, Napoleon appeared in Roland's first dream falling off the mountain. If the ego is inflated by female unconscious energy a great amount of creative energy is realised. However, creative energy needs arms to transform dreams into reality. Moreno calls this spontaneity. If the spontaneous factor is lacking, a certain kind of megalomania, manifested here in the figure of Napoleon, appears. Napoleon is known for his genius, as well as for his fall.

This is the reason for introducing now, in the real situation at Roland's work, a dream figure into the psychodrama. Roland reverses roles with Napoleon who is standing in his room next to a big map. In his role reversals he uses a hat similar to that worn by Napoleon.

NAPOLEON: I conquered almost the whole world. I am a man of great importance. I am going to constitute a Grand-France. Well, people, what can be done to make France greater?

Roland, in the role of Napoleon, gives many different orders. He also asks others for suggestions. He uses the whole room and the group assists him playing soldiers and the crowd.

NAPOLEON: I want to expand. France, it is not big enough for me and you. However, we can't take Spain because it is too big.

SOLDIERS: No, we can't take Spain, but we can take Prussia.

NAPOLEON: That is a good idea. I will send you to Prussia and you will build an empire there.

SOLDIERS: But we have heard that they are going to occupy Paris.

NAPOLEON:	Are you frightened? I have wonderful plans. Look at this plan. I am disappointed with you all. Where can I get brave people?
DIRECTOR:	Tell me about your death Napoleon.
NAPOLEON:	Well, it all began splendid, but the end was not too good!
DIRECTOR:	Why?
NAPOLEON:	I died in exile. My plans failed. My people did not want me any longer. Maybe there was some conspiracy. I died of a broken heart. But it was fun in the beginning.

Napoleon is being brought to the school where Roland works. This is a good example how surplus reality may be used, and how the psychodrama now has the same components as a dream. That is, the differentiation of time, as well as the differentiation between fantasy and reality, is no longer valid.

Napoleon angrily stands in front of the door to Roland's office.

NAPOLEON:	(to the group) What a ridiculous name: *Tageskollegium* (day college), is there also a *Nachtkollegium* (night college). Why is this door locked? Let me in!

Roland stands in his room with some former drug addicts and there is also the flipchart.

NAPOLEON:	What does this mean? Let me in!
ROLAND:	Who is it?

Napoleon breaks the door down and stands there like mad in the room with a surprised group of people. He sees the flipchart and screams as loud as he can and tears the plan into pieces.

Roland is now in the role of Napoleon. Roland is played by a group member

ROLAND:	This is my plan. It was a lot of work.
NAPOLEON:	This plan doesn't work. It is not practicable. It is only a soap bubble. All these former drug addicts and prostitutes are still on drugs. They are absent from school every day. How can this low life be included in your flipchart? It doesn't work. Mr Berger, I am talking to you and you are going to listen.
ROLAND:	I don't like you tearing this plan into pieces.
NAPOLEON:	All these prostitutes who can't make up their minds about anything. This is a *Wolkenkuckucksheim* (Cloud-Cuckoo-Land). The plan is just like soap bubbles.
ROLAND:	But I did have something to do.
NAPOLEON:	That doesn't mean anything.
ROLAND:	People were impressed.

Inflation means, to be filled with hot air and to be puffed up. Napoleon is reminding Roland about the risk inflation imposes to the ego. This is opposite to enthusiasm, which means to be filled with God. Enthusiasm must be integrated in small doses, otherwise the risk of inflation occurs. Megalomania, one could say, is the extreme of an inflated ego.

NAPOLEON: If I were you, I would not be here so often at this job. Why don't you go to conferences? Read some books! Learn something!
ROLAND: I take a book with me every day.
DIRECTOR: What would make more sense?
NAPOLEON: Build up some other things, your private practice, for instance. Otherwise you will not have any energy. I was a gambler and a lot has been happening around me. I invaded Russia. The end was not like this.
ROLAND: I am already tired when I enter this place and this work.
NAPOLEON: There is only empty air here. You can only become sick of it. How often have I tried to help you? I tried to give you great plans, the practice, but you are only killing time!
ROLAND: One has to live on something.
NAPOLEON: I taught you, how to be a new Napoleon. I have invested a lot in you; and what do you make out of it?
ROLAND: Your plans are somewhat out of this world.
NAPOLEON: They are great. Next year you will not have a single client.

The ego is in pain because it is running out of energy and steam. Enthusiasm raises self-confidence, spiritual growth and inspiration. However, it can only be taken in small doses and adapted. If the ego becomes too inflated and gets swamped by the unconscious it will be passive and not in a condition to make decisions and to discriminate. It will also lack initiative.

Our protagonist is struggling inside the ego. The ego, which usually longs for one-sidedness, that is to say either/or, is now torn apart. One can also see how the shadow figure, Napoleon, is confronting Roland's ideas. It is also paradoxical that Napoleon is talking this way, but dream figures are paradoxical. As a rule, integration of the shadow figure brings energy.

During this scene the protagonist reverses roles several times with Napoleon. This encounter is also a major point in the psychodrama. The protagonist, who is usually a quiet and introverted person, is expressing himself spontaneously. The cathartic experience in psychodrama is not to find a solution or a cause. It is rather to give a person a stage and an area where he feels free to express himself. One can't stress enough the importance for people to be able to have a dialogue with their inner figures.

DIRECTOR:	How does Napoleon come to this prognosis?
ROLAND:	Because people don't have to pay for their therapy themselves. That means next year is endangered.
DIRECTOR:	You will be needing this job?
ROLAND:	Nobody is interested if I sit here or not.
NAPOLEON:	I am interested. I am disappointed in what you are doing. Start with your ideas.
ROLAND:	I am not interested. in your advice. It doesn't seem to help me. How many people had to die because they followed you. Everything went wrong for you at the end and you died in jail.
NAPOLEON:	But I had energy. I did something.
ROLAND:	I am doing something. What I do is enough. I read the sports news. The Cologne team has won. This is very important. When I am here I can do what I want. I can take my time in the morning. Nobody gets on my nerves. This place is important for me because of its security. The job gives me money.

When people are confronted with their shadow too forcefully, they tend to regress. Right now the protagonist is becoming defensive, rejecting his complicated situation and struggle within his ego. One way for the ego to get rid of painful or unpleasant feelings of ambivalence quickly is to become one-sided by making a stubborn decision.

From a directorial point of view the director has to watch this process. At this point it would be important to break off the scene because the protagonist's ego can't integrate more shadow material.

DIRECTOR:	How do you see the difference between you and Napoleon?
ROLAND:	Well, security was not important to Napoleon, it is important to me. But on the other side, Napoleon had more steam in his bones (courage).
DIRECTOR:	Where does Roland have steam in his bones?
ROLAND:	At the sportsclub. In his psychodrama group. In the practice.
DIRECTOR:	I think it would be advisable to talk to Napoleon about the way you feel he influences your life.
ROLAND:	Napoleon, you make me feel dissatisfied when you look at me with your great plans. On the other hand you give me steam and liveliness. You have too big plans and when they don't come off you get disappointed and critical.

The protagonist decides to look at the duality of Napoleon. In a certain sense one can say that Napoleon also represents a Dionysian energy. Dionysus is really the god of joy and, therefore, adds flavour to life.

However, this joy can turn into a destructive madness as well. From the myth of Dionysus we know that the people who rejected the Dionysian madness became mad themselves, whereas for the people that followed him a greater, more rewarding life was to come. Dionysus is also famous for his primitive wildness and, therefore, can take his own brutal course if the ego rejects him. Worship the gods for what they are. Our protagonist has decided to do so.

Napoleon leaves the stage and we are back at Madame Blanche's room where Günter repairs the mirror. Madame Blanche, Roland and Günter are standing around the mirror. Günter turns out to be a person in the protagonist's real life that he can't stand. We are still dealing with the shadow and projections of the shadow. Günter is a person that functions as a projection hook for the protagonist.

The protagonist is asked to take the role of Günter. In the role presentation we can see a description of Günter certainly contains a great amount of projections of a negative character. The presentation is stereo-typical, very negative, and would be absolutely contrary to how Günter would present himself. Eros, the god of love and relation, is lacking. Moreno spoke of tele as the opposite to projection. Tele is two-sided, its fundamental process is reciprocity (of attraction, rejection, etc.), and it contains Eros. Tele is based on a sense for and recognition of the *real* situation of others. This is certainly not the case in Roland's presentation of Günter.

GÜNTER: I am unemployed. I am more a mother than a man. Frankly, I almost have tits. Also I have an extremely high and screaming voice. The tits I got from sports. A couple of years ago I was a sports champion, but that was 20 years ago. I have long ugly greasy hair. In general I look like a pig or a slut.

The protagonist is very excited and dresses as Günter. A wet towel represents the greasy hair, and pillows, pushed under the protagonist's jumper, represent his tits. The protagonist is full of energy and is acting out spontaneously. Always in psychodrama when people act out the shadow, the entire human being is there.

MME BLANCHE: I think Günter can repair that mirror! He is very practical.
ROLAND: Günter is ridiculous, and, by the way, he has tits.
DIRECTOR: What happened to you Günter?
GÜNTER: Well I grew up, got married and then had children. I am unemployed and married to a physician. My marriage is bad and I have to clean up the house before she comes home.
DIRECTOR: Well, Günter, that doesn't sound too good. Could you show us a scene of how it is when your wife is coming home?
GÜNTER: (still played by Roland) Sure!

Full expansion of a psychodrama means to be able to act in the role of the other. In surrealist psychodrama, these do not have to be scenes that the protagonist has experienced himself. The protagonist is now acting out a scene he has in his mind, a scene where he himself as Roland is not included. To act out such scenes is to act out the shadow. The protagonists, in general, have fun and a sadistic pleasure in their performance.

As a rule, when something is coloured by the phenomenon of projection the protagonist will refuse to see that the presented material has anything to do him. Insight doesn't help, but action does. The protagonist is acting out shadow material; one can say it boils off through the action. After a while or in a later session, the protagonist will automatically make certain connections to own traits.

The scene shows Günter at home with his wife and children.

THE WIFE: God, what an awful day in the clinic. I can't stand it and now I have to come home to this shit I happen to be married to. I do all the work and he doesn't really do anything. He is a *Schlappschwanz*! (literally that means: soft tail or soft cock; in English the words softie, wet or weakling would be an appropriate match)

GÜNTER: Hello, how was work?

THE WIFE: The house looks a mess. What did you do all day? Go and clean up. I am tired of doing everything. The children get on my nerves, I am tired and I don't want to be disturbed. Is that clear?

GÜNTER: Come children, mother is tired!

THE WIFE: Put on your socks and stop walking around. This is not a zoo here. I need a rest. (monologue) My God, I really was married to a champion once and look what happened. Why am I putting up with this?

GÜNTER: Well you are bankrupt. Your practice doesn't bring in anything. It is all over with you.

THE WIFE: How dare you even talk to me that way. If it wasn't for me we would be on the streets. You cannot support your family at all.

The director brings Roland once more back to the scene in Madame Blanche's house and encourages the protagonist to encounter Günter over the mirror.

One can see clearly now that the scene includes hidden fears of not being a man. How a man can be dominated and lose his male identity and be under the dominance of a woman. This image is adequate when the male ego is not in control of consciousness but is rather ruled by the anima. The marriage between the male and the anima turns into slavery rather than into a fruitful union.

DIRECTOR: Could you please express your feelings towards Günter and
            also express your relationship to him!
ROLAND: You have dominated everything. I am tired of you. Just look
            at the kindergarten where our children go to. It is all on your
            terms, your ideas about picnics, building houses for the
            children, etc. Already after half a year nobody can stand you.
            You have these Napoleonic ideas.
GÜNTER: You are a typical psychologist. You say nothing and you don't
            do anything. You are a failure.
ROLAND: A failure?! Just think about the kindergarten house that you
            were going to build. What happened? Nothing!
GÜNTER: Everybody left me and I had to build it alone. What can you
            do with others? What do you have to offer?

Günter, who reflects the shadow, is now touching upon a great problem
for the protagonist, who is an introverted person and has big problems
with extroversion. Introverted people have also a great longing for
participation, but that includes giving up some of their inner world and
expectations in favour of the collective. The problem for an introverted
person is the balance between the inner and outer world. They either feel
overwhelmed by people or control them. This certain energy for a free
flow between people is lacking.

Our protagonist has brought up this issue several times, but as many
introverted people, comes to the conclusion: It is too much work and it is
better not to do anything.

ROLAND: I can work together with my wife, and I have a brain you don't
            have (the protagonist hesitates and then turns quiet)
DIRECTOR: What is on your mind?
ROLAND: He has more courage than I have. He has the courage to do
            something even if everybody laughs at him. He is a child and
            loves what he is doing with full energy. But then everything
            goes wrong. And everybody can see his ups and downs, *only
            a few people know mine.*

Slowly, the protagonist is making the connection with his own shadow and
feels it. The action is not an intellectual insight but a dramatic one,
experienced in the moment and, therefore, we can see a therapeutic effect
of the psychodrama. To be aware of one's own shadow is impossible and
its integration into the ego is a process that is often related to a great deal
of suffering and pain called *katabasis* (the Dionysian journey into the
underworld), or, as the proverb says: 'One has to bear one's cross
patiently'. Awareness of the shadow is not related to its integration. At
best it could be a beginning. Many people in psychotherapy, including
psychotherapists, usually end the psychotherapeutic work at this starting

point, that is to say, they end where psychotherapy actually starts. However, this awareness of the shadow gives the client a feeling of profound work on himself. The difference between awareness and integration of the shadow is the same as, for example, two people talking about Paris: one has seen Paris on postcards and pictures, another went and lived in Paris for a year.

Günter has left the stage and Roland stands with Madame Blanche on the stage in the hallway of Madame Blanche's residence. Madame Blanche looks at him and then at the mirror.

Roland is playing himself and a group member plays Madame Blanche.

MME BLANCHE: Well, I don't think the work is too good. I would like it to have been perfect.

ROLAND: *I can't do it that well! I can't do it as you want it. If you want it perfect you have to get a professional. However, I like doing it for you because I like you and it won't be bad. I am good.*

MME BLANCHE: Well, I would have liked it to be perfect.

ROLAND: (monologue) If I had a mirror like that I would like the work to be perfect. She has the right expectation, but it makes me depressed.

MME BLANCHE: I have my ideas of how things should be done.

ROLAND: I have done as well as I can and I also need your appreciation, but you can also adapt to me, the person I am and what I am! Your criticism hurts and just gives me a feeling of not being capable of doing anything right. I want to be good.

MME BLANCHE: I am sorry, I am really sorry. I have to admit if I had done it myself it would have been worse. I am sorry.

Roland leaves the stage. This is the end of the scene and the psychodrama. The dream psychodrama doesn't turn back to the role of the sleeper. The psychodrama ends when there is an emotional closure. The Liechtenstein school doesn't make the traditional distinction between dream life and daily life. However, it should be noticed that there is a difference between Roland the dream ego and Roland the creator in the dream psychodrama. In a certain sense we have followed the dream ego on its journey through the dream. However, many aspects of the psychodramatic dream production were not in Roland's dream itself. This would include the aspect the surrealists called the 'never seen' and its relation to the unknown. It is a surrealist opinion that we experience the never seen by its absence. Dream evolution would refer to this aspect where the dream ego leaves the remembered dream and brings up aspects that were not there. With an orthodox analytical mind one might say this is to play out a hidden aspect of the dream; but this is not the case.

We actually don't know or have nobody to confirm whether a scene is a hidden aspect or not. The purpose of the psychodramatic dream production is not necessarily the understanding of the dream but *to experience the dream and experiment with it*. This turns people into creators, not only the protagonist, but also the group. The dream is not produced, as in the classical dream psychodrama, as an absolutely personal experience for the protagonist.

The word protagonist in psychodrama refers to the session's main character. It is his or her story that will lay the foundation for the spontaneous dramatisation and the drama will be presented from his or her point of view. However, this has been quite misunderstood nowadays. If a psychodrama is presented *only* from his or her point of view, the juice goes out of the session. The group and the auxiliary egos will only be background figures and the psychodrama session would be rather untherapeutic and the word protagonist would then also have lost its heritage to the Dionysian theatre.

The Liechtenstein school does not regard the dream as particularly the protagonist's dream. Rather, it emphasises the aspect of the *non-personal* related to the gods and the collective. Therefore, the dialogue in the dramatic production is, to a certain degree, unrestricted for the auxiliary egos.

The protagonist's creative experience is achieved with and shared by a group. Group members participate in the dream production and develop their own relation to it. Therefore, the sharing phase is, from an emotional point of view, essential in this form of psychodrama.

NOTES

1 In theological matter this word is often used in the meaning: The soul departs the body.
2 In-divi-duality means: indivisible two (natures). We see here that this word also refers to the law of the opposites, which is very important in Jungian psychology and will be referred to later.

REFERENCES

Cowan, L. (1982) *Masochism – A Jungian View*, Dallas: Spring Publications, Inc.
Moreno, J.L. (1914) *Einladung zu einer Begegnung (Invitation to an Encounter)* Vienna: Anzengruber Verlag.
Sjölin, J.-G. (1981) *Den Surrealistiska Erfarenheten – Upplevelsen*, Århus: Kalejdoskop.
von Franz, M.-L. (1978) *Time – Rhythm and Repose*, London: Thames & Hudson.
—— (1980) *Projection and Re-collection in Jungian Psychology*, La Salle: Open Court.
Watkins, M. (1990) *Invisible Guests – The Development of Imaginal Dialogues*, Boston: Sigo Press.

The interpersonal dimension

Chapter 11

Cornerstones of role reversal

Commentary

Role reversal has been described by Zerka Moreno as the engine that drives the powerhouse of psychodrama. In this chapter, Peter Kellermann gives an eloquent testimony of its power in a moving clinical example in which the circularity becomes transformed into a better ending and a new beginning. The exposition of the different kinds of role reversal will help guide students and practitioners alike as they develop their skills at using this most wondrous of all Moreno's professional creations. With applications outside the clinical setting, this technique has much potential for shifting unspontaneous situations into a new gear, with new information, counter spontaneity, impact and insight, all of which are the cornerstones of role reversal.

Role reversal in psychodrama

Peter Felix Kellermann

Mary stands facing her mother with her hands outstreched and weeping, urging her mother to look at her. But mother doesn't respond. Mary says: 'Look at me, mother!' But her mother is preoccupied with herself and looks away. The daughter is asked to take the role of her mother and, in that role, she says silently: 'If I only knew how to convey my love to you, I would hold you.' And with tears rolling down her cheeks, Mary looks at the person in front of her who is herself and embraces her for a long while, and while holding on to the person who again becomes her mother, Mary is finally able to let herself feel maternal affection.

This is role reversal, a technique typical to psychodrama, and it is one which is considered by many practitioners as the single most effective instrument in therapeutic role-playing. According to J.L. and Z.T. Moreno (Moreno *et al.* 1955), such a procedure is important not only for interpersonal socialisation with others, but also for personal self-integration. It may thus facilitate the often painful separation of children from their parents and parents from their children, leaving both free to love the other for whom they really are. As such, role reversal resembles a re-enactment of the process of separation and individuation (Mahler 1975).

In this Chapter, I will briefly sketch the history of the concept and technique of role reversal, clarify its meaning, indicate the abilities necessary for its proper use and differentiate between two forms of the technique – the reciprocal and representational role reversals – which have somewhat different goals and may be regarded as functioning within two different theoretical frames of reference.

HISTORY

As with most techniques borrowed from the theatre, role reversal has a long history; it has been used in fairy tales, mythology, drama and in literature throughout the centuries. Furthermore, role reversal has always been a natural and integral part of children's role-playing. It is therefore not surprising that the young Moreno started to experiment with role reversals when he played with children in the gardens of Vienna around 1908. According to Marineau (1989: 46), Moreno later used some role reversal when he put himself in the role of Zarathustra's 'self', thus adapting Socrates' method of teaching through dialogue in a protocol called 'The Godhead as Comedian'.

According to Carlson-Sabelli (1989), the first actual referral to role reversal was described, but not named, by Moreno (1914) in his poem on encounter;

A meeting of two: eye to eye, face to face
And when you are near I will tear your eyes out
and place them instead of mine
and you will tear my eyes out
and place them instead of yours
then I will look at you with your eyes
and you will look at me with mine.

(Moreno 1914)

This poem may be regarded, not only as the spiritual foundation of role reversal, but also as the philosophical basis of Moreno's existentialist view of life, reflecting his deep belief in direct, reciprocal meetings between people who take the roles of one another. Buber's treatise 'I and Thou' conveys a similar message, urging people to encounter one another as if 'I-act-You and You-act-I' (Buber 1923: 73).

After his move to America in 1925, Moreno became greatly influenced by the social psychologists and pragmatists J.M. Baldwin, W. James and J. Dewey who emphasised the social nature of human development and C.H. Cooley and G.H. Mead who talked about the self in terms of roles acquired by the outside world (Moreno 1953: lx). While pointing out certain differences between his own theories and the theories of these scholars, Moreno seems to have been greatly inspired by them (see Abele-Brehm 1989; Hare 1986), and he started to operationalise the concept of role reversal and apply the technique, first in educational and industrial settings (Moreno 1953: 325) and later, within psychiatry, as a way of 'objectifying' a psychotic patient (Moreno 1940: 123).

In 1955, the Moreno family published a joint paper, 'The discovery of the spontaneous man' (Moreno et al. 1955), which described the technique of role reversal as an aid in child-rearing. It contains many examples of role reversals between the child Jonathan and his parents, e.g. a three-way role reversal between a busy father who talks on the telephone, a child who demands immediate attention and a mother who takes sides with her son. The paper is concluded with twenty-six hypotheses regarding the dynamics of role reversals, most of them remaining empirically untested to this day. At the time of the publication of Zerka Moreno's (1959) central paper on the basic principles and procedures of psychodrama, role reversal was already established as the *sine qua non* of this method.

Since the pioneering work of J.L. and Zerka T. Moreno, role reversal has been applied to a wide range of settings (Kipper 1986: 161), including, for example, the clinical (e.g. Alperson 1976; Blume 1971), educational (Carpenter 1968), industrial (Speroff 1955; Kelly *et al.* 1957), in the training of interpersonal communication (Johnson 1971b), in the dynamics of bargaining, and in the study of attitude change (e.g. Johnson 1967, 1971a; Johnson and Dustin 1970; Muney and Deutsch 1968). However, in her reinterpretation of the literature, Carlson-Sabelli (1989) found that most research on role reversal involved individuals playing roles of fantasy characters and that there is still insufficient research supporting claims about role reversal between real people.

DEFINITION

Strictly speaking, role reversal means precisely what it says: a reversal of roles: a daughter reversing roles with her mother, a husband with his wife, a student with his teacher or a persecutor with his victim. While the (social or 'sociodramatic') roles involved in such role reversals are usually complementary and interdependent – one does not exist without the other – they are also opposites that strive for unity. Each side is encouraged to understand the point of view of its own counterpart and to find a peaceful way of co-existence. According to Brind and Brind role reversal:

> naturally compels the protagonist to deepen and to widen his empathic identification with the opponent, just as this same process compels him to see his own self-enactment through the eyes of the adversary or the adversary substitute (auxiliary) who now portrays him.
>
> (Brind and Brind 1967: 176)

It is clear, however, that, within psychodrama, the meaning of role reversal has widened to include also non-complementary, psychosomatic, psychological, psychodramatic and spiritual roles which, according to J.L. Moreno (1953: 75) all together comprise 'the tangible aspects of what is known as "ego"'. Any or all of these 'tangible aspects' may be reproduced within another person and the aspects of the other person may be reproduced in oneself. Blatner and Blatner suggested that 'we are all role-reversing all the time in our minds in a kind of ongoing process for maintaining a sense of social bonding' (Blatner and Blatner 1988: 119). However, while such imaginary role reversal is an essential aspect of all mutual relationships, the particular and unique characteristic of psychodramatic role reversal is that it is done in action and not only in imagination. The daughter actually puts herself in the physical place of her mother and imitates her mother's body posture, her manner of speech and her outer behaviour, while her mother does the same with her daughter. Such externalisation and concretisation of inner representations facilitate experiential learning, a process which is mostly non-verbal and physical in nature (Bohart and Wugalter 1991).

To 'reverse' means to convert something to an opposite character or position. What is converted or transposed, however, is not entirely clear. Because, though the technique of role reversal seems remarkably simple (Kipper 1986: 161), further examination reveals a complex intrapsychic and interpersonal process involving at least three interdependent processes: (i) empathic role-taking; (ii) action reproduction; and (iii) role-feedback.

First, when two individuals try to enter into the personal worlds of one another, they use whatever empathic skills they have – emotional, cognitive and behavioural – to take the role of the other and 'become' him or her for a while. Such role-taking may start with a superficial imitation, mirroring or modelling, to become a more deep and complete impersonation, identification and introjection of the other person. Like empathy, role reversal begins with the perception of some subtle cues from the other and proceeds through a co-ordinated use of certain mental abilities, including memory, fantasy, and awareness of one's own feelings and thoughts in the role of the other. The first phase of role reversal thus rests largely on intrapsychic experience, involving some comprehending or perceiving what another person is experiencing within. But, while empathy is one of the basic principles in the technique of role reversal, Moreno emphasised that empathy alone cannot explain the process of role reversal: 'concepts like "spontaneity states", "the warming-up process", "tele" and "clustering of roles" are necessary for a proper interpretation' (Moreno 1972: 259).

Second, whether correct or incorrect in their comprehension, the individuals involved in role reversal try to reproduce and report in a subjective manner what they perceived in the other. In the words of Moreno, the person taking the role of the other 'is not only feeling but doing; he is both constructing and reconstructing a present or an absentee subject in a specific role relation. Often it matters little whether the reconstruction is an identical copy of a natural setting, as long as he projects the dynamic atmosphere of the setting; this may be more impressive than its identical copy' (Moreno 1972: 259).

Finally, role reversal involves responses which are based, not only on how I perceive you, but how I perceive how you perceive me, and so forth (cf. Laing 1961). In the third phase of role-feedback, the individuals are required to reflect on their own as well as the other person's responses and on the mutual interaction. The 'observing self' must watch and notice behaviour 'from the outside' both when being in their own role and in the other person's. As Moreno pointed out, at the same time as people become emotionally involved in one another, 'they are required to observe themselves in action very closely; to register continuously as they warm up to the role what this role does to them and what they do to it' (Moreno 1972: 259).

Obviously, complete role reversal is impossible. We can never fully conceptualise the feelings, attitudes and motives of another person, and much less reproduce what we perceived. We all differ in our ability to put ourselves in the position of another person and in our skill to reproduce the inner experience of that other person in action. The ability to role-reverse is not only dependent on a certain degree of intellectual, imaginative, emotional and interpersonal functioning, but also on role-taking and role-playing skills which are insufficiently developed in many persons. While some people may learn to take the role of another through playful warm-up and spontaneity training, others will have difficulty in role-reversing because of 'mental rigidity' (Sylvester 1970) or unwillingness to suspend disbelief.

The ability to role-reverse properly was viewed by J.L. Moreno and Z.T. Moreno (1955) as essential for the social growth of the child, developing around the age of 3 years when the child leaves the egocentric phase and is able to recognise a 'you' (Leutz 1974). It can only develop if the child itself has received proper doubling and role reversal from the parents (Z.T. Moreno 1975) and it is then 'an indicator of the freedom from the auxiliary ego, the mother and the mother substitute' (J.L. Moreno 1972: 63). The corresponding and congruous psychoanalytic theories of psychosocial development were formulated by, for example, Freud, Klein, Kohut and Mahler who also have important links with social psychology although their proponents do not specifically acknowledge those links.

A further requirement for proper role reversal seems to be a balanced personality, a certain degree of ego strength and ordinary sensory perception. Role-reversal ability grows with personality development, and especially the separation of 'I' and 'You' – the achievement of personal identity and sense of separateness from parents – described below in terms of object relations theory. Moreover, the process of role-feedback requires a differentiation between 'I' and 'Me' – the ability to exist both in the present and to reflect on the experience through an observing self as described below in terms of social psychology. Patients who have severe defects or conflicts in these areas, such as narcissistic, paranoid, psychotic, autistic or severe personality disorders, will have difficulties to role-reverse with real people (J.L. Moreno and Z.T. Moreno 1955; Starr 1977). With such populations, role reversal should be used sparingly or not at all so as not to confuse their limited sense of self. Rather than using role reversal with these patients, Goldman and Morrison (1984) suggested that the auxiliary be put in role with a 'main message' of the significant other.

Finally, while differences between people may be the very reason for role reversal in the first place, such differences will make it more difficult to role-reverse. In the words of Moreno and Moreno, 'the technique of role reversal is the more effective the nearer in psychological, social and ethnic proximity the two individuals are' (1959: 155). For example, in a recent open session on psychodrama, Barbara who was born in London had difficulty in role-reversing with Li from Vietnam, because she did not understand Li's cultural heritage.

THERAPEUTIC VALUE OF ROLE REVERSAL

The therapeutic value of role reversal is unclear. While most psycho-dramatists of the classical tradition maintain that role reversal is effective in a wide variety of situations, some psychoanalytic psychodramatists dispute its benefits. For example, according to Basquin and co-workers: 'role reversal is useless, even calamitous, because it disdains the patient's defenses, does not ease the expression of unconscious needs and thus it threatens to block the thematic development' (Basquin *et al.* 1981: 82). In a strong refutation of their thesis, Kruger says that 'role reversal is a means to reduce defense by projection and identification. By structuring and integrating interpersonal processes it leads the individual out of isolation and dissociation' (Kruger 1989: 45).

However, while role reversal should be rightfully regarded as one of the most effective techniques of psychodrama, it should not be used indiscri-minately in all situations and for all protagonists. For example, in a case report of a sexually abused adult, Karp was careful not to role-reverse the young woman into any of the male abuser roles because:

> to understand the reasons behind their action was not the task of this session. Too many victims get lost in an attempt to understand and forgive. They can trap themselves in a sea of rationalizations from which they may never return.
>
> (Karp 1991: 109)

TWO FORMS OF ROLE REVERSAL

Two major forms of role reversal were differentiated in the literature. The original form, called 'in situ' (Z.T. Moreno 1959: 241), 'proper' (Moreno *et al.* 1955: 141) or 'classical' (Carlson-Sabelli 1989) role reversal, involved at least two real persons, both present, reversing roles with each other. The second form was called 'incomplete' role reversal by Carlson-Sabelli and Sabelli (1984) because one of the persons involved in the interpersonal situation was absent and represented by a stand-in ('the auxiliary'). I prefer to use the more descriptive terms 'reciprocal' and 'representational' role reversal to differentiate between the two forms, because it is my feeling that the earlier designations: proper/improper, complete/incomplete and classical/modern, convey an unnecessary and erroneous value judgement about the interaction taking place.

The two forms of role reversal have somewhat different goals and may be regarded as functioning within two different theoretical frames of reference. Reciprocal role reversal, based on social psychology, is used mainly as an aid for dealing with people in the outer world, as a way of correcting biased perceptions of other people and receiving feedback of oneself and as an interpersonal conflict resolution technique. Representational role reversal, based on object relations theory, is used more as an aid for the externalisation and interpolation of the inner world of one protagonist. The two forms of role reversal will be further discussed below.

Reciprocal role reversal and social psychology

Reciprocal role reversal aims at facilitating the process of socialisation, the process of social learning by which people (usually children) come to recognise, practise and identify with the values, attitudes and basic belief structures of the dominant institutions and representatives of their society. As such, reciprocal role reversal may be used to assimilate the social norms (group-defined standards concerning what behaviours are acceptable or objectionable in given situations). The most suitable rationale for this technique may be found within social psychology.

Social psychology maintains that children develop in interaction with their environment and especially with certain important others who either stimulate or inhibit their emotional and cognitive growth as well as their sense of self. These significant others convey an outer social reality with which the child can identify. In the dialogue with this outer social reality, the child becomes an object for itself; thus developing a self as object ('Me'). The self as object, or the social self, is the first conception of a self and grows from the perceptions and responses of other people. Cooley (1902) used the term 'Looking-glass Self' to describe this aspect, which develops from the reflective experience of a person looking at him- or herself through other people as in a mirror. Similarly, Moreno and Moreno (1959) described how children use their parents as natural untrained auxiliary ego objects who help the infant get started in life through mirroring.

Sooner or later, however, the child starts to question its view of outer social reality and the self as subject ('I') develops. This subjective part of the self responds from within, in the here and now, on the spur of the moment. While self as object is conventional, demanding socialisation and conformity, the self as subject breaks out in spontaneous, uninhibited and sometimes impulsive actions. Mead pointed out that 'it is through taking the role of the other that a person is able to come back on himself and so direct his own process of communication' (Mead 1934: 253).

Indeed, while socialisation is a necessary part of all interpersonal functioning, strengthening the self as subject is an important part of psychodrama. Moreno felt that 'taking the role of the other is a dead end. The turning point is how to vitalize and change the [conserved] roles, how to become a "rolechanger" and "roleplayer"' (Moreno 1953: 691). In reciprocal role reversal, the dialectic process between 'I' and 'Me' is re-enacted so that both objectification and subjectification can again merge and differentiate so that a new intrapsychic balance is achieved. According to Carlson-Sabelli and Sabelli:

> role reversal allows the protagonist to become aware of his interpreta-
> tions and hold them up for re-examination, thereby providing a way to
> go beyond them. We often uncritically accept what we believe while we
> interpret and critically evaluate the ideas of others. Through the role
> reversal, the protagonist sees himself as an object and experiences
> others as subject.
>
> (Carlson-Sabelli and Sabelli 1984: 166)

From this theoretical basis, reciprocal role reversal may be used to modify biased person perception, to resolve interpersonal conflicts and to increase interpersonal functioning and empathy. These applications will be further discussed below.

Correction of biased perceptions

The first and most obvious application of reciprocal role reversal is to help two persons understand one another better and to modify whatever erroneous conceptions they may have about the other person. For example, William seemed to be looking at everybody 'from above', as if he felt that he was better than everybody else. But when Eva reversed roles with him, she felt that his apparent distance was more a sign of his low self-esteem and fear of being compared to others in the group. This result of reciprocal role reversal involves a change of the perception of *another* person.

In contrast, reciprocal role reversal can also change the view we have about ourselves. In such cases, the immediate feedback and mirror image of how we are seen by others and why we are treated in a certain manner make our own roles more clear. For example, in a recent psychodrama group, Tom kept interrupting every other group member who was talking. This behaviour annoyed Carin who had difficulties expressing herself in the first place. In a reciprocal role reversal between them, Tom understood and sympathised with Carin's position and later altered his dominating behaviour. Carin, in her turn, experienced the joy of being the centre of attention which gave her some incentive to later share with the group her old dream of being an actress.

Ideally, role reversal produces a shift in perception so that both persons can see the other and themselves in a new and fresh way. The goal is not 'insight' or awareness in itself, but spontaneity; to look at an old situation differently, or to reorganise old cognitive patterns in a way which facilitates more adequate behaviour (Yablonsky and Enneis 1956). In the words of Zerka Moreno:

> the patient has 'taken unto himself' with greater or lesser success, those persons, situations, experiences and perceptions from which he is now suffering. In order to overcome the distortions and manifestations of imbalance, he has to reintegrate them on a new level. Role reversal is one of the methods par excellence in achieving this, so that he can reintegrate, redigest and grow beyond those experiences which are of negative impact, free himself and become more spontaneous along positive lines.
>
> (Z.T. Moreno 1959: 238)

Many examples of reciprocal role reversals reported in the literature concern child-rearing situations between parents and their children. For example, after an argument between a mother and her daughter regarding what clothing the child should wear, role reversal produced the following remark by the mother: 'Am I really as aggressive as Kay portrayed me? My poor Kay!' (Z.T. Moreno 1959: 241). This implies a shift in position of the parent. In contrast, Leutz (1974: 47) reported a situation in which a son did not want to go to bed. After role reversal, the son seemed to accept the position of the mother and went to bed with a smile. Thus, while some of the examples emphasise changing the point of view of the parent and others emphasise a behaviour modification of the child, ideally the procedure will produce a widening frame of reference in both of them.

In a variety of interpersonal situations, people rely on simple judgemental strategies which tend to mislead them. Nisbett and Ross (1980) traced the source of many such inferential errors to the tendency of people to overutilise pre-existing 'knowledge structures,' or 'schemas', which frequently lead to biased judgements about people, to transference, prejudices, stereotyped attitudes and to other faulty causal attributions of behaviour (Heider 1958). In such cases, the aim of reciprocal role reversal is to widen the perceptual field and to correct the earlier 'narrow-minded' interpretations of the world. According to Williams (1989), changing old code books and establishing new ideas is a prime goal of psychodrama. By exploring the belief aspect of a role through role reversal, various attitudes, assumptions, prejudices, convictions and expectations which guide the members in their behaviour are revealed and explored.

For example, when Eva chose someone else to become the protagonist, her friend Marianne was very offended. Marianne attributed Eva's choice to her jealousy over Marianne's privileged position with the leader. However, by altering Eva's and Marianne's perspectives through reciprocal role reversal, they changed their causal assessments and cleared up their misunderstandings.

Interpersonal conflict resolution

Reciprocal role reversal is frequently recommended as a remedy for interpersonal conflict resolution. The assumption behind this recommendation is that if antagonists reverse roles with one another, they will be forced to take a new view of the situation and hopefully reconciliate their differences. According to Bratter (1967), this creates a kind of dialectic thesis and antithesis that, if successful, may produce a kind of synthesis or merging of two opposing positions. Williams (1989) argued that the specific value of such a procedure is that it enables a person to embody both sides of the dialectic dyad which is inherent in recurring conflicts.

As an illustration from a psychodrama group, let's consider the following interchange between two group members, Philip and Pamela. It started out by Philip coming late to a psychodrama session. Pamela told Philip that she resented him for not coming in time and that she felt Philip was not serious about the group.

'I don't understand what you are angry about', Philip responded. 'I was in an important meeting and it was impossible for me to come here earlier.'

'Well, then I'll explain', Pamela snapped. 'I expect you to come on time to our sessions, but you always have good excuses for coming late and you don't consider what it does to the group.'

'I'm sorry you are upset', Philip said, 'but you are such a nuisance when you don't get what you want.'

'I didn't come here to be insulted', Pamela yelled, now red in the face and apparently upset. 'You are such an idiot . . . .'.

'Oh really', Philip said with thinly disguised irritation. 'You're not precisely a genius yourself.'

'Don't "Oh really" me!' Pamela answered, leaning forwards in her chair. 'I'm warning you, Philip, if you don't come in time next week, we will lock the door and leave you outside!'

Philip looked at Pamela with wrathful indigation. 'If you want me out of the group, just say so!'

The friction between Pamela and Philip gradually escalated until it reached a point of mutual resentment. What had started out as a personal disappointment rapidly developed into an open confrontation with mutual misunderstandings, insults and a search for revenge. The interaction surprised the group who had no idea what had hit it. The group leader, himself startled by the rapid eruption of tensions, tried to remain calm while reflecting on something suitable to say or to do. In an attempt to work out the differences between them, he suggested that Philip and Pamela reverse roles with one another.

After some initial resistance, Philip and Pamela agreed to reverse roles and, as they slowly warmed up to the role of the other, they repeated the earlier exchange of accusations. Before long, however, they started to argue as vehemently as before, but from their opposite positions. When they had finally ventilated their anger and expressed their fantasies about what was going on within the other person, they became silent, looking seriously at one another. It became clear that something else was going on between them besides the apparent fight; a kind of appreciation and attraction of differences, Suddenly they started to smile and Philip (still in the role of Pamela) said:

'You're a bastard Philip! You don't care about anyone except yourself.'

'Well, I'm glad you care about me', Pamela answered in the role of Philip. 'I wish more people would care as much as you do.'

'I'm sorry I hurt your feelings', Philip responded as himself, now falling out of role. 'I didn't know you cared so much!'

'Well, I do', Pamela said, 'that's why I get so offended when you come late. If you want me to continue to care, please come on time next week.'

The goal of reciprocal role reversal is to generate 'tele'; that almost mystical 'two-way feeling' for the 'actual make-up of another person' (Moreno and Moreno 1959: 6). Tele is not based on transference or other displaced feelings and perceptions. It carries with it an authentic meeting, or encounter, in which people take each other for what and whom they are. As such, it can be characterised as a kind of 'inter-personal chemistry' (Kellermann 1992: 102).

However, reciprocal role reversal does not automatically produce a change of mind in any of the involved persons. Unfortunately, positive outcomes of reciprocal role reversals in interpersonal and intergroup conflicts are rare and reconciliation is usually hard to achieve. Rather, it is my experience that two people who are involved in a head-on collision are stubbornly unwilling to truly reverse roles with one another as long as they conceive the other person as an enemy. If they do agree to reverse roles, they do so for a short period of time, repeating the main message of their opponent and then resort to their old position of 'I am right and you are wrong.' Consequently, Moreno's vision that lasting peace between people and nations will be achieved if the capacity to reverse roles is only cultivated, must therefore be considered naive and utopian.

Moreover, Carlson-Sabelli (1989) did not find enough research evidence to verify the assumption that reciprocal role reversal will promote reconciliation and mutual understanding between parties in conflict (Cohen 1951; Speroff 1955; Rogers 1965; Sylvester 1970; Deutsch 1973). It seems more likely that reciprocal role reversal 'will cause individuals who hold opposing attitudes to come closer together if their initial positions are compatible but will force them further apart if their initial attitudes are incompatible' (Johnson and Dustin 1970: 149). Thus, while we still know too little about the effects of reciprocal role reversal to recommend the blind use of it in all conflictual situations, it is likely that reciprocal role reversal will be more effective in co-operative relations than in competitive ones (Deutsch 1973).

It is my position, dependent on what the fight is all about, that any effort towards interpersonal conflict resolution in psychodrama must take into account at least four levels of intervention (Kellermann 1993): (i) the biosocial–emotional which is based on encounter and the ventilation of aggression; (ii) the intrapsychic which is based on the correction of perceptual distortions; (iii) the interpersonal which is based on mediation and interaction-analysis; and (iv) the group-as-a-whole perspective which is based on sociodrama and group analysis. Reciprocal role reversal would be especially suitable in the second phase in order to reclaim displaced emotions and re-integrate them within oneself (see the following section on object relations theory). It is also suitable in the third phase in which more adequate interpersonal communication can be facilitated, but it should not be regarded as the single, most efficacious remedy for interpersonal tensions.

Representational role reversal and object relations theory

In contrast to reciprocal role reversal which involves two protagonists, representational role reversal is an intrapsychic process, dealing only with one person. The absent other person is portrayed by an auxiliary who becomes the role-reversing partner. Auxiliaries are not only used to portray the roles of absent actual persons, or their inner representations, but also of the protagonist's self (parts or whole), and/or of the inner symbolic world at large. In fact, auxiliaries may portray anyone or anything with whom a protagonist has an inner relationship. For example, in one and the same psychodrama James selected group members to play the roles of his parents, wife and children and also of the part of himself which kept blaming him for not being a good-enough son, husband and father. Later, he also picked someone to play his car, an inanimate object of significant symbolic value. When reversing roles with these inner images, James got an opportunity to externalise his emotional attachments and to learn to deal with them in a more adaptive manner.

Representational role reversal may be understood from the perspective of traditional psychoanalytic concepts and especially from the point of view of psychoanalytic object relations theory (Polansky and Harkins 1969;

Blatner and Blatner 1988; Holmes 1992). Object relations theory has come to refer to a general theory of the structures in the mind that preserve and organise interpersonal experiences. It is based on the assumption that people internalise important people and events which then become representations of anything that was previously perceived; inner pictures or memory images of ourselves (self-representation), of others (object representation) and of the world at large (symbolic representation). Mental representations also include the relations which existed between ourselves and others and the relations between others in varying degrees of veridicality and bound together by affects (Sandler and Sandler 1978). The complete structure of these inner representations, formed in early childhood, develop into an inner drama in which we play all the roles and which continues to influence us in all aspects of life.

Psychodrama, and especially representational role reversal, offers an extraordinarily powerful instrument for the externalisation (and sometimes for the interpolation) of our internalised mental images so that 'they are summoned to life and made to appear in a three-dimensional space' (Sandler and Rosenblatt 1962) as an inner drama on a stage within a theatre. This inner drama may be reconstructed through role reversal so that the images of 'I-and-You' and 'I-and-It' may again be put up for examination.

The main purpose of representational role reversal is not to deal with the realities of the outer world, but to come to terms with one's inner world and to reach some inner peace and self-integration. As a general 'rule', Zerka Moreno suggested that 'the subject must act out "his truth," as he feels and perceives it, in a completely subjective manner (no matter how distorted this appears to the spectator)' (Moreno 1959: 234). This rule, according to Carlson-Sabelli and Sabelli (1984), creates a problem for the psychodramatist who frequently recognises the need of many protagonists to differentiate real perception from misperception. As a general guideline, they agree that psychodramatists should give supremacy to subjective reality but add that objective reality should be given priority in order to enable protagonists to see things as they really are. For example, a patient who was reluctant to receive treatment for a terminal illness had to be helped through role reversal to first recognise objective reality before he agreed to receive treatment (subjective).

Another goal of representational role reversal is to encourage protagonists to take more responsibility for their own decisions. As such, role reversal emphasises the active participation of protagonists in the instillation of change. For example, when Yvonne asked the auxiliary who portrayed her dead mother to forgive her, she was instructed to reverse roles and decide for herself if she was ready for forgiveness or not. In another psychodrama, Eli asked the group leader what to do with his unhappy marriage. But instead of answering Eli's question, the group leader suggested that Eli reverse roles with the leader and, in this role he said: 'Well, first you have to take a more active role in your life and make your own decisions.' A similar focus on self-direction was conveyed by Ruscombe-King who urged alcohol abusers to reverse roles with 'alcohol'. Talking to an empty bottle of alcohol, Tom said: 'You make me feel lousy!' In the role of 'alcohol', he answered: 'I don't force you to drink me!' (Ruscombe-King 1991: 165).

The ultimate focus on responsibility, however, is of course to role-reverse with God himself. In a case report described by Nolte *et al.* (1975), Cinda asked God: 'Why did you take my father away from me?' While attempting to answer her own question in the role of God, Cinda was confronted with her own conceptions of existence and, by making the death of her father more meaningful, she was provided with some comfort in her grief.

Moreno described the dynamics of representational role reversal in the following eloquent manner:

> As the subject takes part in the production and warms up to the figures and figure-heads of his own private world he attains tremendous satisfactions which take him far beyond anything he has ever experienced; he has invested so much of his own limited energy in the images of his perceptions of father, mother, wife, children, as well as in certain images which live a foreign existence within him, delusions and hallucinations of all sorts, that he has lost a great deal of spontaneity, productivity and power for himself. They have taken his riches away and he has become poor, weak and sick. The psychodrama gives back to him all the investments he had made in the extraneous adventures of his mind. He takes his father, mother, sweethearts, delusions and hallucinations unto himself and the energies which he has invested in them, they return by actually living through the role of his father or his employer, his friends or his enemies; by reversing roles with them he is already learning many things about them which life does not provide him. When he can be the persons he hallucinates, not only do they lose their power and magic spell over him but he gains their power for himself. His own self has an opportunity to find and reorganize itself, to put the elements together which may have been kept apart by insidious forces, to integrate them and to attain a sense of power and of relief.
>
> (Moreno 1953: 85)

From the above quote, it is interesting to note that Moreno employed classical psychoanalytic language in his attempt to describe the process of representational role reversal as 'energies invested in inner images'. The emphasis on the internalisation of a good object as a basis for the growth of an independent and integrated self, is apparent. Furthermore, narcissistic processes such as idealisation, splitting, projection, identification and projective identification, which may be viewed both as pathological and as a part of normal development, all have important functions in the process of role reversal (see Kruger 1989). Thus, we may conclude that representational role reversal in itself functions to facilitate and accelerate the separation–individuation process (Mahler 1975) for the not-too-severely-disturbed patient.

EPILOGUE

Mary stands facing her 8-year-old daughter who wants to be held by her. But Mary feels uncomfortable with her daughter's clinging and pushes her away. 'I know it is good for you to be close to me and your need is very real. But every time you cling on me, I feel terrible. And when I push you away, I feel even worse because it makes me feel guilty, like I'm rejecting you.' As if searching for a clue of love in mother's eyes, the daughter looks at Mary with penetrating and reproaching eyes. Mary says: 'I love you! But I can't stand it when you stare at me like that!' In role reversal, Mary looks at herself as if in a mirror. She wants her mother to hold her and to look at her and she stares at her in order to catch a glimpse of her mother's eyes. 'Please, look at me mother . . .'. But, in the middle of the sentence, she becomes silent. Mary is again thrown back to her own childhood and her own mother's rejection. Grandmother is then brought into the scene. Mary says that grandmother has an intuitive, warm relation to Mary's daughter. Mary watches as grandmother and daughter embrace, and then she joins them and they start to move, including all generations of mothers and daughters in their dance.

REFERENCES

Abele-Brehm, A. (1989) 'Psychodrama and social psychology', *International Journal of Small Group Research* 5: 29–46.

Alperson, J.R. (1976) 'Gone with the wind: role-reversal desensitization for a wind phobic client', *Behavior Therapy* 7: 405–7.

Basquin, M., Testemale-Monod, G., Dubuisson, P. and Samuel-Lajeunesse, B. (1981) *Analytisches Psychodrama, Bd. 1: Das Psychodrama als Methode in der Psychoanalyse*, Paderborn: Jungfermann.

Blatner, A. and Blatner, A. (1988) *Foundations of Psychodrama: History, theory and practice*, New York: Springer.

Blume, S.B. (1971) 'Group role reversal as a teaching technique in an alcoholism rehabilitation unit', *Group Psychotherapy and Psychodrama* 24: 135–7.

Bohart, A.C. and Wugatter, S. (1991) 'Change in experiential knowing as a common dimension in psychotherapy', *Psychotherapy: Theory, Research, Practice* 10: 14–37.

Bratter, T. (1967) 'Dynamics of role reversal', *Group Psychotherapy* 20: 88–94.

Brind, A.B. and Brind, N. (1967) 'Role reversal', *Group Psychotherapy* 20: 173–7.

Buber, M. (1923) *I and Thou*, Edinburgh: Clark (English translation, 1970).

Carlson-Sabelli, L. (1989) 'Role reversal – a concept analysis and reinterpretation of the research literature', *Journal of Group Psychotherapy, Psychodrama and Sociometry* 42: 139–52.

Carlson-Sabelli, L. and Sabelli, H.C. (1984) 'Reality, perception, and the role reversal', *Journal of Group Psychotherapy, Psychodrama and Sociometry* 36: 162–74.

Carpenter, J.R. (1968) 'Role reversal in the classroom', *Group Psychotherapy* 21: 155–67.

Cohen, J. (1951) 'The technique of role reversal: a preliminary note', *Occupational Psychology* 25: 64–6.

Cooley, C.H. (1902) *Human Nature and Social Order*, New York: Scribners. (Reprinted New York: Free Press, 1956.)

Deutsch, M. (1973) *The Resolution of Conflict: Constructive and destructive processes*, New Haven: Yale University Press.

Goldman, E.E. and Morrison, D.S. (1984) *Psychodrama: Experience and process*, Dubuque, Iowa: Kendall/Hunt.

Hare, A.P. (1986) 'Moreno's contribution to social psychology', *Journal of Group Psychotherapy, Psychodrama and Sociometry* 39: 85–94.

Heider, F. (1958) *The Psychology of Interpersonal Relations*, New York: Wiley.

Holmes, P. (1992) *The Inner World Outside: Object relations theory and psychodrama*, London: Routledge.

Johnson, D.W. (1967) 'The use of role reversal in intergroup competition', *Journal of Personality and Social Psychology* 7: 135–41.

Johnson, D.W. (1971a) 'Effectiveness of role reversal: actor or listener', *Psychological Reports* 28: 275–82.

—— (1971b) 'Role reversal: a summary and review of the research', *International Journal of Group Tensions* 1: 318–34.

Johnson, D.W. and Dustin, R. (1970) 'The initiation of cooperation through role reversal', *Journal of Social Psychology* 82: 193–203.

Karp, M. (1991) 'Psychodrama and piccalilli: residential treatment of a sexually abused adult', in P. Holmes and M. Karp (eds) *Psychodrama: Inspiration and technique*, London: Routledge.

Kellermann, P.F. (1992) *Focus on Psychodrama: The therapeutic aspects of psychodrama*, London: Jessica Kingsley.

—— (1993) 'Conflict resolution in psychodrama', Lecture presented at the Department of Psychiatry, St Goran's Hospital, Stockholm, Sweden, 17 February.

Kelly, J.G., Blake, R.R. and Stromberg, C.E. (1957) 'The effect of role training on role reversal', *Group Psychotherapy* 10: 95–104.

Kipper, D.A. (1986) *Psychotherapy Through Clinical Role Playing*, New York: Brunner/Mazel.

Kruger, R. (1989) 'Der Rollentausch und seine tiefen-psychologischen Funktionen', *Psychodrama: Zeitschrift für Theorie und Praxis* 1: 45–67.

Laing, R.D. (1961) *Self and Others*, London: Tavistock.

Leutz, G. (1974) *Psychodrama: Theorie und Praxis*, Berlin: Springer.

Mahler, M.S. (1975) *The Psychological Birth and the Human Infant*, New York: Basic Books.

Marineau, R.F. (1989) *Jacob Levy Moreno 1889–1974*, London and New York: Tavistock/Routledge.

Mead, G.H. (1934) *Mind, Self and Society*, Chicago: University of Chicago Press.

Moreno, J.L. (1914) *Einladung zu einer Begegnung*, Vienna: Anzengruber Verlag. Translated by J.L. Moreno.

—— (1940) 'Psychodramatic treatment of psychoses', *Sociometry* 2: 123–9.

—— (1953) *Who Shall Survive?* New York: Beacon House.

—— (1972) *Psychodrama*, vol. 1, New York: Beacon House.

Moreno, J.L. and Moreno, Z.T. (1959) *Psychodrama*, vol. 2, New York: Beacon House.

Moreno, J.L., Moreno, Z.T., and Moreno, J.D. (1955) 'The discovery of the spontaneous man with special emphasis upon the technique of role reversal', *Group Psychotherapy* 8: 103–29. (Reprinted in 1959, *Psychodrama*, vol. 2, New York: Beacon House, pp. 135–58.)

Moreno, Z.T. (1959) 'A survey of psychodramatic techniques', *Group Psychotherapy* 18: 73–86. (Reprinted in 1969, *Psychodrama*, vol. 3, New York: Beacon House, pp. 233–46).

—— (1975) 'The significance of double and role reversal for cosmic man', *Group Psychotherapy and Psychodrama* 28: 55–9.

Muney, B.F. and Deutsch, M. (1968) 'The effect of role reversal during discussion of opposing view points', *Journal of Conflict Resolution* 12: 345–46.

Nisbett, R. and Ross, L. (1980) *Human Inference: Strategies and shortcomings of social judgment*, Englewood Cliffs, NJ: Prentice-Hall.

Nolte, J., Smallwood, C. and Weistart, J. (1975) 'Role reversal with God', *Group Psychotherapy and Psychodrama* 28: 70–6.

Polansky, N.A. and Harkins, E.B. (1969) 'Psychodrama as an element in hospital treatment', *Psychiatry* 32: 74–87.

Rogers, C.R. (1965) 'Dealing with psychological tensions', *Journal of Applied Behavioral Science* 1: 6–29.

Ruscombe-King, G. (1991) 'Hide and seek: the psychodramatist and the alcoholic', in P. Holmes and M. Karp (eds) *Psychodrama: Inspiration and technique*, London: Routledge.

Sandler, J. and Rosenblatt, B. (1962) 'The concept of the representational world', *Psychoanalytic Study of the Child* 17: 128–45.

Sandler, J. and Sandler, A.-M. (1978) 'On the development of object relationships and affects', *International Journal of Psycho-Analysis* 59: 285–96.

Speroff, B.J. (1955) 'Empathy and role reversal as factors in industrial harmony', *Journal of Social Psychology* 41: 163–5.

Starr, A. (1977) *Psychodrama: Rehearsal for living*, Chicago: Nelson-Hall.

Sylvester, J.D. (1970) 'Mental rigidity and the method of role reversal', *Studia Psychologica* 12: 151–6.

Williams, A. (1989) *The Passionate Technique: Strategic psychodrama with individuals, families and groups*, New York: Routledge, Chapman & Hall.

Yablonsky, L. and Enneis, J.M. (1956) 'Psychodrama theory and practice', in F. Fromm-Reichmann and J.L. Moreno (eds) *Progress in Psychotherapy*, vol. 1, New York: Grune & Stratton.

Chapter 12

The dynamics of interpersonal preference

Commentary

In this chapter Adam Blatner looks at relationships and the forces that govern them both in a consciously and unconsciously ordered way. Moreno spoke of the psyche as existing between two people. In psychodrama, the therapeutic process addresses what does and does not happen between people in relationship. Tele was his way of describing human interactions from a non-clinical perspective, as opposed to Freud's more reductionist approach. Blatner describes the usefulness of this concept in dealing with people and places due emphasis on the humanistic perspective that was so much a feature of Moreno's work with clients. He develops the concept in a clear and direct way that brings this sometimes neglected area of Moreno's work back to centre stage and shows how it can illuminate the dynamics in a group.

Tele

Adam Blatner

INTRODUCTION

While Freud addressed repression in the psychodynamics of the individual, Moreno noticed the underlying sociodynamics of groups. He saw that there were interactions which were being ignored and overridden in many group situations which resulted in disharmony and dysfunction. Moreno intuited 'lines' of attraction or repulsion between people, which could be drawn on paper as sociograms representing the 'flow of feeling' he called 'tele'. In this sense, Moreno was an early 'systems' theorist who appreciated that interpersonal dynamics could occur not just in the minds of the individuals involved, but also in a more complex fashion in the space or field between them.

Tele is a term coined by J.L. Moreno to describe 'the process which attracts individuals to one another or which repels them' (Moreno 1937: 213). It refers to the fact that in any group, each individual experiences attraction, neutrality, mixed feelings or repulsion towards and from each of the other people. Yet, such feelings are often not registered consciously and even more rarely openly discussed. The significance of the concept of tele is that it brings these subtle social dynamics into explicit consciousness. 'Finding a name for something is a way of conjuring its existence, of making it possible for people to see a pattern where they didn't see anything before' (Rheingold 1988: 3).

The value of the concept of tele is that it can be used by therapists and psychodramatists in their work and their own everyday lives to: (i) become more explicitly aware of interpersonal interactions; (ii) notice tendencies to avoid these awarenesses; (iii) discuss the origins of such avoidances in terms of family and cultural background; (iv) discuss associated feelings of embarrassment, vulnerability, and concern for evoking such feelings in others; (v) explore the underlying reasons for the various telic reactions; and (vi) help patients to apply the idea of tele in learning how to address all these issues in the group and their own situations.

HISTORICAL ORIGINS

Moreno developed sociometry as a method for bringing these dynamics into the open. Tele's most precise definition is 'what is measured by sociometric tests' (Moreno 1934: 328). Yet, unless one is quite familiar with the method, that definition remains obscure. Moreno's earliest ideas about sociometry addressed the problem of subgroupings formed in refugee camps, schools, and in the workplace by arbitrary assignments from authorities rather than on the expressed preferences of the group members themselves. He noted that when the group could participate in its own formation, greater harmonies and productivity were attained. Ironically, even today this insight continues to be largely ignored.

Sociometry became an instrument of the objective researchers at a time when traditional scientific method had become a value in itself, and because of the phenomenological, subjective nature of tele, they had relatively little use for the term. They generally didn't spend much time working with the groups applying and discussing the results of the testing (Mendelson 1977: 84). Thus, tele is often not even mentioned in most of the professional articles and books about sociometry and psychodrama, and even in those where it is noted, it's generally given only the most superficial and briefest of treatments.

However, in practice, the term is most useful, especially when applied by the people in groups in the course of exploring their own interactions. And so Moreno kept returning to the concept because of its implications for group cohesion, the process of encounter and the essential nature of therapy. Also, he emphasised that the applications of tele and its associated issues transcended the clinical context and included all groups in society. Indeed, he even coined a term for his vision of a more socially oriented psychiatry he called 'sociatry', and the psychodrama journal which he began in 1947 was given that term as its title for the first two years (then changing to *Group Psychotherapy*).

REFLECTIONS ON TERMINOLOGY

Moreno first wrote about tele in 1934 in his major book on sociometry, *Who Shall Survive?* He derived the term from the ancient Greek word for distance: 'Just as we use the words . . . telephone, television, etc. to express action at a distance, so to express the simplest unit of feeling transmitted from one individual towards another we use the term tele' (Moreno 1934: 159; 1953: 314). That is to say that one can experience tele with another person when our eyes meet across a crowded room. Tele operates also when people find themselves in close proximity: our sense of territoriality is offended when others who feel like strangers stand too close, and on the other hand, with certain kinds of very positive tele, we want to hug the other person.

The basic concept of tele is intuitively known even in popular culture. For example, in the late 1960s a song included the phrase, 'She's sending me good vibrations', and a slang word current at the time was 'vibes'. A decade earlier, in the Broadway musical, *Guys and Dolls*, the hero sings to his girl friend about 'chemistry', referring to the mystery of their mutual attraction.

Some other words which allude to telic phenomena include 'rapport', 'click', 'fit', (as in 'goodness of fit'), 'connectedness' and 'resonance'. But a disadvantage of these terms is that they only address the more positive types of feelings and don't allow for different kinds of tele depending on which role or criterion is involved.

Due to the problems entailed by the introduction of a new term, and perhaps in order to avoid the disadvantages of jargon, some writers in the field avoided the use of the word. For example, Hart (1980) in an article on the postulates of sociometry substituted the term 'affiliativeness'. Nehnevajsa (1956) called tele a 'flow of affectivity between individuals'. Carlson-Sabelli and co-workers (1992) referred to 'bonds' and noted the opposing poles of 'choice/attraction' and 'rejection/repulsion'. Still, considering the host of associated concepts to be described, I think it's best that we stay with Moreno's term.

One source of confusion in Moreno's writings about tele is that he used the term in two senses. More generally, he referred to the entire category of preferential interactions including repulsions, indifference, neutralities and ambivalence as well as attractions. His second usage referred to tele in its most positive and reciprocated form in which case it is often associated with such related phenomena as encounter, empathy and group cohesion. In general use, most psychodramatists speak of it in this latter sense, for example, in saying to a prospective auxiliary, 'You seem to be feeling some tele with this protagonist'.

However, we should remember that the term really includes all kinds of interactions, sometimes mixed, sometimes even negative.

NATURAL ORIGINS OF TELE

Tele is an extension of the innate tendencies of organisms to show selectivity. Indeed, Moreno (1934: 158) alluded to a primordial kind of preferential process even at the inorganic level, such as in the process of magnetism, which involves the tendencies of electrons and protons to attract each other and to repel their own kind. Might this be a precursor? In a psychicalistic system of philosophy such as Whitehead's, even atoms 'experience' each other with a quality akin to 'feeling' (Peters 1966). Although we can measure the relative strengths of these interactions, we have no idea *why* this interactive force operates as it does.

In biological systems, even the most primitive one-celled animal will exhibit selectivity over substances it ingests and what environments it moves towards or away from. Higher animals develop their capacities for discrimination in most life functions: eating, choosing a mate, play, etc. In more social species, this selectivity shows greater complexity in matters of territoriality, the herd instinct and patterns of dominance and submission.

Humans exhibit these patterns also, and more, because of the complexity of the nervous system, our species overlays these instincts with elaborate systems of associations, symbols, images, and emotions. The imaginal aspects of instinctual processes constitute the essence of what Carl G. Jung called 'archetypes', and in this sense tele may be considered a psychological function operating at a fundamental level (Samuels *et al.* 1986).

Preference is a fundamental psychological function (Northway 1967: 46–7), and this applies to all manner of activities: food, music, art, hair styles, clothes, religious practices, etc. Tele is an extension of this: 'Just as man has an aversion–affection continuum of biological feeling within himself (liking or disliking certain foods, odours, etc.), he also has a flow of affection or disaffection between himself and others, be they single persons or groups' (Bischof 1964: 364). However, the interpersonal dynamic involving either positive or negative *reciprocity* between persons makes the phenomenon of tele somewhat more complex than mere preference. Reciprocity, a key component of tele, reflects the human capacity to perceive or imagine how others feel about the relationship (Moreno 1956a: 15). The sense of a feeling being reciprocated tends to intensify that feeling, whether it be attraction, indifference or repulsion.

Although the term 'tele' has been applied with regard to objects or symbols (Bischof 1964: 366; Starr 1977: 6), I think it is an unnecessary dilution of the concept because there is no reciprocity with an object and because the term 'preference' can be used just as well. The point, though is that tele is an extension of our basic capacity for preference, and as will be discussed further on, it behoves us to cultivate our awareness of our preferences and to become conscious of the reasons for those preferences.

PSYCHOSOCIAL FEATURES OF TELE

Mental functioning includes more than cognition, which involves such activities as perceiving, co-ordinating, thinking, remembering, symbolising and believing. There is also the category called 'conation', which involves such activities as wanting, willing, desiring, motivation, intention and preference. Conation is more closely associated with affects and feelings, and conative processes emerge earlier in development than cognitive ones. It is clear that tele is primarily an extension of this conative function.

However, it should be noted that as an individual matures, tele begins to include an increasing proportion of cognitive processing (Moreno 1952:

155). In order for tele to be reciprocated, an individual needs to be able to assess the realistic qualities of the other person. This is called 'telic sensitivity' (Moreno 1959a). Here is where role training and perceptual sociometric procedures can be helpful. People need to have some opportunities to explore their interpersonal networks in supportive settings, such as classes dealing with applied social psychology.

Another way to think about tele is that it is the basis of the more spontaneous and informal types of role relationships. These aren't so easily analysed by sociologists, who have mainly addressed the way people relate in 'formal' role relationships, that is, those which can be characterised in terms of their functional expectations, such as parent, employer, team mate, citizen, customer. Informal-role relationships involve those which reflect the processes of peer selection. Groupings at school break-time, in the neighbourhood, those relatives at large family gatherings who break away to chat privately, cliques and clubs, these associations depend on how the group members feel about one another. Thus, while a sociological analysis might outline who are in the formal relations of teachers and students in a school setting, only sociometric procedures could elucidate which teachers or students are more or less popular with others (regarding certain criteria).

Formal relations are determined more by cognitive functions, role definitions, expectations, performances. Informal relations tend to be determined more by conative functions. We may admire someone's skill (cognitive) without necessarily liking that person (conative), and on the other hand, we may find ourselves attracted to someone whom our better judgement warns us against.

In many committees, the actual power of those who are more influential may be based on how well liked or respected they are rather than on their official status. The designated leader in many cases is not the functional leader. In therapy groups, the therapist may at times find that on certain issues or activities another group member exerts more influence than the therapist, perhaps even in a non-constructive fashion.

TELE AS A ROLE-DEPENDENT DYNAMIC

The human psyche is pluralistic, it involves many roles (Blatner 1991). Our tele for others depends on the role relationship in which we find ourselves. This point must be kept in mind. Since tele varies significantly as the nature of the role relationship shifts (Nehnevajsa 1956: 62), a person may feel more preference towards another regarding one aspect of their relationship, and that there is less tele in another area. For example, in a group an individual might select one other group member to work on a project but yet be sexually attracted to a different person and seek the company of a third to attend a sports event. The corollary of this is that any statement about tele needs to be paired with a qualifying statement about the criterion: it lacks precision to say that A 'likes' B, though in certain situations that may be where the process begins. If consciousness is to be raised regarding the nature of that preference, the criterion for that choice must be sought.

Tele also changes according to shifts in needs or context. Lonely people may find that they're less demanding of physical perfection in their prospective dates. Another example would be a traveller in a foreign country who seeks out the companionship of a fellow countryman as the only one who speaks the same language, yet in other settings there would be little else these two had in common.

Not only are external role situations called into more discriminated consciousness: the various inner roles must also be identified. In this sense, a growing sensitivity to one's own tele helps people get in touch with their different 'complexes' or what Rowan (1990) called 'subpersonalities'.

REASONS FOR PREFERENCE

Reciprocity, as mentioned, is just one of many factors contributing to tele in a relationship. Other variables include the following:

- Common goals, tasks, interests, forms of work or recreation
- Attractiveness (e.g., physical, intellectual, social, playful, spiritual, emotional, artistic)
- Role complementarity (e.g., leader/follower, passive/active, dominance/submission)
- Role symmetry, preferring someone who shares similar qualities (e.g., wanting another dominant person, preferring someone who is also easy-going)
- Common background, interests, life style or values
- Intriguing differences which seem 'exotic' or refreshing
- Compatible levels of vitality and ability
- Temperamental similarities or differences
- Familiarity based on consistency or duration of association
- Propinquity, physical proximity, those who are close by
- Transference, similarities to others in one's past
- Prejudices, generalizations based on cultural conditioning

(Blatner 1988b: 131)

Each of these themes in turn contains many subvariables which also overlap, shift with mood and context as well as role.

The first variable mentioned, relating to common interest, leads to a further point of discrimination. Jennings (1947) describes two major subcategories of choices: *sociotelic* and *psychetelic*. Sociotelic choices are based on common interests, such as sharing a certain background or having a similar goal, and they tend to be associated with formal role relationships. Psychetelic choices are based on more personal, idiosyncratic qualities and tend to be associated with informal role relationships. Ann Hale notes that:

> Reasons given for sociotelic criteria tend to be statements about skill, ease in relating, intelligence, quickness or clarity of the person's style and honesty. Reasons given for psychetelic criteria tend to be statements about degree of comfortability, trust, sensitivity, enjoyment of contact and style of communicating.
>
> (Hale 1981: 44)

For example, if a person at a professional conference chooses to attend a workshop because she or he is interested in the topic, her or his relation to the presenter and many of the other people attending the session would be sociotelic in nature. If that person were to choose a workshop because she or he enjoyed the personal qualities of the workshop leader in previous encounters, her or his connection with that leader would be psychetelic.

Psychetelic choices are being made when people group together based on simple mutual attractions rather than any particular role relationship. These occur more readily in relatively unstructured situations, such as at school break-time on a school playground. The value of the distinction between psychetelic and sociotelic choices is that you can more consciously consider which criterion you want to use in a given situation.

Some sociotelic choices are based on utilitarian criteria. The choice of a surgeon for a particular operation might be based on a reputation for technical skill, even if the doctor's bedside manner leaves much to be desired. However, for general care, the choice of family physician might be based on the psychetelic criterion of interpersonal warmth.

On the other hand, there are times when one might decide to affiliate with another person even in situations where there would be negative psychetelic feelings. For instance, you might find yourself organising a political committee with a person whose personality and values differ significantly from your own in order to promote a certain piece of legislation. Socially you would never associate with this person, but practically you need to work together, and indeed, you would seek him or her out because of his or her specific resources or abilities.

TELE AND TRANSFERENCE

One of the most pervasive factors affecting tele is transference, a tendency to overgeneralise on a present relationship based on experiences with similar sorts of people in the past. Transference is a subjective experience, rooted in the individual, and based on fantasy. Tele involves both parties and is in that sense more objective; it is also based more on the realistic elements in both parties and the relationship (Moreno 1959a: 6–10).

In fact, most relationships are a blend of both telic and transferential elements. 'All relationships contain a mixture of reality and fantasy' (Kellermann 1992: 104). In traditional psychoanalytically orientated psychotherapy, most patients develop some degree of transference, the analysis of which is central to the treatment process. Yet these reactions often are based on real qualities or behaviours on the therapist's part, and to this extent are telic in nature (Holmes 1992: 45–6). In everyday relations there are also residues of past expectations which mask the reality of the people involved.

Yet tele is a more general category, one which includes transference, in the sense that the interpersonal relationship includes the reactions of the individuals participating in that field; in this sense, Moreno was a forerunner of what today would be considered a 'systems' perspective (Moreno 1934: 160). From a developmental orientation, tele emerges earlier in life than transference, beginning with the very process of bonding with the parent soon after birth. Transference develops later as the infant becomes able to construct representations of the parent in its mind, and these then become what Moreno might call a 'conserve' which interferes with the spontaneous encounter with what that parent is in the moment.

Positive tele can provoke a positive transference, as liking someone may lead to the development of unrealistic expectations or idealisations. Such interactions, common in romantic involvements, then need to be worked out in time. Negative tele in turn can be magnified into an attitude of hopelessness or hate, especially if the people can find no other roles on which a more congenial alliance can be based.

Countertransference consists of an individual's response to another person's transferential behaviour. Although the term is often applied to therapists in relation to their clients, the process is really broader than that. If someone communicates his expectations to you in a certain fashion that generates a role relationship; if as part of your tendency to 'buy into' that expectation, you also feel some resentment or seduction, that is your countertransference. It is related to another psychoanalytic concept called 'projective identification', which might be more easily understood in the language of role dynamics as 'role reciprocity', Those who fall into becoming helpers to dependent friends, those whose anger becomes triggered by the kinds of 'games' described by Eric Berne (1964), those who react rather than reflect, are caught up in countertransferences. If there is positive tele, that will increase the intensity more than if there is neutral or indifferent tele.

One component of the therapeutic process involves the re-conversion of transferential (and countertransferential) distortions into more realistic, telic interactions. Yet a measure of positive tele is needed in order to create a healing treatment alliance. 'Transference hinders the cure; tele acts in the cure' (Moreno 1955: 319).

DEALING WITH NEGATIVE TELE

Many problems arise because people repress or overreact to their negative telic responses. Helping people to see how this happens is a useful theme in therapy, along with exploring some more constructive ways of dealing with negative tele when it occurs.

There are a variety of response patterns involved. One of these consists of magnifying negative tele into a hostile attitude, and expressing this overtly as rebelliousness or belligerence, or in any of a number of passive–aggressive fashions. Another response is to be placating or even overly friendly, as if good intentions could magically counter this underlying 'poorness of fit'. Perhaps the most insidious and pervasive reaction is unconsciously to fall into the reciprocal role (as mentioned above in the paragraph on countertransference), which reflects a lack of centring in one's 'real self' (Masterson, 1988).

One of the most common issues in therapy is that of fostering patients' individuation. So many have grown up in dysfunctional families or social systems in which as children their natural preferences were discounted. They were expected to acquiesce to the attitudes of their parents – which is part of normal socialisation, but it can be overdone to a pathological degree in families which are egocentrically manipulative. In such cases, the children grow up with habits of overriding their own feelings, and indeed, using reaction formation and counterphobic defences to attempt to be placating and co-dependently friendly even to those with whom they experience (unconscious) negative tele.

Another group of reasons for ignoring tele is that the culture hasn't worked out ways of dealing with it more constructively. This is in part because such experiences are embarrassing, they go against the pervasive attitude that one should (and can) be friendly with everybody. It's helpful to recognise that this is a cultural convention which evolved to foster harmony through denial, but in the light of the technology of group process, such issues can be addressed through the process of encounter and problem-solving. A corollary to the above is that the lack of a sense of how to resolve the implied interpersonal conflict promotes resistance to awareness of negative tele. Therapists can counter these avoidances by helping their patients to learn some specific principles regarding negative tele.

First, instead of overtly or covertly acting out a hostile response or, on the other hand, being overly friendly, behave in a courteous, businesslike, restrained fashion. Know that any attempts to be self-disclosing or close are likely to be misinterpreted.

Second, recognise that since tele is an essentially intuitive response, it is not necessary to justify your emotional reactions. Thus, beware of tendencies to rationalise those feelings, to build a 'case' of various reasons why it's appropriate to dislike the other person. This only consolidates the negative tele and makes it more difficult to resolve the tensions in the relationship. It often exacerbates them. In other words, negative tele need not be amplified into a transferential reaction. There may be nothing wrong with a person to whom you aren't attracted, and there may be nothing wrong with you if someone doesn't particularly like you. This point cannot be overstressed.

A third principle is that although you experience negative tele with another person in one role, it might be possible that other role(s) might be found which could serve as a basis for a more cordial relationship.

Negative tele may also offer an opportunity for personal growth in that one can explore the reasons for a negative reaction, reasons which may involve insights about a variety of transferential reactions as well as personal preferences. For example, in a group which has become somewhat established and cohesive, a sociometric experiment may be suggested, as described by Monteiro and Carvalho. They had the group indicate to whom they would like to give a hug. 'Incongruencies, negative and indifferent mutualities were worked through by having the students explain and clarify their choices in successive pairs' (Monteiro and Carvalho 1990).

Recognising negative tele in psychodrama groups can offer some useful directions. First, a person who has negative tele with a number of other group members or with the director should not become a protagonist until the issues which have generated the negative tele have been resolved. A foundation of support might first be developed by seeing if other roles might be discovered which could serve as the basis of a more positive telic connection. Also, conflicts the person has with others in the group might be examined to see if the underlying issues can be resolved. Sometimes the courage a person exhibits in confronting these problems directly and with a spirit of self-examination can shift the group's attitude and promote a more positive identity in the group.

If only the director experiences negative tele with one of the group members, perhaps a co-therapist could take over the director's role and explore the conflict between the director and the client, seeking to clarify the nature of the underlying issues. (They may represent dynamics which are important in the overall group process.) Alternatively, if the co-director has positive tele with the group member in question, the co-director may simply process the role-playing of that person's issue aside from the relationship with the director.

However, not all relations can be satisfactorily worked out. Therapists who have sustained negative tele with certain patients should refer those patients out, and as a corollary, patients should not stay for months or longer trying to 'work through' a transference with someone whom they've never really taken to. 'It takes tele to choose the right therapist and the right partner; it takes transference to misjudge the therapist' (Moreno 1959a: 12). Sometimes, as in individual therapy, certain patients might do better changing to a group with whom they have a better rapport.

Negative tele may often be only part of a complex of feelings, and ambivalence, neutrality and indifference are also telic reactions which are deserving of attention (Moreno 1952: 162). Especially worthy of note is the way telic reactions are role dependent, and even within a role, each component may evoke a different interactive valence (referring to a variable strength of attractive or repulsive force) (Carlson-Sabelli *et al.* 1992). Exploration of these component roles in terms of their feeling tones and the reasons for those feelings may lead to significant insights. Another strategy is to expand the participants' role repertoires so that new avenues for relating can be found.

Thus, in appreciating the various aspects of the dynamic of tele, people can be helped to face their unsatisfactory telic situations more directly. They may negotiate the critera involved, seek or construct alternative roles which could serve as the basis for a more satisfying connection or more consciously 'shop' for other relationships in which tele would occur more naturally.

TELE AND GROUP COHESION

'There is tele already operating between the members of the group from the first meeting' (Moreno 1956b: 95). This quote is an example of Moreno using the term in its more inclusive sense – the tele may not necessarily be very positive. A group in which the members have few mutually enjoyable telic connections tends to be unstable. Group cohesion grows in proportion to the growth of tele among the leader and participants. Moreno, using the term now in its more positive sense, wrote that 'tele is the cement which holds groups together' (Moreno 1959b: 1380).

Yet, group cohesion also is related to a number of other factors, such as the urgency of their common need, the clarity of the group task, the norms of the group leader, similarities or differences in cultural values and expectations of the group members, the methods used, etc. A group may become closer because they're faced with an emotionally intense unifying force, such as might happen to a military unit in the course of a battle. Sharing the vulnerability of the human condition fosters identification on the level of the inner child, which circumvents the more superficial pretences of the social façade. Although people often feel that they will be rejected if their more shameful secrets are known to others, in most therapeutic groups, it is the disclosure and sharing of just that level of shame-based imagery which tends to generate a greater sense of trust (Nathanson 1992: 252).

When group cohesion develops to a certain point, group members shift in their feeling about their membership in the group from a sense of being part of a mass of individuals to a sense of community. If the group cohesion continues to increase in intensity, the sense of 'we-ness' develops, and the general phenomenon is closer to what might be termed 'communion' (Gurvitch 1949).

A practical application of this principle is that one of the components of warming-up in psychodrama is that of promoting group cohesion (Blatner 1988a: 46). Using exercises which develop the positive tele among the group members while also building their empathic skills, the director structures the session so that people can disclose themselves gradually. For example, working in dyads, the group members interview each other in a given role. They change partners, and repeat the exercise with another role which requires a bit more involvement (Blatner and Blatner 1991). After a number of these dyadic experiences, each person in the group has shared with several others an activity in which some risk-taking and imaginativeness have been required, and as a result feels as if she or he has a number of special connections who will be supportive in dealing with others with whom they are not so well acquainted.

Another application of the tele principle is that in a psychodrama group members play a variety of roles, which in turn allows them to reveal a broader number of facets of their personalities. People can find more criteria for liking one another, and group cohesion tends to be associated with the number of roles which are shared by the members (Moreno 1934: 145).

Another technique for building a positive sense of tele among the group members is to get some consensus about a variety of group norms, such as confidentiality, a willingness to examine oneself, a commitment to deal directly with conflict rather than to keep it to oneself or to engage in gossip, a desire to become more creative and to foster creativity in the others or an openness to allow someone a chance to correct a behaviour which has evoked a negative response. Group norms which reflect superordinate or even spiritual values are especially powerful in promoting positive tele.

In turn, group settings in which the goal is spiritual development benefit from activities which specifically foster group cohesion. Indeed, helping people to encounter each other more authentically partakes of a spiritual quality which the Jewish theologian, Martin Buber, called an 'I–Thou' relationship (Green 1959: 1821).

TELIC SENSITIVITY, EMPATHY AND ENCOUNTER

People are born with a capacity for tele, but it is diffuse and undifferentiated at first. The capacity for assessing how other people might be reacting, whether they might be feeling a similar sense of positive or negative attraction, or even neutrality or indifference, is called 'telic sensitivity'. When two people have divergent feelings towards each other, such as attraction–repulsion, or attraction–neutrality, this is called 'infra-tele,' and reflects a lack of accurate telic sensitivity on the part of at least one of the individuals (Nehnevajsa 1956: 62).

'The sense for tele develops with age. It's weak in children and grows with social awareness' (Moreno 1987: 344). Children reveal some early forms of empathy in that they tend to react to others' joy or sorrow with corresponding feelings. Also, in nursery programs even young children show preferences among their classmates.

In adolescence, telic sensitivity tends to develop more in those who have the natural gifts of 'interpersonal intelligence'. It should be noted that there is a talent for social skilfulness just as there is a talent for music or athletics, and that while some children are innately more adept, so there are others who are less adept at acquiring these abilities (Gardner 1983: 239). And although there is a distribution of this capacity, Moreno believed that it would be possible to increase telic sensitivity at least to some extent in the majority of people through the use of role-training exercises.

For example, Moreno suggested that people practise 'perceptual sociometry', using the following instructions:

> Draw your social atom. Note how you feel towards the various people, and guess what they feel toward you. List the reasons for those feelings. Guess how they're related to each other. Then ask someone who knows you to comment on your assessment, or better, ask the various people in your social network for feedback.
>
> (Moreno 1952: 155)

The area of romance offers one example in this regard. Young people often have crushes on others who do not reciprocate the feelings, an example of 'infra-tele'. In a culture which creates a narrow range of criteria affecting who is and is not desirable, people will tend to admire the culturally accepted clichés regarding attractiveness. What if we helped youngsters pay more attention to those others in one's social network who seem to reciprocate a sense of positive tele? Further, we should encourage young people to address a variety of categories, especially those which emphasise common interests rather than some commercial media-driven image of sex appeal. The implementation of such sociometric principles can help young people mature in learning to assess the reactions of others more effectively.

In psychodrama, telic sensitivity can be cultivated by allowing protagonists and auxiliaries to choose one another. Sometimes someone from the group spontaneously gets up to double for a protagonist because of some identification with the predicament being enacted. If there isn't already a sense of a special bond between the two, this kind of activity tends to foster that telic connection. Alternatively, a protagonist may choose a group member to play a certain role, and afterwards, during the sharing phase, it turns out that the auxiliary in his or her actual life experience had a similar situation happen. This seemingly telepathic connection also arises out of the telic sensitivity of the protagonist who made that choice (usually unknowingly), and again fosters a greater sense of tele among the group members.

Empathy involves an individual's ability to sense into the feelings of another, and the activity of role-taking as happens in the course of the psychodramatic techniques of doubling or role reversal tends to build the skill of more accurate levels of empathy. If the people involved in this process have positive tele with each other, the act of empathy tends to be more effective. While empathy is a one-way process, tele involves both parties interacting with one another (Haskell 1975: 32–3). Because of this, in the act of doubling, auxiliaries should verify their intuitive responses with the protagonist and allow their behaviour to emerge through mutual interaction (Moreno 1954: 233).

On the other hand, if the tele between a protagonist and an assigned or chosen double isn't positive, it's more likely that the doubling itself will not feel 'right' to the protagonist. If this situation occurs, it's best if the director excuses the auxiliary and helps the protagonist to choose another group member with whom there is a greater degree of rapport.

Accurate empathy is a skill which requires a mixture of talent and practice. Some people are naturally more able to sense into others' feelings. Unfortunately, a certain portion of these gifted individuals lack the ethical component of positive tele and use their ability in a manipulative, perhaps even sociopathic fashion. The point is that while positive tele can foster empathy, and in turn, empathy can foster positive tele, still the two phenomena are not identical.

Some people seem almost incapable of being empathic, because they are handicapped by a great deal of egocentricity. This may be due to a lack of native intelligence, sheer immaturity, a pervasive disorder of relatedness (such as autism) or, more commonly, an overabundance of narcissistic traits. Indeed, it may be somewhat diagnostic to have patients in group therapy attempt to role-reverse and see how effective they can be. Whatever the extent to which they succeed, they will likely create a greater appreciation from those whom they are attempting to understand.

Encounter is an even more complex extension of this process of matured telic sensitivity. It involves both parties attempting to empathise with each other. Encounter goes beyond empathy in that there is an associated opening of one's heart, an act of will, an exercise of imagination and an expanding of one's perspective. It requires maturity and sensitivity. Teenagers in love have a goodly amount of positive tele, a modest amount of mutual empathy, yet tend to be limited in the degree to which they can truly role-reverse with each other, which is the essence of true encounter.

Encounter, a term coined by Moreno around 1914, refers to a process in which both parties sincerely attempt to genuinely meet each other. The encounter group, a fashionable personal-growth activity popular in the late 1960s and early 1970s, lost its thrust because it failed to follow this principle. Mere disclosure, often of angry affects, too frequently led to unresolved feelings; inexperienced group leaders didn't know how to have those involved in conflict resolve their differences through role reversal.

Even more than with empathy, encounter fosters tele, and tele in turn encourages people to risk encounter. Referring to its most positive expression, Moreno noted, 'The scientific counterpart of encounter is tele' (Moreno 1960: 17).

PROMOTING INDIVIDUATION

One of the most important applications of the concept of tele is that it encourages people to pay more attention to their own preferences. This in turn increases self-awareness and helps people in their individuation. Karen Horney (1950: 17) wrote of the need to develop one's 'real self' as mentioned earlier. One of the most effective ways of achieving this is to help people pay attention to their preferences, especially with regard to such areas as interests, temperamental styles and imagery. Many people in therapy have little awareness of these dimensions of self-development.

Another practical application of the concept of tele, then, is to have the people in the groups you lead discuss their preferences, including the collectives with which they've chosen to become affiliated, e.g. political, religious, artistic, etc. Have them consider their desired connections, those individuals and groups to which they'd like to belong. Help them talk about not only who is in their social networks, but also who they would want to be included. Talking about how they choose their dates, romantic partners, employment, hobbies and so on, what the criteria were, leads to a gradual emergence of a more authentic sense of self.

Thus, the dynamic of individuation, of helping people find their 'real self' and discover that it can be accepted and enjoyed by others, is facilitated in leading groups when the therapist addresses themes in therapy such as:

- Who is one 'supposed' to admire, based on cultural or family conditioning, versus who one actually feels some tele with. For example, is it okay for a boy to want to be a dancer?
- What did it require to be 'popular' with the other kids when you were a teenager? Was it what you really enjoyed doing?

- If there could have been a club which contained 'your kind of people', what would it be like?

Do sociometric exercises in which group members choose others based on certain criteria, and then allow them to role play or actually enact the activity involved. The activity of choosing should be emphasised, because many people feel awkward about this. They tend to turn to whomever is closest, or wait passively. Fears of not being chosen, the sense of shame when the one most preferred chooses someone else, the difficulty in not accepting a choice which is not preferred, these and other reactions offer a wealth of material for group discussion.

FURTHER APPLICATIONS OF THE CONCEPT OF TELE

One of Moreno's goals was to allow tele to operate more in the organisation of formal relationships as well as informal ones, so that people who enjoy one another's company or complement one another's skills can choose to work on classroom projects, as laboratory partners, or in teams at their jobs. Room mates in a dormitory, committee members, and other groupings should be assigned based on their own indicated preferences rather than some arbitrary criterion imposed by those in charge.

Knowledge of the significance of tele in human relations would also help in structuring community organisations. For example, you might advocate the development of a greater variety of activities and promote the idea of letting children and adults choose their work groups rather than assigning them. To foster individuation, encourage children to discover their own preferences in the home and school (Blatner 1988b: 127–48).

As a group leader, perhaps the major application of the idea of tele is just to use it as a concept, teaching it to the group members so they can talk about their different and sometimes mixed feelings of attraction or wariness with each other. These discussions frequently evoke associations, from childhood onwards, concerning experiences of envy, shame and manipulativeness regarding being liked or disliked, being popular or unpopular and daring to seek a more compatible group (Jennings 1950). The role-based nature of tele will help them to sort out these experiences, and discussion of the various criteria which affect their preferences also deepens shared insights about both individual and group dynamics.

SUMMARY

Moreno discovered that tele is a powerful force at work in the interpersonal field. Having a word for a phenomenon helps people to begin to choose how they want to behave. Enabling people to be aware of this dimension of social interaction has practical implications. Learning to develop positive tele in one's social network promotes individuation, group cohesion, the capacity for empathy and encounter and a context for working through interpersonal conflicts.

REFERENCES

Berne, E. (1964) *Games People Play*, New York: Grove Press.

Bischof, L.J. (1964) *Interpreting Personality Theories*, New York: Harper and Row.

Blatner, A. (1988a) *Acting-in: Practical applications of psychodramatic methods*, 2nd edn, New York: Springer.

—— (1988b) *Foundations of Psychodrama: History, theory and practice*, 3rd edn, New York: Springer.

—— (1991) 'Role dynamics', *Group Psychotherapy, Psychodrama and Sociometry* 44(1): 33–40.

Blatner, A. and Blatner, A. (1991) 'Imaginative interviews: a psychodramatic warm-up for developing role-playing skills', *Group Psychotherapy, Psychodrama and Sociometry* 44(3): 115–20.

Carlson-Sabelli, L., Sabelli, H., Patel, M. and Holm, K. (1992) 'The union of opposites in sociometry', *Group Psychotherapy, Psychodrama and Sociometry* 44(4): 147–71.

Gardner, H. (1983) *Frames of Mind*, New York: Basic Books.

Green, M.R. (1959) 'Chapter 90C: Martin Buber' in S. Arieti (ed.) *American Handbook of Psychiatry*, vol. 2, New York: Basic Books.

Gurvitch, G. (1949) 'Microsociology and sociometry', *Sociometry* 12(1–3): 1–31.

Hale, A.E. (1981) *Conducting Clinical Sociometric Explorations: A manual for psychodramatists and sociometrists*, Roanoke, VA: Royal Publishing Co.

Hart, J.W. (1980) 'An outline of basic postulates of sociometry', *Group Psychotherapy, Psychodrama and Sociometry* 33: 63–70.

Haskell, M.R. (1975) *Socioanalysis: Self-direction via sociometry and psychodrama*, Long Beach, CA: Role Training Associates of California.

Holmes, P. (1992) *The Inner World Outside: Object relations theory and psychodrama*, London: Tavistock/Routledge.

Horney, K. (1950) *Neurosis and Human Growth*, New York: Norton.

Jennings, H.H. (1947) 'Sociometric differentiation of the psychegroup and the sociogroup', *Sociometry* 10(1): 71–9.

—— (1950) *Leadership and Isolation*, New York: Longmans, Green and Co.

Kellermann, P.F. (1992) *Focus on Psychodrama*, London: Jessica Kingsley.

Masterson, J.F. (1988) *The Search for the Real Self: Unmasking the personality disorders of our age*, New York: Macmillan/Free Press.

Mendelson, P. (1977) 'Sociometry as a life philosophy', *Group Psychotherapy, Psychodrama and Sociometry* 30: 70–85.

Monteiro, A.M. and de Carvalho, E.R. (1990) 'Learning through psychodrama and sociometry: two university experiences', *Group Psychotherapy, Psychodrama and Sociometry* 43(2): 85–8.

Moreno, J.L. (1934) *Who Shall Survive? A new approach to the problems of human relations*, Washington, DC: Nervous & Mental Disease Publishing Co.

—— (1937) 'Sociometry in relation to other social sciences', *Sociometry* 1(1–2): 206–19.

—— (1952) 'Current trends in sociometry', *Sociometry* 15(1–2): 146–63.

—— (1953) *Who Shall Survive?* Revised and expanded edn, New York: Beacon House.

—— (1955) 'Psychodrama', in J.L. McCary (ed.) *Six Approaches to Psychotherapy*, New York: Dryden, pp. 289–340.

—— (1956a) 'The sociometric school and the science of man', *Sociometry* 18(4): 271–91.

—— (1956b) 'Fundamental rules and techniques of psychodrama', in J. Masserman and J.L. Moreno (eds) *Progress in Psychotherapy*, vol. 3, New York: Grune and Stratton, pp. 86–131.

—— (1959a) 'Transference, countertransference and tele: their relationship to group research and group psychotherapy', in *Psychodrama: Foundations of psychotherapy,* vol. 2, New York: Beacon House.

—— (1959b) 'Psychodrama', in S. Arieti (ed.) *American Handbook of Psychiatry*, vol. 2, New York: Basic Books.

—— (1960) *The Sociometry Reader*, Glencoe, IL: The Free Press.

Moreno, Z.T. (1954) 'Sociogenesis of individuals and groups', in J.L. Moreno *et al.* (eds) *The International Handbook of Group Psychotherapy*, New York: Philosophical Library, pp. 231–42.

—— (1987) 'Psychodrama, role theory, and the concept of the social atom', in J. Zeig (ed.) *The Evolution of Psychotherapy*, New York: Brunner/Mazel.

Nathanson, D.L. (1992) *Shame and Pride: Affect, sex, and the birth of the self*, New York: W.W. Norton.

Nehnevajsa, J. (1956) 'Sociometry: decades of growth', in J.L. Moreno (ed.) *Sociometry and the Science of Man*, New York: Beacon House, pp. 48–95.

Northway, M. (1967) *A Primer of Sociometry*, 2nd edn, Toronto: University of Toronto Press.

Peters, E.H. (1966) *The Creative Advance: An introduction to process philosophy*, St Louis: The Bethany Press.

Rheingold, H. (1988) *They Have a Word For It*, Los Angeles: J.P. Tarcher.

Rowan, J. (1990) *Subpersonalities*, London: Routledge.

Samuels, A., Shorter, B. and Plaut, F. (1986) *A Critical Dictionary of Jungian Analysis*, London: Routledge and Kegan Paul.

Starr, A. (1977) *Rehearsal for Living: Psychodrama*, Chicago: Nelson-Hall.

Name index

Subject index